"Facing life's last inevitable journeys: AGING and DYING, is often difficult and frightening. What we all want is a guide, a companion, a Medical expert who cares for the body with compassion and for the mind and spirit with creative care. Our guide, our trusted companion, is Rick Holm, MD and the road map for these journeys is in his book. In sharing his own personal journeys of aging and dying, Holm willingly partners with our journeys. We don't have to go it alone. This author and this book are a gift for anyone aging or dying, or for their caregivers."

—MAGGIE CALLANAN, RN, coauthor of *Final Gifts: Understand the Special Awareness, Needs, and Communications of the Dying* and author of *Final Journeys, A Practical Guide for Bringing Care and Comfort at the End of Life*

"Dr. Holm has tended to legions of patients and long advocated best practices to live well and enjoy good health. Now, diagnosed with pancreatic cancer, he taps into his medical expertise, faith and zest for life to share valuable insight and expertise. Holm knows his subject firsthand and writes with the comforting tone you would expect from the Prairie Doc. *Life's Final Season* is—literally—what the doctor ordered."

—AMY DUNKLE, University writing teacher, Author of *The College on the Hill*

"Dr. Holm's readers will find his writing comprehensive and interesting but never condescending. He speaks directly to the reader in an accessible and conversational manner. As the caregiver for my late beloved wife Patti, I heartily endorse Dr. Holm's words on caregiving and caregivers in chapter four and elsewhere. On all of his topics his writings are clear, comprehensive and entirely accessible."

—MAURICE MONAHAN, Professor Emeritus (Math) SD State University, Eighty-four-years-old

"We all are aging people, and we all have much to learn from this wonderful book. Dr. Rick Holm is full of wisdom, insight, personal experience, practical advice and, most of all, inspiration."

—JOHN E. MILLER, historian and author

"This book is both personal and professional, is remarkably informative, inspirational and truly a book to live by. It is creatively written with important ideas and philosophies made concrete and real through vivid figures of speech and deep-hearted storytelling. The book is a powerful dramatization of the great value of holistic thinking and being, and it expresses invaluable universal truths with clarity and conviction."

—CHARLES L. WOODARD, Distinguished Professor Emeritus of English, SD State University

"In *Life's Final Season* Dr. Holm brings a perspective on life and death that fuses his experiences as a physician, teacher, father and patient into a very readable and understandable book. Not just for the elderly, this book will be enlightening and life-improving no matter your station in life. It is like a reference book that can be read and reread as one's life circumstances change. I highly recommend it."

—JIM ENGELBRECHT, MD, Rheumatologist

"In *Life's Final Season* Dr. Holm distills the knowledge he has accumulated during his lifetime as a respected and caring medical provider, and more recent cancer patient, by putting this information into a very readable and practical guide for living. The author's energy and enthusiasm are palpable on every page of this wonderfully written book that deals with the everyday bumps on the road of life for both the sick and the well."

—GEORGE WALDMANN, MD, Family Medicine

"In *Life's Final Season*, Dr. Holm explores, in easy to understand terms, the many aspects of caring for the elderly. Throughout an often complex topic, his language is clear, his reasoning thoughtful and his Socratic guidance plainly helpful to caregivers, and more especially to patients and their families."

—HENRY (PETE) TRAVERS, MD, Pathology

"I've known personally and worked closely with Dr. Rick Holm for nearly twenty years. In *Life's Final Season*, Dr. Holm brings his experience, intuition and lovely manner to bear on the myriad issues of aging in America. A roadmap to living and aging well, this book will be essential for everyone reaching the golden years."

—PETE LOOBY, MD, Orthopedic Surgeon

"Dr. Holm addresses the issues facing the most populous and wealthy generation in history in a most wise and pragmatic way. If a single word could characterize this passage of time, it would be change. Change is inevitable. His commentary on end of life decisions should be read by all of us, not just the Boomers. His words ring true, 'Running away from the aging and dying process is to invite suffering.'"

—MICHAEL E. MAFFETT, MD, Internal Medicine/Anesthesiology

"The words, thoughts and insights Dr. Holm has shared, in this lovely read, really hit home with me. I agree with Holm's guidance that in our living we should explore all of our gifts and reinvent ourselves on a recurring basis. When the challenge of dying brings your life into focus, you will need to take Dr. Holm's advice and get your affairs in order and wishes known to your loved ones. This will help family to celebrate your life rather than be bedeviled by the details that could easily have been avoided."

—JOHN LANGDON, MD, Internist, Gov. Emeritus, Florida American College of Physicians

"Dr. Holm's keen insights from more than 40 years of clinical practice gives one a 'do the right thing' approach to both living and dying. He sees death as a natural part of our existence and exposes the taboos and the dark secrets that have made death the last pornography. By his reflections on facing his own death, Rick's musings bring us the imperative to come to grips with our mortality and even embrace it. Rick can now add 'theologian' to his long list of credentials. I consider it a must read."

—MIKE LIPSITT, MD, FACC, Cardiologist

"Knowing Rick since he and I were high school students has allowed me to see his far-reaching compassion and his doctoring skills. This book takes you through all the stages of life into aging and beyond. Given his pancreatic cancer, I've appreciated his insights, especially as he is facing his own death with grace."

—JEANNIE VAN DYKE CECIL, Retired Assistant Vice-President for Sales & Marketing of Student Loans

"Dr. Holm has a gift for explaining the importance of good preventive healthcare in helping us to lead long and satisfying lives. He is a wonderful storyteller, a very spiritual person and a top-notch physician. We can all benefit from reading this book."

—MICHAEL PETERSON, MD, Radiation Oncologist

"Dr. Rick Holm's enthusiastic zest for life is well known. His 40 some years of homespun prairie medical wisdom has benefited his patients, television viewers, radio listeners and newspaper readers. Now, all this experience, plus his ability to write very readable prose, are evident in this truly remarkable book. Much like a modern-day Montaigne, he uses his own medical and spiritual issues to discuss a series of honest observations, essays and practical suggestions for graceful living while dealing with the complexities that occur during the fourth or final stage of life. *Life's Final Season* is Dr. Holm's gift to all of us."

—JOHN D. BARKER JR. MD

"Required reading for anyone who wants their next years to be better years."

—DAVID M. HYINK, PHD, Scientist, University Professor, and devoted friend

"A book filled with great insights to help us all be the healthiest versions of ourselves, no matter what season of life we are in."

—JEREMY BEIREIS, Family Practice, (the one who suggested writing this book)

"Dr. Rick Holm brings deep knowledge and humanism to the practice of medicine. More than this, though, Rick brings joy and empathy into his clinical partnerships with his patients. I have listened to Dr. Holm speak for the need for this book to help patients for several years now. I know he wrote this book in the spirit of helping his patients, and others, navigate their personal journey though health and illness and the healthcare system. Thank you, Rick, for allowing me to work with you over the years in these conversations with our patients and our community."

—JUDITH R. PETERSON, MD, Physical Medicine and Rehabilitation, photography for *The Picture of Health, A View From the Prairie*

"Dr. Holm's skill in translating medical complexity into practical person-centered advice is once again demonstrated in *Life's Final Season*. His book is filled with insights that will help you *live* the rest of your life."

—DAVID BRECHTELSBAUER, MD, emeritus faculty, Sioux Falls Family Medicine Residency Program

"Dr. Rick Holm perfectly blends his clinical and scientific expertise with emotion and compassion. While *Life's Final Season* provides evidence-based information for those experiencing aging or the aging of a loved one, Dr. Holm's skillful writing surrounding these difficult topics truly makes this book a valuable resource for anyone and everyone."

—ELIZABETH REISS, Staff Editor, SD Medicine and Director of Communications, SD State Medical Association

"Life is a journey distinct to each and defined by the random challenges we face. Healthcare is a part of everyone's life and will, at some point, be relevant to each one of us. Dr. Holm brings together life's experiences and health care in a way that is easy and comfortable to understand. This book is filled with hope and brilliant observations."

—ARDEN WALLUM, General Manager/Chief Engineer, Mission Springs Water District

"For the half century I have known him, Dr. Rick Holm has been an energy-packed dynamo—the absolute embodiment of how to squeeze the most out of a life in all of the best ways. It comes as no surprise that he would perform a generous service to his aging peers with his wonderful insight on the end of life expressed with that same vibrancy within these pages."

—RICHARD L. HAKES (Writer/retired Publisher)

"Do you want to read a book that will truly change your life? Then, read this one. Dr. Holm takes you on a personal journey to better health by sharing his forty-plus years of observations and caring for others. It isn't your run-of-the-mill health tome. Along with being educated and entertained, it might even save your life!"

—V.J. SMITH, Best Selling Author of *The Richest Man in Town* and Noted Professional Speaker

Regarding Holm's metastatic cancer, "Obviously, none can speak with any experiential voice until they have actually been where he's been, living daily with the hope, fear, emotional roller-coaster of this experience. This book is quite special and 'sacred ground.'"

—WILLIAM FRYDA, MD, Oncologist, Catholic Priest, Medical Missions E. Africa for 40 years

Life's Final Season

Life's Final Season

A Guide for Aging and Dying with Grace

Richard P. Holm, MD

O Mother-Father God, now hear our prayers,
It's you who lives where rising sun brings hope,
Where summer sun brings growth, and might to fight,
Where autumn storms give range for full-grown sight,
And winter, old sage wisdom gives us worth.
We thank you for your blessings and our roles
And for the strength to face time's change, to cope.

We pray in harmony as love consoles,
O sacred hoop of life, please touch our souls.

Table of Contents

The Hourglass—Extending the length and quality of one's life

The key to longevity is lifestyle. This includes daily walking and exercise, a lower calorie balanced diet, sensing spiritual love and connectedness with friends, family, and a spiritual higher center.

Chapter Two 29

Drugs, Supplements and all those Side Effects—Truth about the dangers of medicines and supplements

People are taking too many drugs (polypharmacy). We need to go back to scientific-based values of medicine instead marketing-influenced prescribing. Supplements use and the history of vitamins and their promotion is also presented here.

Chapter Three. 85

The Graying of America—Baby boomers: great expectations and great danger

Baby boomers, like a pig in a python, are coming into their geriatric years, and this should change society in powerful ways. Boomers are in danger of suffering from excessive health care at the end of life. This is because many grew up getting their way and thus can be a demanding group. They are at risk for expecting everything done at the end of their lives, even when futile. This is also why advanced directives are especially important for boomers.

Chapter Four 105

The Fountain of Giving—Valuing yourself, too

Meaning and purpose comes from enhanced valuing of others and of self. Listening helps bring people to this valuing. This principle can make caring for an elderly or disabled person rewarding.

Chapter Five 123

The Golden Rule—An ancient and modern guide to making tough choices

This explains how doctors and others should use ethical virtue principles when providing care for vulnerable persons.

Chapter Six 159

Memory Lapse-Alzheimer's, Parkinson's and other causes for dementia

This chapter addresses different kinds and causes of dementia. Also presented are treatment options for those facing dementia and for their families as well.

Chapter Eight 213

What is Suffering? The prevention of suffering near the end of life

When the end of life is certain and due to advanced age, or multiple medical problems, it is important to understand how to reduce suffering at this time.

Case Study: The case of Grandma, certainly dying, arms tied so she wouldn't pull out the tubes 213

Chapter Nine 245

A Silent Shame—Elder abuse: The new and old epidemic

Causes for abuse and bullying are discussed. The elderly, or anyone who may be emotionally or physically at risk of abuse, can be protected by preventive efforts addressed here.

Foreword

IF YOU ARE READING THIS then you are getting old. Aging is one of the blessings of being alive, allotting us knowledge, experience and wisdom. Lines and wrinkles are not enemies, but the rivers and mountains which dot the map of our life's journey. Contrary to what some may think, getting old is not a curse, but a blessing; one that most people throughout history did not have the luxury of experiencing. At the dawn of the 20th century, the average human life expectancy hovered close to fifty years. Advances in medicine and technology, since that time, have increased that number to almost eighty years. This does not change the fact that all of us will one day pass from this earth. Death is the common denominator that unifies all living things. The good news is that the amount of life each of us can expect, short of tragedy or misfortune, has increased considerably. So how do we best enjoy all this extra time, and how do we ensure we are healthy enough to do so? Most importantly, how do we ensure that when the end draws near, we are ready to depart on our final journey with courage, dignity, and grace?

In his book, *Life's Final Season*, Richard Holm, MD, endeavors to help us answer these questions. Growing old can be a perilous voyage, fraught with obstacles and unknowns. Dr. Holm has spent his entire professional career helping people navigate these potentially turbulent waters. This book is the culmination of over 40 years of medical experience caring for the elderly, be it in the hospital, nursing home, or hospice. In addition to his clinical experience, Rick also draws wisdom from his many years spent serving as the president of Healing Words Foundation, a nonprofit organization dedicated to improving public health by providing honest, science-based information via publication, radio and television.

You can usually find Dr. Holm spending time either seeing patients at a long-term care facility, meeting with the hospice committee, producing health-care information on the radio or television studio, working in Cook's Kitchen on writing projects, with his family or on his sailboat at Lake Poinsett. If he's not there, you might find him in the classroom teaching medicine, philosophy or journalism. His genuine compassion and charisma puts patients at ease and inspires would-be doctors and laypersons alike to be better, healthier people. Dr. Holm knows that the medical science surrounding our personal health can be difficult and confusing. That is why he has dedicated his life to treating and educating the public, presenting complex medical science in easily understandable ways and empowering his patients, viewers, listeners and readers to take a more proactive stance on their own wellness. Rick firmly believes that one of the most powerful medicines in existence is our ability to help ourselves.

Over a lengthy career, Dr. Holm has become keenly attuned to the concerns, questions, and needs that people often have toward the end of their lives. The decision to write this book was the result of Rick seeing a number of patterns emerging in his patients during their later years. Immobility, polypharmacy, poor quality of life and prolonged suffering at the end are just a few of the worrisome trends he has seen. While this can be disheartening, Dr. Holm notes that many of these things are often within a person's own power to prevent or correct. He thus decided that there was a need for a guide—something to help individuals successfully navigate their fourth season with as much ease, health and enjoyment as possible. Throughout his career, Rick has seen what works and what doesn't; what helps and what hurts; and how to properly handle difficult decisions and end of life matters. Dr. Holm pulls from a lifetime of experience in geriatric medicine and public health education to give you *Life's Final Season.*

This book is meant to be a guide to help you or a loved one experience your final years in the healthiest, happiest and most fulfilling way possible. It is a balanced mixture of practical advice, medical education, philosophical musings and answers to many frequently asked questions about growing old. Are you concerned that immobility will keep you from enjoying your senior years? There's a chapter for that. Do you think the number of pills you are taking might be hurting your pocketbook and health? There are sections for that as well. In addition to addressing many of the common concerns regarding aging, Dr. Holm also addresses less obvious topics, such as designing living accommodations for persons with limited mobility, or spotting and addressing the common yet underreported occurrence that is elder abuse.

Though this book's emphasis is on aging, it is not directed solely toward the elderly. Readers at any stage of life can reap the benefits of what's presented here. Several of the suggested activities to maximize happiness in our later years can be incorporated at any age. It is not only the experienced who will face the challenges presented by an ever-increasing population of seniors. There are several sections in this book that provide perspective and wisdom to young adults, preparing them for many of the common difficulties they might encounter as their parents grow older and supplying them with advice on how to assist their loved ones in their later years.

Rick also invites us to have a discussion about dying—a dialogue on death. He encourages us to be courageous and not shy away from something that doesn't have to scare us. The unfortunate reality is that much of the pain and suffering which occurs at the end of life stems from an inability to discuss the matter before it becomes imminent. Dr. Holm has seen, first hand, how medical interventions designed to prolong life (artificial hydration, feeding tubes, etc.) have been used inappropriately, to keep alive people who are ready to die, prolonging the suffering of all involved. You will read later in this book a personal incident in which his own grandmother, at ninety-six years of age, suffered a terrible stroke. That, among many other ailments, left her with an abysmal quality of life. Ready to die after a long, fulfilling life, she continued to pull out a feeding tube which had been placed once she decided to stop eating, only to have it continually replaced, denying her the ability to pass naturally and peacefully. This type of tragedy is one that Dr. Holm has seen too many times, and he hopes that by addressing this and many other all too common issues, we may be able to prevent them from happening as frequently in the future. But how are we supposed to know what constitutes a peaceful and natural death? How are we supposed to know when to intervene and when to let go? And how are we supposed to know that our personal wishes regarding our own health care will be followed when we are no longer able to properly convey them? All of these difficult questions, and many more, are discussed in depth in the pages that follow.

In his book, Dr. Holm also reminds us that growing old does not have to be a bad thing. He firmly believes that our final years can be some of the most enjoyable and rewarding of our lives. It is more about how we approach our elderly years that matters. Rick reminds us again and again that we do not have to be the victims of old age. How we age has much to do with our attitude and willingness to put in the work as it does genetics or luck. Several chapters of this book are dedicated to discussing how we might go about investing in our own wellness to promote the healthiest and happiest future possible.

Over the course of his career, Rick has been called many things, the majority of which have been positive. But one thing that no one ever expected to call him was a cancer patient. About a year after beginning this book, Rick was unexpectedly diagnosed with pancreatic cancer. And while I understand that no one ever anticipates a cancer diagnosis, he was one of the least likely candidates: a medical doctor/philanthropist who maintains a vigorous exercise regime, meticulous diet and numerous happy and healthy relationships. With a good natured, if not slightly morbid, sense of humor, Rick candidly commented that of all people that could get pancreatic cancer, he was among the most emotionally and mentally prepared. After all, was he not currently writing a book on how to both age and die with grace?

Now it would have made a nice hook—focusing the book around Rick's battle against pancreatic cancer and him coming face-to-face with his own mortality. And while there are certainly aspects of that journey included here, it was never the driving inspiration for writing *Life's Final Season*. This book was and is designed primarily as a guide to help people get the most out of their final years. If anything, Rick's personal experience with pancreatic cancer only serves to highlight an already recurring theme in his work: that even if we make all the right decisions, we are not guaranteed a long life. What's truly most important, Rick says, is enjoying the years that we have. This, fortunately, often involves doing the same types of activities that also prolong life. It's a win-win, really, but not a guarantee.

This book was not inspired by Dr. Holm's own potential mortality, but by his need to address the many recurring questions and concerns he finds common among the patients he treats and the people for whom he cares. We all have several questions about end of life matters, and Rick hopes that this book will provide you with at least some of the answers. It is organized in such a way that it can either be read cover-to-cover or used as a reference that can be quickly and easily consulted. Rick does not claim to have all of the answers. He does not claim that his book holds the recipe for immortality, or that reading it will prevent every difficulty that might be encountered during our later years.

What he presents is a culmination of advice and wisdom gained from a lifetime of working in public health, treating and caring for the elderly and his own personal experiences with life and death. It is Rick's most sincere hope that this book will help you or a loved one enter and exit your fourth season with a sense of grace, dignity, and peace.

~ KYLE HAIN, MS
Research Associate at Montana State University
and Freelance Editorial Consultant

... public health ...

Introduction

THIS BOOK WAS WRITTEN for those who are aging. Everyone. It addresses issues to help the well, the sick, those dying and those caring for elderly persons in the fourth season of their lives. Although many issues about aging are presented within this book, let me begin with a story about death. Fear of dying is a unifying experience in which only humans suffer. The question remains: do we have to suffer?

THE CASE OF THE AUTHOR WITH PANCREATIC CANCER

This is one tale I never thought I would tell. I was a half-marathon-running, spiritually healthy, family man, in my late sixties. I had abundant friends, more interests and activities than I could accomplish. I was a person at minimal risk of an early death, or so I thought. I was surprised with the diagnosis of cancer of the pancreas at sixty-seven years of age during the early stages of writing this book. What does the cancer diagnosis have to do with the question, "Why read this book?"

THIS BOOK: MORE ABOUT LIVING THAN DYING

Although chapters Eleven and Twelve are written to reduce the fear of death, dying is not the only topic covered in this book. Each chapter starts with a real case study, followed by health information content, and is capped with an essay that summarizes salient information. Finally, a question and answer segment has been added.

In the beginning, the intent of this book was to **help a caregiver** provide aid to an elderly person, but the book evolved. Now, it's just as much a **guide to help the aging individual,** the elderly person, in her or his quest in aging and to eventually face dying with grace and dignity. For the purposes of this book, **the caregiver is a family member,** a friend or a nursing assistant hired to give care, to an elderly person. **A care provider is a physician, nurse practitioner, physician's assistant or nurse.** Thus, for this writing, there is a difference in definition between caregiver and care provider.

Chapters One through Three describe methods for staying healthy as we age and the appropriate use of medicine and supplements. Chapters Four through Seven prepare us for aging and explain how best to care for another who is medically compromised. Chapter Eight explores how to deal with suffering, Chapter Nine addresses elder abuse, and Chapter Ten deals with a variety of geriatric problems. Chapter Eleven helps a caregiver as a loved one dies, and Twelve helps the reader face her or his own death. The reader of this text has an exposure to a broad scope of information about aging and the end of life. This depth of information comes from the life experiences of a geriatrician who is aging himself and who is, personally, looking into the face of death.

RICK HOLM, THE PRAIRIE DOC®

I grew up in De Smet, South Dakota, (pop. 1,600), the "Little Town on the Prairie,"[1] of Laura Ingalls Wilder fame, where Dr. Bob Bell, MD, a family physician, was my mentor. I attended undergraduate and the first two years of medical school in South Dakota and transferred to finish my medical training at Emory University School of Medicine in Atlanta, Georgia. After residency, I taught, did research, and collaborated on five chapters in medical texts[2,3,4,5,6]

---

1   Wilder, LI. Little Town on the Prairie. HarperCollins Children's Books, 1941, 10 East 53rd St., New York, NY 10022

2   Rock C, Holm RP: Nutritional History. In Clinical Methods: The History, Physical, and Laboratory Examination (2nd Ed), HK Walker, DW Hall and JW Hurst, editors. Butterworths, Boston, MA, pp. 477–485, 1980.

3   Rock C, Holm RP, Hall DW: Body Size: Height and Weight. In Clinical Methods: The History, Physical, and Laboratory Examination (2nd Ed), HK Walker, DW Hall and JW Hurst, editors. Butterworths, Boston, MA, pp. 521–528, 1980.

4   Holm RP: Surgery in the Obese: Diagnostic and Therapeutic Considerations. In Medical Management of the Surgical Patient, MF Lubin, HK Walker and RB Smith, editors. Butterworths, Boston, MA, pp. 447–460, 1982.

5   Holm RP: Poisoning with Tricyclic Antidepressants. In Medicine for the Practicing Physician, JW Hurst, editor. Butterworths, Boston, MA, pp.1853–1855, 1983.

6   Holm RP: Leg Ulcers. In Medicine for the Practicing Physician, JW Hurst, editor. Butterworths, Boston, MA, pp. 1893–1896, 1983.

and two papers in journals.[7,8] At Emory, I especially loved providing a lecture course to the Emory University's physician's assistant (PA) students on the medical science and art of taking a History and Physical Exam (H&P).

In 1981, I returned to South Dakota to practice and brought my Floridian wife, Joanie, with me. She is a certified pediatric nurse practitioner (CPNP), and we have practiced in Brookings, SD in a multispecialty clinic since 1981. I explain all of this to give you a sense that what I say in this text comes from an academic tradition followed by a clinical and practical perspective. True science should be the basis for what medical professionals do. I should say that in caps: TRUE SCIENCE SHOULD BE THE BASIS FOR WHAT WE DO IN MEDICINE.

Joanie and Rick, 1979[9]

The icing on the cake for a rewarding life of medical practice has been the opportunity to teach. At Emory, my teaching

7   Holm RP, Taussig M, Carlton E: Behavioral Modification in a Weight-Reduction Program. J Am Dietetic Association 83(2):170–174, 1983.

8   Cooper K Jr., Owen SL, Holm RP, Pruit AW: Blood Pressure in School Age Children in Georgia. J of Med A of Georgia 70(5):345–347, 1981.

9   Photo of author and future wife Joanie Smith, walking St. Augustine, FL beach, December, 1979. Private collection

experience involved lecture courses, overseeing residents in internal medicine and making rounds with fellows, residents, interns, medical students and PA students. In comparison, South Dakota teaching has been that of practicing medicine while providing one-on-one exposure to students in all disciplines. They would shadow, observe and practice under supervision, and thus, learn to care for patients. All styles of teaching have been a great joy for me and have allowed me to improve my own skills in providing medical care for people.

MY EXPERIENCE IN CARING FOR THE ELDERLY

Older people, in the fourth season of life, require a special touch. The very elderly often suffer from multiple medical problems and are extra sensitive to medication. They are also at a higher risk for infection and blood clotting. Making this situation worse, the elderly are often taking too many medicines and vitamin supplements, are frail and weak from age, and are at risk of falling. I was not surprised when the new medical subspecialty of geriatrics evolved in 1988. In the following ten years, I took and passed the board test required to become board certified as a geriatrician. This important subspecialty, which gives appropriate attention to the particular needs of the elderly, has improved the care they deserve.

Caring for people in assisted living centers and long-term care facilities (nursing homes) has provided me a great perspective about my own life. Change is something we all must face in life, and I have observed that those who embrace change seem to flourish. When our community hospital developed Home Health and Hospice agencies, I was honored to become the Medical Director. Although I have stopped seeing patients in the hospital and clinic, I am still practicing and prescribing

for patients in local long-term care facilities, still the Hospice Medical Director for our Brookings Health System and still hosting and writing for radio and television.

Ninety-one-year-old mother of author, 2012[10]

BROADCASTING EXPERIENCE

In the early 1990s, I was invited to be a talk show guest on a local AM radio station which evolved into a weekly show that continues today. In 2002, we started something similar on television utilizing the help of South Dakota State University. At the time of this writing, we are into our 17th season of "On Call with the Prairie Doc®," a live, call-in, medical-information show that airs weekly throughout South Dakota and the bordering states. I am the host, topic developer and I invite the guests. Our volunteer physicians, and health-care guests are local and international experts. At the end of each television show, I provide commentary about the medical topic of the week, which some liken to Andy Rooney's essays. These 400-word essays are printed weekly in more than 50 newspapers throughout South Dakota and the region. In 2008, along with artistic photos by artist philosopher,

---

10   From private collection

Judith Peterson, MD, I put together a compilation of many of the essays.[11] My essays since 2008 are the backbone for this book.

. . . AND THEN CAME CANCER

In late September 2016, my belly started aching, and I turned the color of a pumpkin. We hoped gallbladder disease was the diagnosis, but when the surgeon operated to remove my gallbladder, she discovered pancreatic cancer blocking the bile duct. (Illustration-1) There have been some rough seas, but I've tried to remember the old proverb, "A smooth sea never made a skillful sailor." The treatment plan, before surgery, started with big-time doses of triple chemotherapy with all the side effects one would expect. Once chemo was done, radiation followed with accumulative icky-belly-feelings that continued to grow worse even for a couple of weeks after radiation. Traditionally, the patient rings a bell after the last dose of radiation.

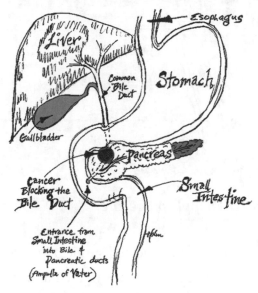

(Illustration 1) of pancreatic tumor[12]

---

11   Holm RP, Peterson JA: The Picture of Health, A View from The Prairie: South Dakota Agriculture Heritage Museum Publisher (SD State University), Brookings, South Dakota, Sept. 2008.

12   Illustration by author, 2017, private collection

Although some people skip the bell, I rang it hard, loud, long and, maybe, with a little anger and relief.

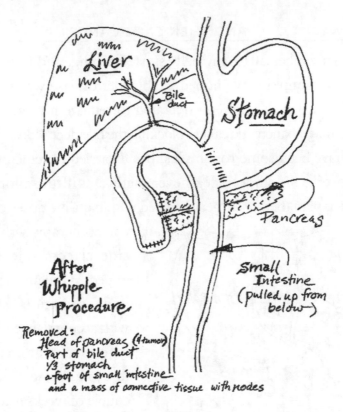

(Illustration 2) after Whipple procedure[13]

In May, 2017, a long, intricate and complicated surgical procedure called the Whipple was performed to remove the remaining cancer. (Illustration 2) After the surgery, I experienced significant pain and profound weakness. I took about four months along with a fair amount of pain medicine to recover. I like to think that the whole experience has made me "a more skillful sailor."

---

13   Illustration by author, 2017, private collection

It has brought me to sense, for my patients with cancer, empathy where there was once only compassion.

However, the storm is not over. The cancer has returned and I am back on chemo. The chances are significant that cancer will bring about an earlier-than-wanted death. From the beginning, the diagnosis of pancreatic cancer carried a paltry 3 to 8 percent chance of cure, and, even with all that treatment, risks remain very high. All that said, I am still alive at this writing, two years after the diagnosis. Although I remain hope filled, I have good reason to look at the dying experience from a more personal perspective.

VOICE OF REASON

I'm a physician and teacher who has spent 40 years caring for the sick, elderly and dying, as well as writing and providing public health broadcasting for these people. The diagnosis of my own pancreatic cancer gives me an unusual perspective which, I believe, positions me as a voice of reason for those in the final season and for those caring for the elderly. You might enjoy this book from beginning-to-end, or you might dip into its tailored chapters for specific needs and use this text as a reference source. My deepest wish is that this book will help you, or someone you love, to face aging and death with courage, dignity and even enthusiasm . . . a voice of reason for those in their final season.

Chapter One

The Hourglass

Extending the length and quality of one's life

Case Study:
The case of the woman in a motorized chair and worsening weakness

AN ELDERLY PATIENT OF MINE decided she wanted, as she put it, "one of those scooter chairs." She believed the heart attack had left her disabled to a degree that would justify such a thing. I was struck at how dangerous this might be for her as the scooter would result in less walking and exercise which is the exact opposite of what she needed. I strongly discouraged such a purchase, but, regardless of this advice, she called me a few weeks later to announce that she had purchased a used scooter.

Six months later, I received a call from her daughter who was upset about how profoundly weak her mother had become. I asked myself if her weakness was progressive heart disease or could the frailty be a result of decreased physical activity due to dependence on the scooter? People who stop any physical activity, especially walking, become weakened quickly.[14] After further testing, the evidence pointed toward the scooter as the culprit, and the family, with my help, convinced the patient to get off the scooter and start walking again. Fortunately, the elderly woman was eventually able to recover and return to normal functioning, but it took many months

of rehabilitation. Inactivity is, appropriately, becoming known as the "new smoking."[15] This is not just criticizing the habit of sitting too much, this is stating, loud and clear, that poor conditioning and inactivity are dangerous. Too often, people come to my office and complain about weakness, and, too often, the cause is simply couch-potato disease. People can become totally incapacitated by inactivity.

Person on mobility scooter[16]

---

14   https://www.ncbi.nlm.nih.gov/pubmed/20046119

15   https://theconversation.com/why-sitting-is-not-the-new-smoking-72568

16   Photo from Phasmatisnox at English Wikipedia from https://commons.wikimedia.org/wiki/File:Mobility_scooter_zoo.jpg

Studies show that a twenty-year-old person has a one in four chance of becoming disabled before she or he retires. Estimates show that over 37 million in the U.S., or about 12 percent of the population, are classified as having some form of disability and will need at least some health care support if they are unable to work.[17] Caring for someone who is disabled is important, but we shouldn't "kill 'em with kindness." The core element of rehabilitation is to make every effort to help people develop or regain their independence and function. The goal for every patient should be to obtain the highest level of self-sufficiency and autonomy possible. Making life easier for the patient can be doing them a disservice. We must go the second step, which is to encourage rehabilitation and recovery. Rarely the easiest path, the work of rehabilitation is almost always the best way to go.

This is in no way meant to sound like an all-encompassing criticism of motorized wheelchair devices. They can provide mobility for people who are otherwise permanently and significantly disabled, allowing them exactly the independence we should encourage. Look into the reference[18] written for people with multiple sclerosis, a condition that can progressively disable people. The reference describes a wide scope of options for assistive devices that are available. **Caregivers should try to achieve a balance between providing loving support and encouraging independence.** Mary Pipher's advice for parenting, in her book

---

17   U.S. Social Security Administration, Fact Sheet. Feb. 7, 2013, and U.S. Census Bureau, American Community Survey, 2011.

18   https://www.nationalmssociety.org/NationalMSSociety/media/MS NationalFiles/Brochures/Brochure-How-to-Choose-the-Mobility-Device-that-is-Right-for-You.pdf

Reviving Ophelia,[19] suggests children thrive when parents provide a balance of clear and understandable discipline along with unconditional love. Caregivers, and family members, must cook a stew which includes compassion marinated with the kind of tough love that provides the elderly firm and achievable goals. For healing to occur, it is critical for the patient to regain as much independence as possible.

Seeing a person so utterly disabled by a scooter chair shows how remarkably harmful inactivity can be. Of all the cacophony of advertisements that I oppose: the selling of this drug, that supplement, this wrinkle remover and that way to make life easier, the scooter chair lesson is possibly the most important message in this book. When possible, getting up out of that chair and walking, moving and exercising will bring anyone a more thriving, favorable and healthy life.

The emotional cost of physical dependency for the elderly is significant. Independence fosters healthy self-esteem and purpose. To gently encourage activity and rehabilitation for our elderly selves, patients and loved ones is challenging, especially when they are tired and weak, but the rewards of an improved quality of daily life can be enormous.

19   https://www.amazon.com/Reviving-Ophelia-Saving-Selves-Adolescent/dp /1594481881/ref=sr_1_1?ie=UTF8&qid=1514829976&sr=8-1&keywords =raising+ophelia

THE QUESTION OF HOW WELL AND HOW LONG
ARE WE GOING TO LIVE

"Hematuria (blood in the urine)? What?" I thought.

The kidney specialist (nephrologist) told me, "The blood in your urine might be just minimal change disease." I knew this was a slowly progressive type of kidney failure. He reassured me, "It could be up to seven years before your kidneys quit. That is good news." His "good news" almost brought me to my knees. These were shocking words to a thirty-year-old, unmarried, junior-faculty physician. I was teaching medical students and residents at Grady and Emory Hospitals, in Atlanta, Georgia. Like most young adults in the U.S., I had never seriously considered becoming ill or facing my own possible death. Later that week, I remember praying and desperately asking for just 20 more years of life. "If I can just make it to fifty, I will accept my own death. Please don't take me now as I want to have a family. Please just let me live to fifty, and I will be satisfied." By looking into the bladder through a scope, the hematuria proved to be the result of jogging, not kidney stones, not malignancy and not kidney disease. What a relief! True story. Now at sixty-nine, 19 years past my bargained end of life of fifty, I have the diagnosis of cancer of the pancreas. I should feel lucky, right? Actually, I do feel lucky.

What about you? Have you ever asked the uniquely human question, "How long will I live?" Of course, there is no method that can guarantee a long life, but there are simple, inexpensive, powerful and scientifically solid principles that can truly improve people's chances of a long, healthy and happy life. I will outline them here. However, there is still no guarantee. Perhaps, asking, "How well will I live?" is the better question.

PREVENTING THE NATURAL AGING PROCESS
OF HARDENING OF THE ARTERIES

Many conditions that affect the elderly are not diseases but are the undeniable natural aging processes which involve all organs and arteries. Getting old cannot be stopped. However, a reasonable goal would be to prevent PREMATURE aging. With this goal in mind, efforts to prevent atherosclerosis (hardening of the arteries) should take center stage. Many catastrophic medical issues stem from the failure of proper blood flow. Blocked arteries will result in heart attacks, strokes, kidney failure, loss of legs from diabetic vascular disease and other organ problems. These words are also undeniable: preventing premature atherosclerosis saves lives.

What causes atherosclerosis? Atherosclerosis is defined as inflammation and damage to the endothelial (lining) cells of the arteries with the resulting buildup of scar tissue. Like skin cells, which scar and lose elasticity from age or exposure to the sun's radiation, arteries scar and lose elasticity from age or exposure to poisons in the environment. For example, smoking and high blood sugar levels (diabetes) both directly damage blood vessels causing arteries to stiffen, thicken and scar. This is premature atherosclerosis, an accelerated aging process from toxins.

There are several ways to prevent toxin-induced aging of arteries. Avoiding cigarette smoke, and, if diabetic, keeping the blood sugar controlled will help. There is a group of medicines called statins, related to red yeast rice, which reduces cholesterol production by the liver. Although they are heavily promoted to reduce atherosclerosis or hardening of arteries, statins are disappointing and **only minimally effective.** In addition, they carry some risk for harm especially in the elderly.

I believe exercise is an exponentially more powerful tool to prevent toxin-induced problems.

Author running on the beach March 2018[20]

A recent study on preventing Parkinson's disease supports this assumption. The experiment involved injecting chimpanzees with a chemical toxin which is known to cause a premature brain-aging condition that behaves like Parkinson's disease.[21] After all were injected, the chimpanzees were divided into two groups: one pushed to exercise and the other left to relax. The experiment revealed that the exercising chimpanzees were

20 From private collection

21 Ahlskog JE: Does vigorous exercise have a neuroprotective effect in Parkinson disease? Neurology. 2011 Jul 19; 77(3): 288–294.

protected from the brain poison while the couch-potato chimpanzees developed the disease. Similar studies in mice, humans and other animals support these findings. While there are unavoidable toxins in this world of ours, movement and motion can soften the harm of the premature aging toxins around us.

A recent study found that for people who walk three miles a day (or run 45 minutes three times per week), the death rate lowers 37 percent. This is better than for those who walk one mile; however, the lion's share of benefit (31 percent) comes with that first mile.[22] Side effects of daily walking include increased strength and energy, stronger bones, improved mood, better balance and superior sleep. Longevity is increased, but increased quality of life should be the strongest motivator.

Bottom line: While there are unavoidable toxins in this world, physical activity can soften the harm. Walking, stretching and keeping our bodies in motion is the best way to avoid premature aging, and you don't have to be a chimpanzee to reap those benefits.

EATING LESS AND THE VALUE OF EATING BRUSSELS SPROUTS

My sister and I were among the many baby boomers who were not allowed to leave the dinner table until we finished our Brussels sprouts. Our dog wouldn't eat them, either. The word at our house was, "Eat your vegetables because there are starving kids in . . . (fill in the foreign country)." I still remember picturing very hungry kids somewhere out there trying to survive on Brussels sprouts.

---

22   https://www.ncbi.nlm.nih.gov/pubmed/25844730

Brussels sprouts[23]

The problem we currently have in the U.S. is not one of eating inadequate amounts of vegetables, but rather about eating too much, too much of everything. Since the mid-1930s, nutritional scientists have revealed that rats live 20 to 60 percent longer when they are fed 40 percent less than the rats enjoying the "all you can eat" diet.[24] There exists a great deal of scientific support that shows this holds true for almost every insect, reptile, amphibian, bird and human. The reason eating too much food (too many calories) causes premature death is likely related to rust-like damage that occurs within our cells from too much of a good thing (such as free radicals and oxidative stress to our mitochondria).[25]

23   Photo by MOs810 from https://commons.wikimedia.org/wiki/User:MOs810
24   J. Nutr. 1935 10:1 63–79.
25   https://www.ncbi.nlm.nih.gov/pubmed/20872368

The butter, eggs, highly processed food, type of fats or even high-fructose carbohydrates are not the culprits. Science points to excessive total daily calories as probably the most important cause for premature aging. The corollary supports the point: a reduction of excessive food, although very difficult, is the most powerful extender of life.

Excessive food (measured by calories) brings on, or worsens, sleep apnea, reflux esophagitis (destructive acid rolling up into the esophagus), hypertension, diabetes and begets all the manifestations of vascular disease to include stroke and heart attack. In short, **too much food causes premature aging.** (Note that I am not claiming "you have to lose weight.")

More recent data would suggest that, specifically, **eating less processed carbohydrates** is an important component to the proper diet, especially if one is diabetic. Perhaps, in contradiction to this recommendation, science also supports a **daily balanced diet** that includes at least two servings of fruit, and at least three servings of nonstarchy vegetables (corn and potatoes are starchy) and one serving of something green. However, the strongest and oldest data speaks to **less food (calories)** as the principle key to longevity and health.[26]

Again, notice I am NOT writing about weight reduction for obesity. The goal is to eat less, and this may not cause weight reduction. Repeated scientific studies have shown how **ineffective** long-term **weight loss programs** can be. Although losing weight would reduce sleep apnea, make breathing easier and make exercise more achievable, very few people can lose weight

26   Nature August 29, 2012, 489, 318–321

and maintain that weight over time. (Repeated studies show the best weight loss programs are about 30 percent effective,[27,28] and after one year, only 10 percent have kept the weight off, and after five years, 5 percent have kept it off. Other studies have said 0 percent at five years)[29,30] My best recommendation is to learn to count calories and, subsequently, eat fewer total calories. If counting calories is unwieldy and intimidating to you, consider simply "eating less" at each meal and in between. If eating less food and fewer calories results in weight loss, great, but don't depend on it.

Bottom line: Eat less; this is an important and difficult challenge in a world of excess. Maybe we would all be better off if everything tasted more like Brussels sprouts.

THE VITAMIN E STORY

In the '80s scientists discovered that cellular oxidation (discussed earlier) was responsible for at least some of the aging process, and there was early evidence that vitamin E might prevent that oxidative (aging rust-like) process. (Thus, the scientists came up with the word antioxidant.) The theory spread and scientists all over the world started taking vitamin E supplements. That is until in 2008 when the results of the Physicians' Health

---

27   https://www.consumeraffairs.com/nutrition/nutrition.htm

28   Rosenbaum M, et al. Obesity. N Engl J Med 1997; 337:396–407

29   Rosenbaum M, Leibel RL. Pathophysiology of childhood obesity. Adv Pediatr 1988;35:73–137

30   Wadden TA. Treatment of obesity by moderate and severe caloric restriction: results of clinical research trials. Ann Intern Med 1993;229:688–693

Study II[31] came out comparing use of vitamin E in supplement form (as well as several other supplements) in 14,000 male doctors over an eight-year period of time. The study showed vitamin E supplements did NOT reduce cancer, eye disease, heart attacks, strokes, cardiovascular deaths or the aging process. Instead, Vitamin E, in pill form, slightly increased the risk of hemorrhagic (bleeding) strokes. Note here that the study was looking at supplements not food.

Nutritional experts agree that getting one's **vitamins from food and not from pills** is optimal. In other words, vitamin E supplement is NOT an effective antioxidant (antiaging agent). Presently, I believe the only effective antioxidants available to us is the avoidance of too many calories and exercise. Currently there is **NO** significant scientific evidence that any vitamin supplement, self-proclaimed antioxidant pill, powder or chelation treatment makes any difference in the aging process. (Chelating agents are legitimately prescribed for heavy metal poisoning, but there is no scientific evidence that they prevent atherosclerosis or aging.)

There are always people who always want to sell you an anti-aging supplement and will claim their pill does just that. Presently, there is no law stopping them from making false claims. I repeat: nothing in supplement or pill form works to prevent premature aging, period. What does work: 1) eating a balanced diet with enough vegetables and fruit while eating fewer calories; 2) being involved with daily physical activity; and 3) having friends. Sellers of pills, vitamins, supplements, statins or other lipid-lowering agents will tell you otherwise. Don't buy it.

31   JAMA. 2008;300(18):2123–2133

EMOTIONAL HEALTH: ON THE VALUE OF FRIENDSHIP

What is a friend? The dictionary defines a friend as a person with whom one has a bond of mutual affection that is exclusive of sexual or family relations. The word comes from the German *freund*, which, in turn, originates from an Indo-European root meaning "to love." There are many more definitions of friendship. Friends listen, care, support, open-up and, when it counts, are loyal. Almost like the ethics of medicine: friends try to benefit and not harm their pals, try to do this honestly and try to respect the other person's freedom to choose.

*Friends: Mike Lipsitt, the author, Mike Maffett
(residents together at Emory 1975–1979)[32]*

---

32   Photo by author, private collection, spring 2018

There are a lot of great quotes about the value of friendship. An unknown author said, "A friend is someone who knows the song in your heart and can sing it back to you when you have forgotten the words." Charles Caleb Colton said, "True friendship is like sound health; the value of it is seldom known until it be lost." Emily Dickenson professed, "My friends are my estate." And of course, Lennon-McCartney wrote and Ringo Starr sang, "I get by with a little help from my friends."[33]

University of South Dakota students on spring break, enjoying friendship, March 2018[34]

---

33   https://www.goodreads.com/quotes

34   Photo by author, private collection, permission granted

In this social media age with such things as Facebook and Twitter, the number of people one has "friended" is apparently a sign of influence and popularity. Isn't it ironic that the technology of the Internet has, instead, isolated people?[35] Several studies have even indicated the Internet may be a major reason why there has been a decline in the number and quality of friendships nowadays.

Humans are hardwired to have friends. Through the ages, anthropologists tell us a troop (also called a community, a tribe, or a congress)[36] of chimpanzees is typically limited to 50 individuals because, with shared grooming as the social language, they are limited by time to know a maximum of 50 other chimpanzees. Hunter-gatherer human tribes were typically limited to the size of about 150 people because that's the maximum number of friends one could get to know when limited by human verbal skills.[37]

The challenge of true friendship is more than just being one of the 150 acquaintances within the tribe. A fulfilling and healing friendship requires more. Friendship calls for many ingredients including listening, unselfish giving, honesty, freedom of choice by both parties and, on top of those, a big dose of forgiveness.

The health advantages of friendship are enormous. Solid scientific studies find those with strong friendships have better mental and physical health, increased longevity and a deeper

---

35 https://relevantmagazine.com/culture/tech/6-ways-social-media-ruining -our-friendships

36 https://www.quora.com/What-do-you-call-a-group-of-chimpanzees

37 Wade, N. *Before the Dawn: Recovering the Lost History of Our Ancestors*, The Penguin Press, 2006.

sense of happiness. The opposite is also true: those friendless have an increased risk for heart disease, infections and cancer. Of course, these illnesses come to people with friends, too, but survival is longer and easier for those who are connected.[38,39,40]

In this tough and tumble world, don't you know, "We get by with a little help from our friends."[41]

BLUE ZONES, THE REPORTED PLACES IN THE WORLD WHERE PEOPLE LIVE THE LONGEST

The original "blue zone" research about longevity, marked by circles of blue on a map, was on the Island of Sardinia where more people on certain areas of that island survived into their nineties and even past one hundred-years-old. This was first published in *Experimental Gerontology* in 2004,[42] and since this original real scientific research, the words "blue zone" have been used to define areas of the world where people live longer. I should add, one of those blue circles goes around a region in western Minnesota and eastern South Dakota where

---

38   Yang YC, t al. Social relationships and physiological determinants of longevity across the human life span. Proceedings of the National Academy of Sciences. 2016;113:578.

39   Thoitis PA. Mechanisms linking social ties and support to physical and mental health. Journal of Health and Social Behavior. 2011;52:145.

40   www.mayoclinic.org/healthy-lifestyle/adult-health/in-depth/friendships/art-20044860

41   https://www.youtube.com/watch?v=75Oct1Qv8x0

42   Poulain M.; Pes G.M.; Grasland C.; Carru C.; Ferucci L.; Baggio G.; Franceschi C.; Deiana L. (2004). "Identification of a Geographic Area Characterized by Extreme Longevity in the Sardinia Island: the AKEA study". *Experimental Gerontology*. 39 (9): 1423–1429.

I live. I would speculate that the longevity in this region is due to the work ethic, a northern European heritage and a lifetime of vigorous activity.

Dan Buettner made the term "blue zone" popular. He is a college graduate, bicyclist, explorer and professional fundraiser; and his book, *Blue Zones: Lessons for Living Longer from the People Who've Lived the Longest,*[43] was well received. His book springboards from first-hand observations of elderly people in areas of Japan, Costa Rica, Greece and California.

The book explains that the key to living a long and healthy life results from things like performing daily moderate exercise, eating a low-calorie plant-based diet, being connected to family and community, having spiritual and purpose-driven goals and avoiding tobacco smoke. Although his words about each region are speculative and not scientifically proven, his general principles for enhancing health are generally supported by other more rigorous scientific data.[44]

A healthy lifestyle gives everyone a better chance to live a long life, but there are no guarantees. Our genetic codes have an influence over which we have no control, but experts say that genetics account for only 20 to 30 percent of the influence on life span.[45]

43   Buettner, Dan (21 April 2009) [2008]. "Contents". *The Blue Zones: Lessons for Living Longer from the People Who've Lived the Longest* (First Paperback ed.). Washington, DC: National Geographic.

44   www.nia.nih.gov/research/publication/global-health-and-aging/living-longer

45   https://www.semanticscholar.org/paper/Genetic-influence-on-human-lifespan-and-longevity-Hjelmborg-Iachine/9a59c6ddbb59e21eec09b2597a-da7d2316ffc110

We decide when to get off the couch and what we put into our mouths. Prevention is mostly about lifestyle choices.

I presented some of this "blue zone" information to our hospice committee one day just after discussing several cases of dying patients. The advice sounded hollow to this group of caregivers who provide for individuals, not populations, and for people often dying of cancer. I repeat, individual lifestyle changes do not guarantee a long life for any individual. No writer worth her or his salt should go without adding this distinction between a population versus an individual. While noting the improved longevity benefit from an active lifestyle, I believe the most important benefits of being active are better sleep, mobility and a sense of strength and well-being. Staying physically active helps us get around and feel good and should be something we do even if this doesn't give us a better chance of living longer.

So, which lifestyle advice is best? Every day there appears another study advising something which contradicts what we used to think: eat less salt, now salt more; don't eat butter, now eat butter; don't eat eggs, now eat eggs; don't exercise too much, now more; don't drink alcohol, now drink a glass of wine every day; and so on. This recalls the adage, "Do everything in moderation" (including taking advice about living longer). No question, many of us have lifestyle advice fatigue.

Bottom line: I have developed a bias in my years of practice as a general hospitalist and outpatient internist. First, I believe the core of health comes primarily from regular and significant physical activity, and I believe that point is supreme. Second, I also believe eating fewer calories is central to living longer. Third, developing social connections gives meaning and quality to life. Exercise, less food, and friendship, together, constitutes my "pound of cure."

Personally, I have developed the habit of walking a mile a day, vigorously exercising three days a week, avoiding excessive calories, steering away from smoke, staying connected to family and friends, singing in a choir and enjoying my work. Maybe I will live longer, and maybe I won't, but I don't do any of those things to live longer. I do them because they help me feel good and give me meaning.

ONE MORE THING

I would be remiss if I didn't address spiritual health at this time. One author stated clearly, "Spiritual health is that aspect of our well-being which organizes the values, the relationships, and the meaning and purpose of our lives. Patients and health-care professionals have experienced a growing recognition of the importance of spiritual health as a foundation for physical health and well-being."[46] A recent compilation of 30 surveys identified five positive characteristics of spiritual people (people searching for something sacred through religion, meditation or higher power). Spiritual people are 1) Gracious (grateful and generous), 2) Compassionate (care for others), 3) Flourishing (have self-esteem and purpose), 4) Self-actualize (try for personal improvement), 5) Take time to savor life experiences (reflect on smaller pleasures).[47]

---

46 https://www.ncbi.nlm.nih.gov/pubmed/10127982

47 https://www.psychologytoday.com/us/blog/cant-buy-happiness/201302/why-be-spiritual-five-benefits-spirituality

As I face my pancreatic cancer and high likelihood of a sooner death, I have been thinking about the younger times of my life when an innocent spirituality filled my heart, when I felt I knew my maker, when I first sensed the ethical drive to do good. Although I yearn for that clear, black and white strength of direction, what I have now is a skeptical but earnest love of this world with all of the good and bad that comes along. I am grateful for my past and current life, and I am ready for the next turn of events. (See **Chapters Eleven and Twelve.**)

An essay
Amazing medicine reverses aging

FOR A FUN ROMP about the value of exercise, go to a YouTube presentation called *23 and a half* by Dr. Mike Evans.[48] His ten-minute whiteboard visual and verbal teaching is very entertaining, full of facts and is the most powerful encouragement for activity I have ever seen. The following essay, written somewhat in the style of the late TV sales pitchman Billy Mays, is meant, not only as an overture to exercise, but also as a parody of an overpromising, almost-shouting method of sales. Although the cornball tongue-in-cheek style is a bit over the top, I believe the exercise issue is so important it warrants such a presentation!

I bet I hear, once a week, someone say, "It's hell to grow old!" Of course, growing old is something all will do unless we die first. Alas, the future can look quite sad

---

48   http://www.evanshealthlab.com/23-and-12-hours/

and depressing, especially if you think about the flab, falls, pain, blues, anxiety, thin bones, loss of libido, weakness and memory loss that can come with aging.

But wait! Listen to the exciting news. Just out! There is a powerful potion that can help prevent the aging process. That's right, guaranteed to slow aging. Researchers have observed that shortly after starting this terrific tonic, flab turns to muscle, falls are reduced, chronic pain and fibromyalgia seem magically lessened, depression and anxiety disappear, bones are strengthened, sexual function is enhanced, people experience new strength, energy, power and, most importantly, memory is magically improved.

What's more, this special medication has also been shown to reduce diabetes, heart attack, stroke and breast and colon cancer. That's not all. If you take advantage of this fabulous offer today, my plan will improve your appearance within weeks. Sounds too good to be true? My plan is scientifically proven, beyond a shadow of a doubt. And no other treatment plan comes even close. Nothing!

You would expect the price for this magnificent medication that brings about all these benefits to be more than the sum of one-third of your income, or at least many thousands, if not millions, of dollars. But no! This medicine is equally available to the rich and poor alike, requiring only an extra effort on your part.

You could expect to work many extra hours each day to achieve these wonderful benefits. But no! You don't have to work an extra two hours at the beginning or end of your workday. You don't have to work even one extra hour.

Starting today we have a special opportunity. For spending, only an extra half hour every day walking twelve blocks—yes that's right, just twelve blocks, or whatever distance you can make in 30 minutes—you will receive most of the benefits I mentioned earlier. That's right, only a half hour! But wait, this offer only lasts for a short time. The longer you delay, the less you will get. If you start today, the benefits begin sooner and last longer. That's right, guaranteed to slow aging. Exercise is the bargain of a lifetime.

One can argue this exercise message is not provided enough by physicians and care providers, yet, I believe, this is probably the most important communication physicians could provide. Changing one's lifestyle is a big challenge, but not impossible. Unfortunately, prescribing a pill is far easier than taking the time to persuade patients to change their ways of living, their activity levels and their eating habits. Care providers should know better and so should their patients.

THINGS YOU SHOULD KNOW: Q & A

Questions and Answers about:

The Hourglass—Extending the length and quality of one's life

Question: I hate walking, let alone running, biking, weight machines or stationary exercise machines. They bore me to death. I am working in my house doing all sorts of activities, and hardly sit down all day. Do I have to exercise?

You read what was written earlier about the chair or couch being as dangerous, or more dangerous, than smoking cigarettes. The sedentary lifestyle is what causes trouble, and this is, apparently, NOT your problem. If you are up cleaning, cooking, gardening, fixing, moving stuff all day long, this must be close or better than a regular exercise program.

In 2016, I collaborated with South Dakota State University researchers to develop a project involving nearly 100 seventy-year-olds, or older. They were divided into two matched categories, and, in groups of under ten, we taught people of both categories calorie counting, nutritional issues and the value of daily walking. While one group was taught stretching, balancing, hopping and strengthening exercises, the control group was simply encouraged to walk every day.

What we discovered was that when the seventy-year-old subjects pushed themselves to walk every day, after twelve weeks, they began including their spouses, and walking became an enjoyable routine. As one of our group, a retired ninety-four-year-old college professor said, "Walking makes me feel so much better. If they only knew how much better they would feel, everyone would do it."

You are already very active; however, you would benefit from more. My recommendation for you is to get started slowly and gradually increase with a goal of at least 30 minutes of walking, or whatever kind of exercise you are most likely to do daily. Try partnering with a spouse or friend. Getting out the door is much easier when held accountable by a friend. This should be in addition to your important home-based activity. If you can persist in a daily program, after three months, walking will become habit. No question, the exercise will make you feel and be so much better.

Question: If what you say about antioxidants is true, how can they state on the bottle that the supplement is an antioxidant, and how can they claim all the benefits? Isn't there a law that requires they tell the truth?

As pointed out in the September 2016 issue of *Consumer Reports*,[49] companies that produce a supplement are NOT required by the FDA, or any government agency, to prove that their supplement is safe, that the supplement works as advertised or that their package contains what the label states. Further, because of this lax policy, supplements can pose risks for contamination with bacteria or other microscopic living creatures, heavy metals, or illegal drugs, all with potential harmful side effects and dangers to consumers. Another cause for caution results from the risk that

---

49   https://www.consumerreports.org/cro/magazine/2016/09/index.htm

supplements can sometimes change the absorption or effectiveness of *prescription* medication. People too often do not realize this potential danger. *Consumer Reports* points out that each year 23,000 people end up at the emergency room (ER) as a result of problems related to taking a supplement.

The law of the land allows the manufacturer and seller to decide what is a drug and what is a supplement simply by the label and specific claims that are made. If the label states, "This product is not intended to diagnose, treat, cure, or prevent any disease . . ." then what is within is a supplement. If stated on the bottle that the product IS intended to do those things, then what is within is a drug. Something is not right when the seller, not the content of the pill, determines which is a supplement and which is a drug.

The seller of supplements can make unconfirmed claims. When you see the words "innovation," "quick cure," "miracle cure," "exclusive product," "new magical discovery," "affects structure and function" or "secret formula," you can bet you're looking at a supplement. How do the supplement companies and the pharmaceutical industry get away with this? They have the most powerful lobby in Washington, and they have effectively prevented or reduced such protections.

There is debate about when and how much we should expect of our government to regulate anything, let alone supplements. Personally, I believe that the government should protect us when there is evidence that bad characters are selling pills or supplements on false promises and that these pills or supplements are repeatedly and significantly causing harm. The 1994 Dietary Supplement and Health Education Act needs overhauling. An enforced purity and quality standard for supplements, which is at least something close to what we now have for drugs, should be enacted and enforced. In 2016, people of the U.S. spent more than $30.2 billion on vitamins and supplements.[50] **All companies providing any kind of supplement for sale should be playing by the same rules and the rules should be there to protect the consumer.**

We should expect our government to protect us from unscrupulous profiteers.[51,52] (Please also see **Chapter Two.**)

Question: I am concerned about my general health, especially since I have a bad relationship with my dysfunctional family. My father was abusive in my childhood, and my mother enabled him. Does this mean I'm going to face more health risks in general?

---

50   https://nccih.nih.gov/research/results/spotlight/americans-spend-billions

51   https://ods.od.nih.gov/factsheets/mvms-healthprofessional/

52   consumerreports.org, Consumer Reports, September 2016, pp20-33.

(Please see **Chapter Nine**.) The National Coalition for the Homeless estimates that ten million children are exposed to domestic violence every year,[53] and that children exposed to such hostility grow up to be three to four times more likely to become abusive, or to be abused, than people raised in families without it. Not all of those ten million growing up with dysfunctional families go on to face abuse or mental and physical health troubles. While one in three abused children grow up to become abusive, two in three do not.

You cannot go back in time and undo the abuse heaped on you as a child, but please realize that the abuse was not your fault. You don't have to let that part of your past bring you down. The most important health risk you face, or your family faces, is from abuse. Additionally, you are at risk for posttraumatic stress syndrome and all the psychological problems that can follow.

Realize, if you are an adult, you chose your own path. You can forgive and make time to be with your dysfunctional parents. You can also inform them that you will choose to avoid visiting unless they make their home more emotionally comfortable when you visit. Remember that the definition of domestic violence and abuse is, "negative control of one person by another in any relationship by means of physical,

53 https://www.goodhousekeeping.com/life/relationships/a37005/statistics-about-domestic-violence/

sexual, emotional or economic abuse." You are not abusing your parents when you make rules about fair play when you are visiting.

Most importantly, you should endeavor to make the family, created by you and your spouse or partner, one of shared responsibility, unconditional love and fair discipline. My favorite book[54] on parenting advises teaching children by example, especially by how you treat your partner. All the rest is minimally important. Supporting your partner with respect and fairmindedness teaches your children how to treat others and provides for a mentally healthy home. Overall health is deeply affected by abuse, so make every effort to make your home safe for all family members. After that is secure, then consider safely reconciling with your parents.

---

54   Nolte DL, Harris R. Children Learn What They Live. May 1998, Workman Publishing Co.

Chapter Two

Drugs, Supplements and all those Side Effects

Truth about the dangers of medicines and supplements

Case Study:
The case of the falling elderly woman with a broken hip

AS A KID IN COUNTRY SCHOOL, she ran faster than others, fell a lot but always was able to pick herself up. This active, happy, young woman seemed to have perpetually skinned knees. She stayed busy and active her entire life until retirement and arthritis settled in and movement became markedly reduced. Now in her eighties, she's been falling again, but this time it's not from playing hard. Falls started happening after medications were prescribed for a leaky bladder. This added another drug to her already long medication list including pills for blood pressure and chronic pain. She had asked her doctor for the bladder pills after seeing the advertisements on TV. Before she knew it, between late-night TV advertisements, the encouragement of her daughter and the enthusiasm of a supplement store sales person, the pill count mounted as did the side effects.

No surprise! She fell in the bathroom, couldn't get up and remained there until a neighbor checked on her many hours later. Too many medications resulted in dropping blood pressure whenever she stood, resulting in a fall and a broken hip. Following surgical repair and recovery time in the hospital, she moved to a long-term care facility (nursing home) and lived there the rest of her life. Others had come into the nursing home with a fractured hip, embraced rehabilitation, recovered and were able to go home. Countless others were able to live many years in their home without a fracture because they got off the couch, took walks in the neighborhood, stretched daily, swam at the local pool and (this is the important point) avoided too many pills. Moderate exercise is essential in order to avoid falls and fractured hips, and so is the avoidance of pills that have side effects.

Advertisements that encourage yet another pill have powerfully influenced the prescribing of too many medicines. They have also pushed the use of brand-name medicines when generics would be cheaper and would work equally well. With more medicines come more side effects. In my opinion, drug and supplement advertisements (and the excessive prescribing that has followed), have resulted in much more harm than good. I was practicing medicine before this kind of promotion was allowed, and I saw firsthand how drug advertisements negatively affected the health of my patients. We are one of two countries in the world that allows direct-to-consumer advertisement for medications,[55] and, in my opinion, nothing good has resulted from this "freedom".

---

55   http://knowledge.wharton.upenn.edu/article/prescription-drug-ads/

The pharmaceutical industry does this because advertisements and promotions sell drugs. You can't blame them. Last year the entire pharmaceutical industry (pharma or big-pharma) spent more than $4 billion in the U.S. promoting their drugs directly to consumers. Add to that the promotion they aimed at health care professionals, and the total, in 2016, reached $23.3 billion spent for advertising and promoting drugs in the U.S.[56]

Remember that the goal of direct-to-consumer pharmaceutical advertisements is to get you to ask your doctor to prescribe their pill. Your doctor or care provider simply wants you to get better and also wants you to be happy, and so, too often she or he prescribes the requested pills. You may ask about a medicine you see advertised, but, please, NEVER push for it. Tell the care provider not to prescribe it unless it is necessary. This goes for supplements and vitamins, too, as global sales of herbal and dietary supplements reached $132 billion in 2016 and are growing rapidly.[57] (More about these later in this chapter.)

Bottom line: Don't be influenced by advertisements for pills, don't push your care provider for them, realize the dangers and side effects from drugs and supplements and realize that too many medicines compound the dangers.

---

56   https://www.statista.com/statistics/470460/pharmaceutical-preparations -industry-ad-spend-usa/

57   https://globenewswire.com/news-release/2017/01/11/905073/0/en/Global- Dietary-Supplements-Market-will-reach-USD-220-3-Billion-in-2022-Zion -Market-Research.html

PILLS CAUSING SPILLS AND BROKEN HIPS

More than one-third of Americans older than sixty-five experience a fall at least once every year with nearly two million of them ending up in the emergency room for injuries due to those falls.[58] Once in the emergency room (ER), 30 percent of patients who've had a fall are admitted to the hospital for evaluation, bone fracture care or head trauma care, either because they have a problem that caused them to fall or have a problem resulting from the fall. Falls by the elderly commonly cause fractured vertebrae, wrists, hips, legs and arms and can also cause brain damage. The mean age of those visiting the ER for fall-related incidents is seventy-nine, and most are women (76 percent).

More than 300,000 people over sixty-four years old need major surgery every year because of hip fractures. Unfortunately, 25 percent of them, even those who were healthy prior to the fall, die within a year, most frequently from blood clots or pneumonia related to the fracture. About 20 percent of those with new hip fractures, who were previously living in the community, must move into a permanent nursing home. Chances of fracturing a hip doubles every five years after the age of fifty; so, by ninety, one in four women and one in eight men will have had a hip fracture. Fall-related injuries, such as hip fractures, cost our society billions of dollars every year ($50 billion in 2015),[59] not to mention the physical and emotional cost to

---

58   https://www.aafp.org/afp/2000/0401/p2159.html

59   https://www.cdc.gov/homeandrecreationalsafety/falls/fallcost.html

the individual who must endure the pain and disability resulting from the accident.[60,61]

A gentleman who required long-term care after a fall. He said he appreciated the care. [62]

Falls are more common in the elderly for many reasons. People in this age group are especially sensitive to medications which can potentially make them less steady. Older people also have slower reflexes, balance problems, reduced muscle strength, poorer vision and are more often plagued by generalized illnesses. With age comes a higher incidence of neurological conditions such as stroke, Parkinson's disease and decreased mental alertness, all of which increase the probability of falling. Alcohol consumption, by people of any age, decreases reaction times, contributes to balance problems and induces people to take risks that can lead to falls. However, for the elderly, the consequences of a drunken stumble can be much more severe.

Fall prevention begins with reducing pill numbers and increasing exercise. Naturally, it's not quite that simple. Medications

60   ncbi.nim.nih.gov

61   Ther Adv Drug Saf. 2013 Aug:4(4): 147–154

62   With permission from patient, from private collection, 2015

for anxiety, high blood pressure (HBP) and pain are just a few commonly prescribed medicines **which can cause fatigue** and can make even moderate exercise seem like too tall an order. Add to that, this irony: sustained moderate exercise can keep the conditions at bay (anxiety, HBP and pain) which were why the pills were prescribed in the first place. It can be a complicated vicious cycle and reminds us that exercise, as a natural part of our life, is critical to healthy aging.

Whatever the cause, too often elderly people are not exercising and not stressing their bones. This results in weakness and a softening of the skeletal structure making these individuals at a higher risk for a fracture. Studies show that exercise, **not a pill or a shot,** is the best way to prevent falls because it improves balance and reaction time, all the while making bones stronger.

Of course, strong bones are built by a combination of bone stress from exercise, like walking, running or weight exercises, and enough vitamin D (2000 International Units or IUs of vitamin D3/day) to help calcium be absorbed from the food we eat. This cannot be repeated enough: aside from vitamin D, there is no medication or supplement that can come close to exercise in strengthening bones and preventing fractures. (More on this later.)

Although there are some studies that support calcium supplementation, there are some that show **increased long-term risk of vascular disease following the use of a calcium supplement. I encourage calcium-rich food but not calcium tablets** even in those people with osteopenia or osteoporosis. I also recommend a blood test for a calcium level and a vitamin D level if there are signs of thin bones. I repeat a calcium level once every year-to-five years, especially if one is taking calcium supplements.

The risk of stumbling and falling also increases in the presence of loose rugs, cluttered floors, poor lighting, exposed electrical cords and stairs with no handrails. Everyone should do what they can to change risk factors for falls among themselves or their loved ones, especially as aging occurs. (see **Chapter Three.**)

Let me say it again, the most powerful way to prevent problems in the elderly is to prevent or stop overmedication (polypharmacy). Despite this proven truth, the number of medications prescribed for the elderly seems to be increasing every year. One reason for too many medications results from government and health insurance rulemakers who evaluate the quality of care by how care providers are following protocols, many of which add another pill. Protocols for treating a certain condition are like recipes for baking a cake and are developed with the good intention of bringing the quality of care across the country up to the best level that science knows.

However, I believe many of these protocols are misdirected. Medical conditions have too many variables to be contained in one universal recipe; textbook medical conditions are always unique to the individual and the circumstance. Physicians and other care providers may benefit from knowing or learning about a standard protocol but should **always tailor it or toss it** according to the unique situation happening before them. Unfortunately, protocols have become more than a recipe to consider and tailor, they have become required, and have become a misguided way to judge the quality of a care provider. More than that, the quality of the protocols themselves may not always be so good.

According to a *Mayo Clinic Proceedings* report January 2014,[63] 11 percent of those protocols, also called clinical practice guidelines, written by physician committees, were based on level A data meaning there was very good scientific data to support the guideline. Here is the problem: the rest were based on level B or C (mediocre or poor) scientific data. That means **89 percent of the protocols directing care in this country are based on mediocre to poor scientific data.** Even worse, **at least 45 percent of the physician experts, developing treatment with prescription medicine guidelines, had recorded five or more conflicts of interest involving the pharmaceutical industry. Thus, almost half of the people developing these guidelines were being incentivized by Big Pharma to encourage care providers to prescribe another pill.** Sadly, there is no reason for this to have improved since the study was conducted in 2014. I believe the pharmaceutical industry is the dominant culprit in the continual encouragement of care providers to prescribe more drugs. Following protocols, a method used to define the "quality of care provided by a health professional", often requires adding another drug. Therein lies the rub.

If I have a criticism of my profession, it is that we are guilty of overprescribing medications. "Polypharmacy," which literally means "many drugs," has become a popular new word in the geriatrics literature because of the problems that can result from too many pills. Despite the push of the pharmaceutical industry, prescribing care providers must take the responsibility for patients

---

63   http://www.mayoclinicproceedings.org/article/S0025-6196(13)00872-0/fulltext

being on too many medicines. Well-meaning care providers add medicines in response to protocols or to each new complaint and forget (or are reluctant) to take away the old ones. No question, geriatric studies show we are overprescribing opioids, other pain medicines, antibiotics, blood pressure medicines, antianxiety medicines, sleeping pills and major tranquilizers. Often a new drug is prescribed to treat the side effects that are the result of a previously prescribed drug. A better answer would be to simply stop the first drug.

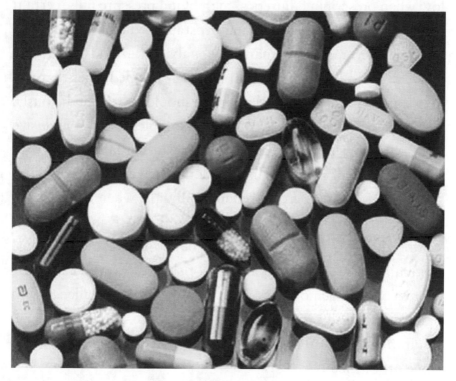

Pills[64]

64   Photo by RayNata from https://commons.wikimedia.org/w/index.php?title=User:RayNata&action=edit&redlink=1

More than 20 percent of people over fifty-five years of age are taking more than four prescription medications, and the numbers climb dramatically in older populations. During my medical career, I often inherited patients who were taking fifteen drugs or more. I was amazed at how often a patient would tell me they felt better after I reduced their medications.

My personal experience has taught me to **avoid** prescribing any benzodiazepine-type sleeping pills and most urinary incontinence medicines. I am **very watchful** for the blood pressure dropping too low when prescribing diuretics, high blood pressure pills, certain heart medicines, alpha-blocking prostate medicines, digoxin (a heart rhythm medicine), narcotics, gabapentin and pregabalin (Lyrica).[65] The last two drugs are antiseizure medicines that can help some with neuro-based pain but should be used judiciously. The drugs listed above are common examples and not inclusive of all the drugs that have potential for causing falls.

One study of people living in a long-term care facility found that there was a 66 percent reduction in falls when benzodiaze-pines (benzos) or benzo-active medicines (like Ativan or Ambien) were reduced or stopped.[66] These benzo-active medications, originally designed to treat anxiety or sleep disorders, can cause depression and memory loss. However, the biggest challenge with benzo-active medications is that when they are stopped, they will result in withdrawal anxiety, and therefore, many people never come off of them.

---

65   Please note that generic meds (e.g., pregabalin) will not be capitalized and brand names will be capitalized (e.g., Lyrica).

66   https://www.stayonyourfeet.com.au/health-professionals/what-works-to-reduce-falls/check-your-medicines/

If a patient is experiencing chronic stress and anxiety, and nonmedicinal antianxiety efforts are not enough, antidepressants in the selective serotonin reuptake inhibitors (SSRIs) group or the Serotonin and Norepinephrine reuptake inhibitors (SNRIs) group may be more helpful (along with exercise). Examples of the SSRIs include sertraline (Zoloft) or fluoxetine (Prozac) and examples of the SNRIs include duloxetine (Cymbalta) or venlafaxine (Effexor). If nonmedicinal sleeping aids fail, and a sleeping medication is still indicated, mirtazapine (Remeron) or trazodone (both nonbenzos) can help. These are closer to being in the antidepressant group and not in the benzo-active group. I believe that there is rarely a place for the long-term use of benzodiazepines, especially in the elderly. Don't hesitate to speak to your care provider about alternatives. Realize the difficulty in getting off the benzo-active medications.

Also, beware of over-the-counter medicines which contain diphenhydramine (Benadryl) due to their significant side effects in older patients. Over-the-counter melatonin is a naturally occurring brain hormone that usually rises at bedtime and is safer than other sleep aids. Take it about two hours before bedtime,[67] and read the reference from Johns Hopkins' health letter.[68] One can take Benadryl for occasional sleeplessness, but stop it if you don't find improvement, and don't use it if you are pregnant, breastfeeding, have an autoimmune disorder (like rheumatoid arthritis), seizure disorder or are depressed.

67

68 https://www.hopkinsmedicine.org/health/healthy-sleep/sleep-science/melatonin-for-sleep-does-it-work

Don't get me wrong, medications can be very helpful for many conditions. Medication lists should be carefully reviewed at every health care visit, especially after any fall. The advantages of medicines must always be balanced with the risks. Pills can cause spills and can result in broken bones. Talk to your doctor. **Ask if there are any pills that could be stopped, but please don't stop them on your own. Let this begin a conversation with your care provider about avoiding polypharmacy.**

In summary, there are many reasons for increased falling in an older adult. Better to take appropriate precautions and stay standing rather than find yourself on the ground unable to pick yourself up.

TAKE-HOME MESSAGES:

1. Falls in the elderly cost individuals and society a lot of suffering.
2. There are many reasons for falls, but family and physicians should start with the possibility that medications could be the cause.
3. Every effort to prevent falls (and polypharmacy) should be taken and should be tailored to the individual.
4. In the end, probably the best way to protect yourself or your loved one is to find an internist, family physician or another care provider whom you trust. Do NOT stop any of your medications on your own, but never hesitate to ask if some medications could be reduced.

THE STORY OF INDIAN HEALTH, HERBAL WISDOM, THE GROWTH OF THE PHARMACEUTICAL INDUSTRY, AND QUACKERY IN THE U.S.

There is a long history of America's love affair with medications. In his historical text, *Frontier Medicine,*[69,70] author and historian David Dary described how western Europe and European Americans in the 1600s and 1700s came to almost worship medicine. It started with the assumption that the superb health of American Indians resulted from their understanding of the healing properties of the natural flora and fauna of the Americas. This misleading mind-set was given credence by the Indian knowledge of a few truly effective herbal therapies like cinchona bark for malaria and willow bark for fever. Dary points out that these herbal therapies were taken to Europe, developed further and their use in Europe spread and spurred the development of the world pharmaceutical industry.

As valuable as these new medicines could be, herbal therapies were not the central reason for the fabulous physical health of the prereservation American Indian. John Wesley, who started the Methodist Church in England, and who was visiting for a short time in the Americas, described the vigorous physical activity required to live in the wilderness. He correctly surmised this as the reason for the superb health of American Indians. Many have also speculated that the hunter-gatherer diet of vegetables, fruit and lean wild meat was another factor

---

69   Frontier Medicine, From the Atlantic to the Pacific, 1492–1941 by David Dary. Knopf, 2008.

70   Holm RP: JAMA Book Review of Frontier Medicine, From the Atlantic to the Pacific, 1492–1941, by David Dary. JAMA 2010 Jan, 20; 303 (3); 3–4.

in the early American Indian's remarkable physical condition, and I would agree.

John Wesley portrait from the University of Texas Library, Utopia Portrait Gallery[71]

People wanted to believe there was an easier medicinal way to achieve wellness which would allow the avoidance of all that native-lifestyle work. This trend of thought encouraged Americans and Europeans to develop patent medicines. It is interesting to note that traveling medicine shows of the 1800s moved about the country selling unproven herbal and alcohol-based concoctions. These wagons of vagabond salesmen often had some person dressed in Indian garb as a pretense that their bogus product was a credible American Indian herb. Patent medicine concoctions of the time included Kickapoo (Joy Juice,) Hamlin's Wizard Oil, Grove's Chill Tonic, Lydia Pinkham's herb medicine and the first two nonalcoholic, or "soft," health tonics we know now as Dr. Pepper and Coca-Cola. It is disquieting, but believable, that Coca-Cola, which originally contained cocaine, was sold as a tonic to improve one's health.

---

71   From the U.S. Public Domain, from https://commons.wikimedia.org/wiki/File:Wesley.jpg

Driven by the profit motive of the supplement and pharmaceutical industries, we seem to have completely swallowed the almost magical hope that to beget good health an easy pill can replace physical activity and the effort it requires. No pill will do. The same misdirection has infiltrated standard health care education and protocols where medicines are pushed instead of lifestyle changes.

This is NOT a call to all older people, or the younger people who are caring for them, to stop any prescribed medicines without first consulting their care provider. However, it IS a call to encourage care providers, patients and families of an elderly person to consider the use of fewer medications, especially when alternatives—such as exercise and dietary changes—are available.

David Dary's *Frontier Medicine* was a book that covered many more historical American medical topics worthy of discussion, and I highly recommend it.

PRESCRIPTION MEDICATIONS, TRUE AND FALSE PROMISES

No question, the people of this country and era expect medications and supplements to provide a shortcut solution for almost any problem. Why wouldn't people think this way? There are miraculous cures from certain medicines: antibiotics reduce infections in people who would otherwise die; antidepressants return people from a world of black-and-white to one of color; gastrointestinal acid-blocking medicines allow people to swallow easily rather than suffer from intolerable reflux. What people only 100 years ago would consider miracles are now treated with modern medicine, but have we come to expect too much?

The anticipation that prescription pills are effective has spread to vitamins and supplements. One-half of all Americans take a daily multivitamin, and one in five take herbal supplements. Like the comic book characters of the '50s, Donald Duck's nephews, Huey, Dewey and Louie, learned from their Junior Woodchuck Manual that taking special vitamins would allow them to accomplish some challenge without having to stop for food or any sustenance. That is comic book thinking! Food is the best source of most vitamins.

Hucksters are not new. There have been unethical people who have taken advantage of others since the dawn of time. In ancient Greece, there were salespersons at the Temples of Asclepius who would lure rich and desperate people to their island of healing. After a payment, the perpetrators would sedate the sick with a medication that would bring about a deep sleep with wild dreams and hallucinations. When awakened, the ill realized something almost magical had happened. Keepers of the temple would then provide comfort and entertainment while convincing their patients that they were getting better. Historians believe that the success of the Asclepius temples resulted mostly from the placebo effect.

For a modern take on false promises, turn on morning news shows, the evening news or late-night TV, and you will be bombarded with infomercials promising miracle cures. Also, in an almost comic-book-way, we think there is a pill to restore hair, to reduce weight and to reverse aging if only we send in our money. It turns out that hope is extremely profitable. Even though people suspect they might be hearing a false promise, they become lured in by the second false promise of a special money-back guarantee. What is even more frustrating to science-based physicians and care providers is the profit-driven and minimally helpful motivations coming from within our own scientific and pharmaceutical community. All physicians and pharmaceutical companies should have the same ethical promise to do good, do not do harm, be honest and respect choices. Money should not be the driver.

Island of Kos, ancient Temple of Asclepius[72]

It has come to this: the responsibility to dissect out the truth is on us, the public/patients. Dishonest people will always find a way around regulations. People need to learn to know the difference between science and sales. We must be careful to look with a critical eye at everything we see and hear, especially when

---

72　photographer: Heiko Gorski (Moonshadow), from https://commons.wikimedia.org/wiki/File:Kos_Asklepeion.jpg

something seems too good to be true or is obviously promotional and highly profitable. Use common sense. When that little red flag goes up, research the issue on reputable Internet sites and talk to your doctor or care provider who isn't profiting from selling that same product.

Bottom line: We must learn to know the difference between science and marketing, even when the advertisements sound like they come from the scientific world. Be aware, careful, skeptical and ask questions.

VITAMINS AND MINERAL SUPPLEMENTS, TRUE AND FALSE PROMISES

Americans spend close to **$35 billion a year on underregulated supplements, pills, powders or patches.** There are great benefits gained from taking vitamins, minerals and nutrients; however, for the most part, that which most of us need is found in food. There is a rich history of how scientists, investigating malnutrition, discovered the value and importance of vitamins (micronutrients). For example, vitamin C deficiency was discovered when scientists were trying to understand what caused scurvy. This is a deadly illness that results in profound weakness and lethargy, gum deterioration, hair changes and bleeding into the skin. Scurvy-riddled sailors, of all countries, would be out to sea for months at a time. The British sailors had a huge advantage over others starting in the mid-1700s when Dr. James Lind determined that citrus fruit containing vitamin C could help the British "Limeys" avoid scurvy. It worked and subsequently England won many more battles on the sea.[73]

Vitamin B1 (thiamine) deficiency was discovered while analyzing why a neurodegenerative illness called beriberi affected Japanese sailors. This occurred after those providing the food for sailors switched from brown rice to white. By removing the brown coating, the Japanese unknowingly removed the vitamin B1-laden protein coat. In the early 1900s, scientists discovered it was thiamine in the rice coating (they called it the "vital amine") that would prevent beriberi, and now all white rice is fortified with thiamine. It is interesting to note that "vital amine" is the origin for the word vitamin.

Micromineral iodine deficiency was discovered while analyzing why goiter (a thyroid enlargement condition) and cretinism (a childhood condition of mental deficiency) both occurred in landlocked areas in the world. Epidemiologists (those who study diseases in populations) realized that people suffering from goiter and cretinism were low in iodine due to a lack of exposure to iodine-rich seaweed and deep-sea fish in their diet. Scientific studies showed that by iodizing salt these debilitating conditions can be prevented in millions of people and children throughout the world. The similar condition of vitamin D deficiency has been countered with the addition of small and safe doses of Vitamin D to most dairy products. (However, even with Vitamin D-fortified milk, many of us may still need an extra vitamin D supplement.)

Too much of a good thing, of certain vitamins and minerals, can be as bad, possibly worse, than too little. Scientists discovered

---

73 https://askabiologist.asu.edu/explore/sailors-called-limeys

that **elevated doses** of iodine and other minerals, as well as the fat-soluble vitamins A, D and E, can be dangerous. As defined by *Consumer Reports*,[74] certain doses of certain supplements, which include chaparral, coltsfoot, comfrey and yohimbine can cause liver damage, heart trouble and an increased risk of cancer. Obviously, the whole nutritional supplement story is very complicated. Before starting any supplement, you should talk to your physician or care provider. Any research about supplements should come from a reliable source **that is not selling the product.** Examples of excellent and reliable sources are the National Library of Medicine[75] and *Consumer Reports*.[76] We should be skeptical about any research which comes from the seller of the supplement. Remember that there is a big difference between evidence-based science and marketing. A balanced diet with enough fish, nuts, fruits and vegetables should supply all of us enough of those needed vitamins, minerals and nutrients.

In 2011, the "Iowa's Women's Health Study"[77] occurred where more than 38,000 women older than twenty were asked for information about their supplement use from 1986 through 2008. After 22 years in the study, researchers noted a slight increase in the death rate of those taking a daily multivitamin and an iron supplement when compared to those who took neither.[78] I should repeat that I have stopped encouraging women to take calcium

74   consumerreports.org, Consumer Reports, September 2016, pp20-33

75   medlineplus.gov

76   consumerreports.org

77   Arch Intern Med. 2011 Oct 10;171(18):1625–33

78   http://www.ncbi.nlm.nih.gov/pubmed/21987192

supplements because, in the same "Women's Study", there were increased heart attacks and strokes in those having had long-term calcium supplements. Although other research data are mixed (some good, some bad), I encourage good calcium intake **by a food source** and not by supplement.

After reading this study, I believe that multivitamins are of no help for most of us except when used by those who are malnourished or pregnant. On the other hand, I believe there are enough data to support regular use of vitamin D, and, if neurological symptoms, vitamin B12. For those living north of the 41st parallel (north of Omaha, Nebraska), we simply do not have enough sun from fall equinox to spring equinox to provide for our vitamin D needs. (Other places on about the same latitude of Omaha include Chicago, Illinois, Providence, Rhode Island, the Northern border of California and Pennsylvania.) For those north of Omaha, I recommend taking 800 to 2000 international units (IU) of vitamin D3 (cholecalciferol) on a daily basis for at least six months out of every year. (I take 2000 IU daily 12 months out of the year.) I also often advise taking 1000 micrograms (mcg) of vitamin B12 on a daily basis when neurologic symptoms are present or measured levels of the vitamin are low. Examples of neurologic symptoms for low B12 levels would include numbness, weakness, walking trouble and confusion. Other nonneurologic symptoms would include paleness, anemia, swollen tongue and jaundice.

Bottom line: The best plan should be to exercise daily; eat a balanced diet with enough fish, nuts, fruits and vegetables; take vitamin B12 if you are troubled with any neurological symptoms; take vitamin D3 for at least the darkest six months of the year, especially if you live north of Omaha. Also, maybe you should think twice about joining the British or Japanese Navy!

PAIN RELIEVERS AND ALCOHOL

Pain relievers or painkillers are some of the most commonly consumed medications in the U.S. These range from common over-the-counter (OTC) medicines like aspirin, ibuprofen (Motrin, Advil), naproxen (Aleve, Naprosyn) and acetaminophen (Tylenol) to the prescription opioids such as hydrocodone with acetaminophen (Vicodin, Narco, Lortab), oxycodone with acetaminophen (Percocet), hydrocodone alone (OxyContin) and many more. Information about opioids (narcotics and opiates) and cannabis (marijuana) has been placed in this chapter because caregivers, dealing with a patient, and people, dealing with pain, need to be aware of the uses and the potential dangers of such medicines. I include alcohol in this category because of its addictive nature and its common and incorrect use to escape emotional pain.

Opioids (Narcotics)

By definition, the word narcotic comes from the Greek word for "stupor" (dulled senses). The broad definition of "narcotics" (drugs that cause a person to act drunk or stuporous) includes the words opiate and opioid. The word opiate means the drug was processed from the white tears of scored opium poppy fruit (opium, codeine, morphine and heroin). The term opioid was originally defined as a synthetic opiate but now has come to mean the entire class of drugs, replacing the older term narcotic.

Opioids are legal prescription pain medicines which include codeine, morphine, oxycodone, hydrocodone, fentanyl and tramadol. All these alone, or in combination with heroin, meth-amphetamine, cocaine and other mind-altering drugs, are illegally sold on the black market. Opium-like medicines are remarkably effective in treating the cramping pain that happens when a smooth muscle tube is blocked. This type of pain happens when natural peristalsis (like squeezing a toothpaste tube) is trying to push material down any blocked smooth muscle tube in our bodies. The abdomen is chock full of organs that are smooth muscle tubes, and, when something goes wrong and blocks one of these tubes, there will be severe, cramping, abdominal pain associated with nausea and vomiting that is mercifully relieved by an opioid. Examples of such problems include a stone in the kidney, ureter (tube from kidney to bladder), urinary bladder or urethra (tube from bladder to outside); adhesions or tumor blockage in the esophagus, stomach, small intestine, appendix, large intestine, gallstones in a bile duct or gallbladder; an ectopic pregnancy (the fertilized egg is implanted in a fallopian tube rather than the uterus) or even a mature baby ready for birth within a uterus (peristalsis is trying to move the baby out). All these smooth muscle tubes cause severe, cramping and nauseating pain when they are blocked, and peristalsis is not able to move the contents down the tube.

It is important to understand that this is the type of pain most effectively treated by opioids since the fruit of the poppy not only provides some intrinsic pain relief but also slows down peristalsis. Opioids block parasympathetic activity by reducing tears and saliva and slowing the movement of all smooth muscle tubes. Parasympathetic activity is the opposite of sympathetic activity (fight or flight). Parasympathetic activity encourages the "rest and digest" or "feed and breed" activities. When it is time to relax after a tough day, enjoy a nice meal, digest food and get the juices flowing; the parasympathetic system kicks in. When an opioid is taken, it blocks that parasympathetic action, tears and saliva dry up and all the smooth muscle tubes slow down. Constipation, for example, is a common side effect of the action of opioids.

Poppy flowers Lake Poinsett Spring 2015[79]

Care providers, caregivers and patients alike need to know that opioids may reduce or take away the pain of the obstruction of a smooth muscle tube, **but they do not resolve the obstruction.** If the

---

79   Photo from a private collection

appendix is infected and obstructing the small intestine, an opioid injection will temporarily relieve the cramping pain, but then the pain medicine might delay the diagnosis. (I was taught that once the diagnosis is made, and the patient is in line for surgery, THEN provide the opioid but not before the diagnosis is made.) Be careful not to cover-up a diagnosis by providing or taking an opioid.

Also, opioids do NOT effectively provide significant relief for many other types of pain, especially long-term pain. These would include: chronic back pain, chronic headaches, joint pain and fibromyalgia. (Fibromyalgia is a widespread muscular-skeletal pain condition associated with weakness and disorders of sleep, memory and mood.)[80] When opioids are used daily, they lose effectiveness and require higher doses to get the same relief, making them a poor choice to help people with muscular-skeletal pains or for chronic pain of any type. Nonsteroidal antiinflammatory drugs (NSAIDs), like aspirin, ibuprofen (Motrin and Advil) or naproxen (Aleve) are significantly more effective than opioids for muscular-skeletal pain and would be preferred unless the person develops stomach or esophageal irritability. In addition, there are many scientific studies that show acetaminophen (Tylenol) is more effective than many believe, even though it is so safe, cheap and readily available without prescription. (That is why the pharmaceutical industry has commonly added acetaminophen to opioids.)

A recent (March 2018) study was done with 240 veterans **who had chronic pain.**[81] The subjects were treated with: 1) An

---

80   https://jamanetwork.com/journals/jama/article-abstract/2673971 ?redirect=true

81   https://jamanetwork.com/journals/jama/article-abstract/2673971

ibuprofen alone plan (Advil), 2) An acetaminophen alone plan (Tylenol), or 3) An opioid plus acetaminophen plan (Vicodin). Over the year, both nonopioid groups did equal or better in living comfortably than the opioid plus acetaminophen group and with less side effects. Every pain medicine seems to have some rebound pain when reducing the dose, including acetaminophen, and so, in my book, the intermittent use of any pain medicines is always better than the regularly scheduled method (e.g., four times a day).

We are in the middle of an opioid overuse and overdose epidemic. An estimated 16 million people in the U.S. are abusing prescription or black-market opioids including 20 percent of our high school kids. Abuse is one thing, but death is another. The Center for Disease Control and Prevention (CDC) reports more than one-half-million people suffocated to death from opioid overdose between 2000 and 2015.[82] In 2016, it is estimated that 64,000 U.S. citizens suffocated from opioid overdose.[83] One half of these deaths were from prescription medications. Additionally, three out of four heroin users were addicted initially to legal opioid pain medicines prescribed for so-called legitimate reasons. It seems that when they can no longer get a refill of the prescription pain medicine, they turn to heroin. This tragic news is troubling and uncomfortable for the healing profession as we have the prescribing pen and carry at least some responsibility for these deaths.

---

82   https://www.cdc.gov/mmwr/preview/mmwrhtml/mm6450a3.htm

83   https://www.drugabuse.gov/related-topics/trends-statistics/overdose-death-rates

This has happened during the era of the electronic medical record with progressively more government monitoring and discouragement of opioid prescribing and is an example of how oversight has been ineffective in bringing control or change. Causes for the deathly opioid epidemic are myriad. For more than twenty years, physicians have been encouraged to ask patients to rate their pain on a zero to ten scale. Again, quality parameters rate physicians, PAs and NPs poorly if not addressing the patient's pain needs, and care providers are encouraged (by protocol) to prescribe a pain medicine (or increase the dose of what the patient may already be taking). Additionally, our whole culture has been almost hypnotized by pharmaceutical advertisements telling us that the answer to every medical problem is a medicine which is obtained if you "ask your doctor." Take it from me, it is easier to prescribe a pill than to say "no" to a demanding patient.[84]

Part of the opioid epidemic results from the **diversion** of drugs. Diversion means that the person for whom the opioids were prescribed didn't get the medicine, and the opioid was moved (or diverted) to the hands of another. The elder who has an opioid pain medication is often the target for diversion, most often by a family member who steals the opioid and sells it. Those who have such prescriptions (whether elderly or not), should never advertise that they have possession of opioids and should never share them, even when others have legitimate pain. Those with prescriptions of dangerous opioids should always keep them locked up where others don't have access.

---

84 https://assets.aarp.org/rgcenter/general/prescription-drug-advertising-10.pdf

Bottom line: Physicians and patients must say "no." Treatment for chronic pain means listening to provider advice, remaining physically active, returning to function and work and, **most importantly, avoiding opioids.**

Cannabis (marijuana)

About 4,000 years ago, Chinese writings explained the medicinal powers of what is now called cannabis or marijuana, describing its ability to help arthritis, gout, malaria, nausea and psychological stress. The use of cannabis for medicinal purposes, as well as for its intoxicating/recreational effects, eventually spread to India and Persia where it was used by many cultures

especially during religious ceremonies. From there, cannabis spread to Europe during the middle ages.

Cannabis Sativa [85]

In the 1500s and 1600s the Spanish and English brought cannabis to the new world, both for medicinal purposes and for the commercial purpose of making hemp rope. In the late 1800s, cannabis lost popularity for both rope and medicinal purposes, but in the 1920s, it

---

85   Photo by Thayne Tuason from https://commons.wikimedia.org/wiki/File:Cannabis_sativa_2.jpg

reemerged in jazz clubs as a recreational drug. At the time, it was thought of as a better alternative to alcohol since cannabis users didn't seem as disruptive within the community.

During the prohibition era of the 1920s and 1930s, the U.S. Bureau of Narcotics began considering cannabis as addictive and as dangerous as alcohol. Although many people continued to utilize cannabis as a medicine, in 1942 the government made it illegal.[86] Further, under President Nixon's direction, the U.S. Controlled Substance Act of 1970 redefined cannabis as a schedule 1 drug claiming it had high abuse potential and no medical benefit. That placed it side by side with heroin and LSD (lysergic acid diethylamide). It is interesting to note that there is significant historical opinion that Nixon's "war on drugs" was politically motivated to keep both liberal antiwar people and Afro-Americans[87] locked up and unable to vote. If these historians are right, legislation that defined cannabis as a highly illegal drug, had very little, if anything, to do with an effort to help society and everything to do with politics and suppressing votes.

Although these claims about the addictive character and medicinal effect of cannabis have changed, the U.S. laws about cannabis remain on the legal books. Cannabis is still (by the Federal Government) a schedule 1 drug which makes it extremely difficult to do cannabis research. During the Obama administration, the Department of Justice was directed to relax prosecution of cannabis rule-breakers while allowing state rules to supersede

---

86   https://www.entrepreneur.com/article/296559

87   https://www.forbes.com/sites/eriksherman/2016/03/23/nixons-drug-war-an-excuse-to-lock-up-blacks-and-protesters-continues/#16ce38f242c8

the U.S. law. Since the Trump administration has taken over, that directive has been losing ground. What will happen next is undefinable as of this writing.

Questions about cannabis remain. Are there legitimate medical uses for cannabis (or any of its chemical derivatives) such as for seizures in children, chronic pain syndrome, transitioning off opioids, glaucoma, appetite stimulation in wasting diseases and nausea and malaise in cancer patients? Is it right to restrict recreational use of cannabis when we accept alcohol use in this society? If recreational use of cannabis expands, especially to our young people, will this result in long-term "physical and emotional" harms to our people and our society? If we restrict cannabis only for medicinal use, are we limiting access to cannabis for those who can't afford a physician and the increased cost of "medicinal-grade cannabis?" Would this make physicians unhappy gatekeepers for this drug, and make the cost of legitimate cannabis outrageously priced along with almost every other prescription medicine? It is not known what will happen as new U.S. and State legislators are elected, but one might guess that the legitimate use of cannabis will expand, especially as a pain reliever and an antiseizure medication.

We know there is abuse potential with cannabis, as there is with alcohol, and that driving while intoxicated with cannabis increases crashes even if less than half as much as alcohol. Also, we know excessive cannabis use dulls and injures the mind, especially in young and undeveloped minds. Would legalizing cannabis worsen or, with better laws and enhanced regulation, possibly lessen these problems?

Bottom line: Regardless of your stance on cannabis, several studies show successful medical uses of cannabis. There is a time and place for the careful use of opioids, and, I believe, there is also a time to use cannabis. It is important that you, either as a patient or as a caregiver, educate yourself on the medications that you are either taking or administering. The best way to avoid complications with any medication is to be educated.

Alcohol abuse by the elderly or by the caregiver

Why is it that alcohol will take hold of some people and not let go until it's destroyed their lives and the lives of those around them? Perhaps it has something to do with what one dear friend said, "It's amazing how the booze makes you so intelligent!"

My friend described the summer of his twenty-first year, just after returning from the jungles of the Vietnam War, when he stayed drunk all summer and then some. It was two buddies, hot cars, lots of bars, dances and fights and one or two cases of beer a night. He would drag out of bed in the morning, still drunk, go to work driving truck and then do it all over again. This destructive spiraling down cycle ended when he destroyed his car, lost his job and ran out of money. He said it took him two weeks to sober up and, only then, did he realize he'd been drunk for five months. The paradox is that the stuff that makes you feel so smart destroys your judgment. My friend put it this way: "They can't get out of it, 'cuz they don't realize they're in it."

Take this same destructive, alcoholic stranglehold and imagine it on an elderly man or woman. Overall, alcohol consumption seems to lessen some with advancing age; although, for many people, the problem persists throughout life. At least 2 percent of elderly women and 13 percent of elderly men are drinking excessively (more than two drinks a day for women and four drinks a day for men).[88] Clues to unsuspected alcohol abuse in the elderly might include: a new decline in mental function, a skipping of medications or therapies, an increase in accidents, injuries, falls, broken hips, visits to the emergency room, a worsening of gastro-intestinal problems and estrangement from the family.[89] Excessive alcohol in anyone can cause nutritional deficiencies, dementia, pneumonia and premature death. Finally, alcohol excess in elderly people will make them doubly susceptible to fraud and scams.

When the caregiver becomes a victim of alcohol, it may become harmful to those for whom they care. Everyone involved should keep a watchful eye for this scenario, including family members, the persons receiving care, the physician and the social worker. Those abusing alcohol should not be given the important responsibility of providing care and certainly should never drink on the job.

How can we help those who have succumbed to the illness of addiction to alcohol? It will take tough love while always valuing the alcoholic as a person. Don't enable the habit, don't accept it, don't tolerate it, don't live with it and, absolutely, don't provide money. A supportive family may even have to walk away for a while, but they shouldn't go too far. It's likely that those addicted

---

88   Mirand AL, Welte JW. Alcohol consumption among the elderly in a general population, Erie County, New York. *Am J Public Health*. 1996; 86:978–84

89   Rigler, Sally. University of Kansas School of Medicine, Kansas City, Kansas *Am Fam Physician*. 2000 Mar 15;61(6):1710–1716.

will soon find themselves in deep medical, emotional or financial trouble and will eventually need help.

Confront this problem with compassion and hope, respecting the autonomy and rights of the alcoholic individual. We should fully understand they are at high risk for getting themselves back into trouble again. If you drink, protect yourself from the risk of addiction and slipping into gradually higher doses of this dangerous drug and the habits that follow. Seek help from a physician, contact a treatment center, talk with a pastor or call Alcoholics Anonymous (AA) (they're in the phone book). Helping people of any age, or yourself, with an alcohol problem is one of life's greatest challenges. Don't give up.

An essay
Good medicine

THE OTHER DAY an eighty-year-old ill woman came into my office visiting from another state, and, as I was asking her a lot of questions about her symptoms, she said, "Could I get off some of my pills? I take too many," and I agreed with her. We stopped ten of the fourteen she was taking. When I saw her two weeks later, she was clearly feeling better, realized some of her problems came from the pills and told me I was a good doctor. True story.

We live in a pill-taking society. Some of this probably results from the human tendency to try and find an easier way to do things. If we have a choice whether to walk or ride to work, we will likely ride. If we have a choice whether to exercise or take a pill to lower blood pressure, we will likely take the pill. A pill is easier than a lifestyle change.

Clearly drug companies work very hard to convince doctors and patients that drugs work for almost every ailment. Think about how providers are asked by patients to solve a new problem each time and how simple and pleasing it can be to give a pill to satisfy the patient's needs. We have a culture with an inclination to overrely on drugs and overplay their benefits, but, what is worse, we underplay their risks. This is a fact: the more drugs, the higher the likelihood for a significant side effect or a dangerous interaction between medicines.

However, sometimes we have no choice, and certain medical illnesses just call for a number of medicines. It often takes three or four drugs to get blood pressure down, to control a diabetic person's blood sugars and to help a weakened heart continue pumping. If you happen to struggle with a combination of these or other conditions, you can sometimes end up taking a smorgasbord of pills, and there is no way to reduce the pill count.

I am not saying that all medicines are bad, and I'm not encouraging you to stop taking your medicines without careful direction by your doctor. However, the next time you see your provider, ask her or him to review the pills you take and, if possible, try to get the number down. That would be good medicine.

THINGS YOU SHOULD KNOW

Questions and Answers:
Drugs, Supplements, and all those Side Effects—Truth about the dangers of medicines and supplements

Question: I am a seventy-year-old man on three pills for diabetes, three for congestive heart failure, a baby aspirin to prevent stroke, a vitamin D3 2000 IU capsule (since my doctor found that I had a low vitamin D blood level), and Miralax periodically for constipation. Is this polypharmacy? Are you saying I should stop all or some of these pills?

The answer is NO! despite your multiple medicines. Diabetes and heart failure often require a lot of medicine. In no way am I suggesting you should stop any medicines. **I repeat: Do NOT stop any medicine without your care provider's direction.** However, it is a good idea to make your opinions known to your clinician. In your case, it doesn't look like there will be any easy reductions unless it would be in the diabetes field.

Unfortunately, the patient or family is often the driving force that pushes for more medication. Please be a force for less medicine. Again, at every visit be prepared to discuss each prescribed or nonprescribed medication with the care provider.

———⌘———

Question: What medicines best help people with chronic pain?

Of course, every situation is different, but, in this country and in this era, care providers prescribe far too many pain medicines, often combining opioids (narcotics) with acetaminophen (Tylenol) and a muscle relaxer. Unfortunately, when this happens, the pain medicines often provide inadequate help for the person in need. We simply expect way too much from these pills and expect far too little from self-directed and nonpharmacologic remedies such as activity, exercise and physical therapy.[90]

I would add that people who have pains that last longer than twelve weeks and have an unclear cause often may have a poor response to therapy (chronic pain syndrome).[91] Antidepressants (SSRIs and SNRIs) and antiseizure medicines (gabapentin, Neurontin, Lyrica) can help; however, either group of medications **only work for people with chronic pain syndrome if those people are also exercising**. It would be best if physical therapy, activity, meditation, massage and hands-on manipulation were always provided. Experts are recommending that small doses of nonopioid, nonmind-altering, over-the-counter ibuprofen (Motrin or Advil), acetaminophen (Tylenol) or a combination be utilized.

90   https://www.ninds.nih.gov/Disorders/All-Disorders/Chronic-Pain-Information-Page

91   https://medlineplus.gov/magazine/issues/spring11/articles/spring11pg5-6.html

Especially in an elderly person with chronic pain, I would completely avoid dipping into the world of opioids (hydrocodone, oxycodone, tramadol) and muscle relaxants (baclofen, carisoprodol/Soma, cyclobenzaprine/Flexeril, methocarbamol/Robaxin, orphenadrine/Norflex). Opioids and muscle relaxants reduce alertness and memory, are habit forming and may even perpetuate pain. They will also increase the incidence of falling. Some people have chronic pain regardless of what is prescribed or what the individual does. In these situations, the use of medications does far too little to reduce the pain and far too much to increase the chance of untoward side effects. Living with pain, being physically active and moving on with life all remain the best options available.

David Hanscom, MD, orthopedic surgeon, in his book **Back in Control**,[92] advises that a person with chronic pain syndrome should write down free thoughts, any thoughts whatsoever, for 15 minutes once or twice a day as an effective method to relieve pain. In a recent radio interview, Dr. Hanscom stated that this method works, not because the content of the writing is organized or even readable, but rather because the writing releases some inner self-anger or turmoil. Hanscom says that, with his method, people often find relief from suffering when other methods fail. I think that there is

92   https://www.amazon.com/Back-Control-Surgeons-Roadmap-Chronic/dp/0988272997/ref=sr_1_1?ie=UTF8&qid=1522424746&sr=8-1&keywords=back+in+control+by+david+hanscom

hope in this idea, and it might be worth buying his book if you are suffering from chronic pain and not finding help. (For more about opioids go to **Chapter Seven.**)

———

Question: What supplements and medications do you regularly prescribe?

You may have guessed, I am a physician with a fairly conservative style when prescribing medicines. I believe nonmedicinal efforts should be tried first, when appropriate. When medications might be significantly helpful, we know there are those that can be safely used in the geriatric population. These medications should be carefully selected according to the need of the individual. Here are specific classes of medications that I will prescribe for the elderly, but, like any medicine, these need to be monitored carefully.

1. **Anticoagulants (blood thinners):** Warfarin, an anticoagulant, works to prevent the hidden killer pulmonary emboli (blood clots to the lung) and other clotting problems. It is less expensive, equally effective, reversible and allows for more effective monitoring than the newer anticoagulants.[93,94]

---

93   https://www.uptodate.com/contents/direct-oral-anticoagulants-and-par-enteral-direct-thrombin-inhibitors-dosing-and-adverse-effects?search=an-ticoagulation&source=search_result&selectedTitle=1~150&usage_type=de-fault&display_rank=1

94   https://www.ncbi.nlm.nih.gov/pmc/articles/PMC4711523/

These medicines can be critical in preventing stroke, heart attack and blood clots to the lung, and are, therefore, lifesaving. Be careful, these anticoagulants are probably the most dangerous group of drugs we prescribe. Anticoagulation should require scrupulous monitoring because of the major side effect of bleeding. This is why I prefer warfarin over the newer agents; not because it is remarkably cheaper. There is a time in a frail elderly person (especially if the person has been falling) that the risks of falling while on a blood thinner from whatever reason, far outweigh the advantages of the blood thinner, and the warfarin should be stopped.

2. **Antidepressants:** Most prescribed antidepressants are in the selective serotonin reuptake inhibitors (SSRI) family like fluoxetine (Prozac) or sertraline (Zoloft). These are very helpful medications for depression. Depression sometimes follows when death occurs in a family or when tough times occur from any loss, but, even more important, these medicines are helpful when a chronic sadness comes on for no good reason. These medicines may also work for anxiety, pain, loss of alertness, insomnia and may help prevent depression. Side effects are minimal. It is very important to note that the good results of SSRIs are greatly enhanced when combined with an exercise program.

3. **Bipolar and major psychiatric medications:** First it is important to realize that these are conditions

resulting from brain chemical imbalances and not from choice. Probably no other group of medical conditions causes more suffering than these disorders, and I wish we could do more for those affected and for their families. Although I feel we have room for improvement in treating psychiatric disorders, treatments that we do have are very helpful and much better than what we had when I started practicing medicine. These medicines do require careful monitoring, management and artful balancing. Patients with a bipolar diagnosis, or schizophrenia, need to be on board with their diagnosis and be taught the danger of stopping their medications. With acceptance of the long-term benefit of staying on medicines and with a trust between the patient and the physician or care provider, there is a greater chance of recovery and a normal life.

4. **Diuretics (water pills) and blood pressure medicines:** We use diuretics in treating congestive heart failure (CHF, heart weakness, fluid congestion in the lungs) which is a common condition in the elderly.[95] Diuretics are medications designed to increase the amount of water and salt expelled in the urine, and examples include spironolactone, furosemide (Lasix) and torsemide (Demadex). Other types of medicines used to treat CHF

---

95   https://www.ncbi.nlm.nih.gov/pmc/articles/PMC4824339/

include certain high blood pressure pills like lisino-pril, losartan (Cozaar), certain heart medicines like atenolol, nebivolol (Bystolic), carvedilol (Coreg), propranolol (Inderal), labetalol, metoprolol and digoxin (Lanoxin). Each of these medications can decrease the blood pressure in an attempt to help the heart and blood vessels. All of these medications are tricky to balance and require a careful physician or care provider. If you have problems with these medications like dizziness (especially with standing), balance issues or high or low blood pressure, please talk with your provider.

5. **Other medications:** Effective medications have reduced suffering and increased longevity for many people over this last half century. Good drugs work for infections, seizures, reflux esophagitis (acidic stomach contents moving back into the esophagus causing inflammation), major psychiatric illness, heart failure, diabetes (the full scientific term is diabetes mellitus), low thyroid and many other conditions. I am NOT criticizing or trying to reduce the wonderful help these medicines have provided many people. I am, however, making the point that **overuse, and overdosing may cause problems, so use medications judiciously.**

6. **Supplements:** For those older than sixty-five, once every year or two I check blood levels for Vitamin B12 (especially when there is any neurologic

symptom)[96] and vitamin D (especially in heavy people and especially in this northern prairie clime).[97] I often prescribe Vitamin B12, Vitamin D3 and ground flax seed, and I take them myself. (I buy whole golden flax seed at our grocery store, grind it in a coffee grinder and take a tablespoon full with morning cereal. It helps with bowel regularity and is similar to fish oil for heart health.) There are also scientific data to support the use of melatonin.[98] Melatonin is a natural hormone that prepares us for sleep and helps us reset our sleep cycle especially when traveling. (See earlier in this chapter for more on melatonin.)[99] There are scientific data to support eating fish but no good data to support taking fish oil capsules as a supplement (which is close to the same type of oil found in ground flax seed). Good food is the best source for most other nutrients. I advise that people regularly eat mixed nuts, fruits, nonstarchy vegetables and plenty of vegetables and greens. All of these are commonly found in a balanced Mediterranean diet. (We enjoy canned collard greens in our home, spiced with hot pepper vinegar.) As stated in *Consumer Reports*:

96   https://www.mayoclinic.org/drugs-supplements-vitamin-b12/art-20363663

97   https://ods.od.nih.gov/factsheets/VitaminD-Consumer/

98   https://familydoctor.org/melatonin/?adfree=true

99   https://www.hopkinsmedicine.org/health/healthy-sleep/sleep-science/melatonin-for-sleep-does-it-work

"Eating more whole grains, vegetables, fruits and fish resulted in the largest improvements in diet scores."[100] Several studies have shown that canned fruits and vegetables retain more minerals and vitamins than frozen, or even fresh, products. Taste and availability should be the driving force, but at least learning that canned vegetables have excellent retention of vitamins and minerals can mean that eating a nutritious diet doesn't have to be expensive. Just remember mom's advice: "Eat your fruits and vegetables."

7. **Alcohol:** Daily, mild to moderate alcohol intake among men and women appears to reduce over- all death rates unless there is an acceleration in drinking.[101] Mild to moderate intake would mean drinking one of the following on a daily basis: one bottle of beer, a one-and-a-half ounce shot of hard liquor or a four to six ounce glass of wine, depending on the size of the person. Some data even suggest that moderate alcohol intake is better than mild intake.[102]

The other side of the picture is that excessive drinking can kill and disable both the young and old. Because of the real risk of alcoholism, there

---

100   https://www.consumerreports.org/diets/eating-for-longevity/

101   https://bluezones.com/2017/08/longevity-link-how-and-why-wine-helps -you-live-longer/

102   http://www.indiana.edu/~engs/articles/women.html

are those who would advise no drinking, especially for the elderly. My recommendation is to be wary of one's risks, especially for acceleration of alcohol intake. Please stop drinking if there is evidence of such a problem. If not, then one or two glasses of red wine each day are likely to benefit most people, but **please be careful**.

8. **Malabsorption dietary therapies:** If one has a unique gastrointestinal or malabsorption problem (food doesn't completely get absorbed or digested), please let the professionals guide you on the diet or supplements required to resolve it. Particularly bad smelling feces is one of the most telling indications of such a problem. Milk intolerance and Celiac disease[103] are relatively frequent, and some specialists are recommending a gluten-free diet even in those who do not test positive for the condition when there are symptoms of malabsorption. I predict there will be a lot more about this topic in the years to come. Keep alert, monitor and talk it over with your care provider if there is a question.

9. **Aspirin:** I regularly prescribe a daily baby (81mg) chewable aspirin (acetylsalicylic acid or ASA) for those over 50. Originally acquired from willow root and bark, aspirin is now made in a pure and exact-dose form by organic chemists. Daily aspirin

---

103   https://medlineplus.gov/celiacdisease.html

reduces the body's ability to form blood clots. Scientists have shown that low-dose aspirin (81mg baby aspirin) can prevent strokes, heart attacks, colon polyps and colon cancer. However, this is partially countered by the small bleeding risk disadvantage of aspirin which can be devastating if significant bleeding happens in or around the brain. If one has a strong family history of clotting-type strokes or heart attacks, low-dose aspirin may be helpful.[104] The other reason to use low-dose aspirin is to prevent colon polyps and colon cancer. Strong scientific data indicate that a daily 81mg dose of aspirin is better than 325mg and is helpful in preventing colon cancer, especially in those with a family history of colon cancer and in those having certain glandular-type (adenomatous) polyps discovered by a colonoscopy.[105] Talk with your care provider before starting a daily aspirin.

10. **Prostate medicines:** I like three types of prostate medicines for men with noncancerous prostate enlargement (benign prostatic hypertrophy or BPH) and with urine blockage symptoms.[106] However, each of these medications must be used with caution. I usually wait for symptoms to

104   http://www.ncbi.nlm.nih.gov/pmc/articles/PMC3354696

105   http://www.nejm.org/doi/full/10.1056/NEJMoa021735#t=article

106   https://www.mayoclinic.org/diseases-conditions/benign-prostatic -hyperplasia/diagnosis-treatment/drc-20370093

progress before starting this type of medicine. When the guy is having to get up three or more times a night to pass urine, medicines may be indicated. It is important to realize that urinary blockage might also indicate prostate cancer. If there are hard nodules noted on rectal examination, I send these fellows to the urologist.

One group of fast-acting prostate medicines is called alpha-1 blockers and consists of medications like terazosin (Hytrin), doxazosin (Cardura) and tamsulosin (Flomax). They work in one to two days by relaxing the smooth muscles of the prostate and bladder neck. However, alpha-1 blockers only work well for several months to a year and gradually lose their effectiveness. This group of medications can cause the blood pressure to drop upon standing, putting him at high risk for a fall. Falling from dropping blood pressure is a special concern for the elderly, and one must consider this fact when prescribing alpha-1 blockers.

A second group of prostate drugs are the 5-alpha-reductase inhibitors like finasteride (Proscar) or dutasteride (Avodart). Unlike the alpha-1 blockers, these do not result in the same dropping of blood pressure. Instead, they work by inhibiting male sex hormones, thus shrinking the prostate. However, these cause a separate list of problems: sore breasts are common, there may be a higher risk of prostate cancer and sexual libido (desire) and sexual function are reduced significantly. If there are no signs of prostate cancer, if urinary blockage symptoms are significant, and if sexual function is not a concern, then this drug is worth discussing with your care provider. Avodart and Proscar will cause prostate shrinking, and although they take about a month to start working, the benefits are long-lasting.

Mild symptoms of benign prostatic hypertrophy may also be improved by all three forms of erectile dysfunction drugs: sildenafil (Viagra), tadalafil (Cialis) and vardenafil (Lavitra) when used daily in lower doses. They might, at the same time, improve, instead of reduce, erectile dysfunction. These medicines are generally expensive and can cause low blood pressure (hypotension), flushing and headache. Be careful, as they should never be used in combination with nitroglycerin in any form (Isosorbide, Isordil, Imdur, Nitrostat, Nitro-Bid and Nitro-Dur). Sildenifil is now available generically in a lower dose which may result in a cost savings but check with several pharmacies as generic prices can be quite variable.

11. **Dementia medicines:** For patients with dementia, family members should research the Alzheimer's Association, the National Institutes of Aging[107]

---

107 https://www.alz.org/alzheimers_disease_standard_prescriptions.asp

and medlineplus.gov[108] for nonmedicinal ways to approach this catastrophic and heartbreaking condition. Although there are studies that show the importance of brain exercising like solving crossword puzzles or other mind games, some experts suggest that the best brain exercise is simply having a conversation with another person. Early Alzheimer's patients often retain their distant past memory, and caregivers might take the opportunity to ask about early childhood experiences, the stories of their early adulthood or memories of long lost relatives. This kind of exchange might provide a positive and loving experience for not only the person with dementia but also for the caregiver. Since physical exercise also helps the brain, it is also a good idea to exercise with your friends or spouse. (For more on medications for dementia, go to **Chapter Six**.)

〜〜〜

Question: What commonly prescribed medications are you reluctant to prescribe for the elderly?

Before prescribing a medication, I first consider the nondrug options. I compare the potential benefits of the drug with the potential harms from side effects. I also consider the cost to the patient and to society (Medicare, Medicaid and insurance companies).

---

108   https://medlineplus.gov/alzheimersdisease.html

When the benefit outweighs the negative aspects of the drug, I try to inform the patient and family about the medicine and give them the final decision before prescribing. I must admit that the medical profession, myself included, could do better in this regard.

What follows is my personal list of medicines that I am more hesitant to prescribe because, for most elderly, the risks outweigh the benefits. Exceptions do occur and I would ask that no pill should be discontinued without a discussion with the care provider (doctor, physician assistant, or nurse practitioner).

1. **Bone density medicines:** I am slow to prescribe bone density medications. The long-term risks are still pending,[109] and regular exercise is the more important, viable and healthy option to strengthen bones.[110] Vitamin D levels should be checked regularly as deficiency can mimic osteoporosis, and this is especially important in anyone who is considering bone density medications. Remember, pills simply don't compare to even a small amount of daily exercise. There are also concerns about the long-term risk of brittle bones with the alendronate (Fosamax) type bone medicines and the untested long-term side effects of the newer injection medicine zoledronic acid (Reclast). In summary, find a

---

109   https://www.betterbones.com/osteoporosis/osteoporosis-risks-vs-benefits-of-osteoporosis-drugs/

110   https://medlineplus.gov/ency/patientinstructions/000493.htm

way to exercise or a way for the elderly person, for whom you are providing care, to exercise.

2. **Bladder medicines:** I try to avoid bladder-relaxing medicines in the elderly since they provide only marginal help compared to the significant number of side effects and problems. Oxybutynin (Ditropan), tolterodine (Detrol), trospium (Sanctura), darifenacin (Enablex), solifenacin (Vesicare) and mirabegron (Myrbetriq) can all cause dry eyes, dry mouth, confusion, worsening dementia and excessive drinking (to quench thirst and reduce dry mouth). Medicine-induced confusion, along with excessive drinking, may result in worsening of the overactive bladder symptoms. In addition, constipation can also result from these medicines which may, in turn, further aggravate bladder symptoms. This type of medication can come in extended-release forms with somewhat fewer side effects but with markedly increased cost.

   Behavioral interventions should always be tried before bladder medications. These would include pelvic floor muscle training called Kegel exercises, other bladder-training techniques, reduced fluid consumption and absorbent pads. Failing these, the benefits of medication versus the disadvantages must be weighed by the individual with the help of her or his physician. I generally avoid prescribing bladder medicines for any who have a hint of compromised mental function.

3. **High Blood Pressure (HBP) medicines:** A work up for high blood pressure should be done to rule out kidney and metabolic disease and to test for possible sleep apnea. If treatment is started, it should be adjusted slowly and carefully. High blood pressure medicines in the elderly can be dangerous because they can potentially cause severe drops in blood pressure when the patient stands or bends over.[111] The usual systolic (top number of blood pressure) goal of 130–140 range should go up for the elderly to a goal of 150 or so. When there is light-headedness or falling, the patient (or the family) should call the care provider for directions on reducing blood pressure medicines. **One fall causing a fractured hip is a far greater risk of disability or death than the long-term consequences of high blood pressure (HBP).**

    This is not to criticize controlling HBP, especially in young or middle-aged people. However, controlling HBP in the elderly must be approached very carefully since the systolic BP may one day be high one moment (180) and low (90) when they stand. Reducing the 180 with a medicine might cause the patient to pass out and fall, especially when she or he stands up and tries to be mobile. Any light-headedness upon standing should be urgently reported to the

---

111 https://medlineplus.gov/ency/article/007484.htm

doctor. Don't "live with it" and especially **don't let it keep you or your loved one from activity and exercise**.

4. **Lipid medicines:** I am not a big fan of cholesterol (or lipid) lowering medications **especially in the elderly** and especially if there is no history for heart disease in that individual. If an individual is relatively young and has had a heart attack, then treatment is called secondary prevention. In this case, I prescribe a statin (like simvastatin) and carefully monitor the patient for side effects that might be occurring from the statins. In studying primary prevention, meaning in people WITHOUT a previous heart event, only one study using a statin medication has shown any reduction in **death rate**, and that study was done in men only and by the statin drug maker. Realize that in primary prevention, more than 800 men need to be treated with a statin before one is benefited. In my opinion, the benefits of statins for the elderly who have not had a cardiac event are not good enough to justify the significant risk from their use.

Side effects from statins seem to increase with age, and those problems include: generalized weakness, respiratory infection-like symptoms, headaches, muscle and skeletal pain, diarrhea, nausea, insomnia, constipation, flatulence, **memory loss** and the list goes on. These are problems that can occur in the elderly, anyway without statins, making it difficult to detect statin medication side effects. Those suffering from balance problems, memory issues or any suspected side effects, should call their physician or care provider and ask about stopping the drug for a trial of two weeks. Restart and see if there is a significant reduction and a return of side effects. Often the knee-jerk reaction is for your care provider to replace the statin with some other lipid lowering agent but remember all other (nonstatin) lipid lowering medications, have NOT yet been shown by science to **reduce death rate**. I am constantly amazed when I see a marketing push to prescribe a medicine that has NOT been proven to significantly benefit the patient by impartial scientific methods.

In studying and treating people who have already had a heart attack, there is some proof that statins are effective in preventing a second or third event, but results are still disappointing. I should add that statins don't hold a candle to daily exercise like going for a 30-minute walk, eating fewer calories and even drinking a glass of wine each day (if alcoholism is not a problem). Physicians should emphasize these options more and cholesterol medicines less.

So, I have joined many other geriatricians in believing that it is a rare person over seventy-five (who has not had a heart attack) who should be on a statin medication.[112] For a beautifully written summary of the data about statins go to an article written by John Carey in *Bloomberg BusinessWeek* in 2008.[113] Since then, the only new significant cholesterol-lowering medication has been the introduction of an extremely expensive new injectable cholesterol reducer (evolocumab and alirocumab @ $15,000/year). The study supporting its use showed that if **high-risk people** were treated (the study involved 81 percent with a history of prior heart attack, 19 percent with prior stroke, 13 percent with peripheral artery disease), 66 people needed to be treated before one was benefited by reduced "events" such as a stroke or a heart attack. The most important point to me was that **death was no different in the treated versus the nontreated groups**.[114] Maybe one could consider using this drug for those with some very rare congenital lipid abnormality, but this drug **has not been proven to benefit** those who have not experienced a prior vascular event (primary prevention).

Once again, I am advising you talk to your doctor or care provider if you have questions about

---

112   B Han, et al: Effect of Statin Treatment vs Usual Care on Primary Cardiovascular Prevention Among Older Adults, The ALLHAT-LLT Randomized Clinical Trial. JAMA Intern Med. 2017;177(7) July 2017:955–965.

113   https://www.bloomberg.com/news/articles/2008-01-16/do-cholesterol -drugs-do-any-good

114   http://www.nejm.org/doi/full/10.1056/NEJMoa1615664

this. While I am a physician, I am not your physician. You need to have a primary care provider that you trust and one who knows your medical history. That also means you should be able to discuss and disagree with her or him sometimes. This may be a challenge because most care providers in the medical world seem to have been influenced by the tremendous marketing effort that never lets up about cholesterol medications. Cardiologists have been influenced as well, perhaps even more than primary care doctors. I take comfort that most geriatricians agree with me.

Bottom line: Come to your outpatient visit prepared, have courage to discuss the issue, promise that you will improve your exercise and diet and always ask your doctor or care provider if there are any pills that can be stopped.

5. **Benzodiazepam-like medicines:** As I discussed earlier, I very rarely prescribe benzodiazepines or benzo-active medicines (Ativan, Valium, Xanax, Klonopin, Ambien) because this group of sedative-type medications has dangerous side effects and short- and long-term problems with withdrawal.[115] This is true especially for the elderly. If you think you are addicted and desire to get off these memory-reducing benzodiazepines

---

115   https://americanaddictioncenters.org/benzodiazepine/length-of -withdrawal/

(benzos), talk to your care provider for a method to taper off over a six-month period. As discussed earlier, the antidepressant medicines (SSRI or SNRI groups) are much better alternatives than the benzo-like drugs. These often work at the underlying problem that bring on anxiety, and they don't lose their punch over the long haul. Again, trazodone and mirtazapine (Remeron) are much better for long-term sleeping problems and safer alternatives than zolpidem (Ambien, a benzo-like medicine) or any of the benzos. I know of more than one older person who has regrettably told me how they took benzos for years in the middle of their lives and the memory of those years were lost to them. Any benzo-active pills are not good long-term medications.

6. **Opioids:** Opioids (narcotics) can cause constipation, urinary retention, confusion, poor sleep, dry mouth and, in higher doses, suffocation death.[116] They are not as effective as other pain medications for chronic pain including acetaminophen (Tylenol). Opioids are not a good choice in most elderly patients. They should be used conservatively and judiciously.

---

116   https://www.ncbi.nlm.nih.gov/pubmed/18443635

Chapter Three

The Graying of America

Baby boomers: great expectations and great danger

Case Study:
The case of the World War II soldier saved by the atom bomb

DURING WWII, most of the draft eligible men, eighteen to twenty-five years of age, were drafted. The rest were either defined as necessary for the war effort at home or were unable to serve. In the first twelve months after soldiers returned home from WWII, there was a birth rate boom coming almost as a celebration of life and soldier survival. The babies born during a successful postwar economy, between 1946 and 1964, became the generation known as the baby boomers.[117]

A typical boomer was born of a woman who was expected to support her hero soldier (or her hero who was needed for the war

---

117 https://en.wikipedia.org/wiki/Baby_boomers

effort at home) and of a man who had post-war expectations for their perfect home. This has caused the progeny of this couple to have a distinct perspective that is found with boomers. My experience was typical for a prairie boy of the time. I was born in 1949 and was raised in De Smet, South Dakota: a rural farming community of about 1,400 people and home of the famed writer, Laura Ingalls Wilder.

Parents of author: Jody and Earl Holm, 1941[118]

118   Photo from private collection

My dad had been drafted into one of the first groups at the beginning of WWII and was subsequently sent to the newly developed Fort Leonard Wood near Springfield, Missouri. There he met my mother at a dance, and the two were on a picnic the day Japan bombed Pearl Harbor. They heard of the bombing on the radio while driving home and realized what was going to happen. They married before he left for the Pacific Ocean theater of war and met again upon his returning after the war, more than three years later. Dad always said that I shouldn't criticize the atom-bombing of Japan because it had saved his life; and, thus, I could be born. He was preparing to land on Japan, and that would have been a bloody awful killing experience for both sides. He figured he would not likely have survived.

Atom bomb test, 1944[119]

---

119   Photo from a private collection

When Dad came home, he returned to a waiting young wife. He longed for a comfortable home where he would become the breadwinner and where his wife would quit her secretarial job and become the housekeeper to stay home and raise children. I was told it was exactly nine months after Dad returned when my sister was born, and almost three years later when I came along. Our family moved where Dad could get work which was more than 400 miles from any other family support group. They were not near grandparents, aunts or uncles, parents or siblings, and, they were, by definition, a "nuclear family".

There has always been a double-meaning to the words "nuclear family" since it was the nuclear bomb which ended the war ushering in a subsequent period of peace and dread. My dad survived the war and was filled with hope like the many others described by Tom Brokow in his book, *The Greatest Generation*.[120] However, the nuclear threat, which followed the arms race between the U.S. and the USSR, left the boomers fearful. Throughout the first half of my life, the emotional menace of nuclear war seemed ever present like a dark menacing cloud. We discussed in grade school what to do when the atom bomb would drop near us. Because we were so close to the intercontinental ballistic missiles (ICBM) sites out on the western South Dakota plain, many believed those of us out here on the prairie would not survive if the Russians attacked. Bomb shelters became a discussion topic. These shelters were found scattered throughout communities in South Dakota. A large community shelter was obvious when driving into our state capital city of Pierre. I saw them as death caves.

---

120   Tom Brokaw, *The Greatest Generation*. Random House, 1998.

I remember how the cultural influence of this awful death threat even inspired Hollywood to make an unsuccessful comedy with Mickey Rooney.[121] The story was about his accidental driving into an atomic bomb testing range, surviving the explosion and then developing strange nuclear powers whenever he would sneeze. As I recall, I attended the movie with my older sister when I was six or seven. I remember crying during that poorly intentioned comedy and ending up in the cry room (a luxury of yesteryear). For many months after that movie I had terrible nightmares. The threat of dying was the cloud under which I lived growing up in a small, seemingly safe, South Dakota town.

Indeed, boomers were greatly affected by the bombing of Japan and the subsequent threat of nuclear warfare. First, because the war was quickly ended after the atom bomb, saving a great number of American and Japanese people who, likely, would have been lost to fighting during and after the invasion of Japan. Second, because, with the threat of nuclear war, the idea of death came early to kids growing up in the U.S. during this time. One can only speculate how this early glimpse at dying will affect boomers as they face the aging process and their inevitable end to life.

There was another shadow hanging over the new progeny of this era. Many children were raised in an overstressed environment, influenced not only by the threat of nuclear death, but also by the posttraumatic stress disorder (PTSD) of a soldier dad. Add to that the often-suppressed dissatisfaction of a mom stuck at home where she didn't always want to be. It was a time of

---

121   Ted Okuda, "The Atomic Kid: Radioactivity Finds Andy Hardy" in *Science Fiction America: Essays on SF Cinema* (edited by David J. Hogan; McFarland, 2006), pp. 120–129.

financial prosperity, tremendous social change, conflict in many households and unmet expectations of the ideal home with the pressure and expectation of picture-perfect children.

FREUD AND FRIEDAN DUKE IT OUT

Men returning from WWII perceived that their new duty was to come home to protect and provide for their families. It was implied that the wife of the soldier had to stay at home, watch after the kids and not question her husband, who was used to the hierarchy of command with orders being followed. Sigmund Freud (1856–

1939) was no longer living, but his concepts became popular,[122] especially with men who had been surrounded by men for the duration of the great conflict. Freud's words seemed to ring true for these men, "Nature has determined woman's destiny through beauty, charm and sweetness."[123]

Sigmund Freud[124]

---

122   http://www.pbs.org/youngdrfreud/pages/perspectives_women.htm

123   http://studymore.org.uk/xfremil.htm

124   By Tullio Saba from https://www.flickr.com/photos

At the same time, Freud said women who wanted careers ". . . were neurotic and imbued with penis envy."[125] During the war, enormous industrial voids were filled by women, embodied by the iconic Rosie the Riveter. This brought many women gratification, independence and pride in their new-found roles. However, there was a downside. Women, who had filled in for the workforce when the war was going on, often lost their jobs and their independence when the war was over. It is not surprising that women placed the responsibility for these changes on their husbands, no matter how well-meaning and forgivably war affected he may have been.

Woman turret lathe operator for transport planes, Texas 1942[126]

---

125   https://www.livescience.com/54682-is-penis-envy-real.html

126   Photo by Holward R. Hollem, from https://commons.wikimedia.org/wiki/File:WomanFactory1940s.jpg

Along came Betty Friedan (2/4/1921–2/4/2006), American feminist and activist.[127] She remarked upon Freud's error-in-judgment in her 1963 book, *The Feminine Mystique*.[128] Friedan noted that in the early 1900s there had been grand advances made for the rights of women, especially for higher education, for pursuit of a career and for the right to vote. With the exception of the right to vote, much of this went away after WWII when the men returned, and Freud's ideas became pervasive.[129] Friedan claimed

that being forced to stay at home caused great unhappiness in the households of many women and, thus, many men. Injustice and inequality beget disharmony.

Betty Friedan[130]

My mother was one of those very talented women who, I believe, was not fulfilled by her role as a housewife. She eventually began working outside the home doing clerical work for the *De Smet News* and later at the De Smet Insurance Company. This took some of the pressure off at home. I think that the many fights between my parents reflected the consequences of the popularity of Freud's ideas clashing with Friedan's message.

---

127   https://www.biography.com/people/betty-friedan-9302633.

128   https://www.thoughtco.com/friedans-the-feminine-mystique-3528957

129   https://www.newyorker.com/magazine/2017/08/28/why-freud-survives

130   By mender re from https://www.flickr.com/photos

Friedan also pointed out that, "Men are not the enemy but fellow victims. The real enemy is women's denigration of themselves." The Freudian attitude of a stay-at-home wife pervaded the whole society. Some women, perhaps even more than some men, were guilty of stifling career-minded women. The resulting family disharmony greatly affected the boomers. We were born into revolution (the "women's rights" revolution) and in the midst of a nuclear threat. This made the boomers incredibly aware of social problems and familiar enough with change. Perhaps this is why boomers have lead the charge in some of the most important societal issues in America.

THE PIG IN THE PYTHON, A LOOMING POPULATION OF ELDERLY AND POTENTIAL PROBLEMS

Often raised with a soldier-disciplined father and a not always happy work-at-home mother, baby boomers grew up watching too much TV, listening to the Beach Boys, Joni Mitchell and the Beatles, and facing the real threat of atomic warfare. Still, life was quite idyllic for kids during those first 18 years. Up to that time, we were the most privileged group of children to have ever existed. I would say that many of us were spoiled rotten.

After graduating from easy and perfect high school, we were slapped into reality by Vietnam, the draft and the reality of inequality between sexes and races. This generation, often labeled as one of sex, drugs and rock'n'roll, grew into an angry government-distrusting counter culture that fought for social justice, and for causes like feminism, civil rights and stopping the Vietnam War. People of this generation were believers in the American dream and grew up as the radicals and revolutionaries of the time.[131] Did this happen because of frustrated mothers dealing with their own world of unequal opportunity? Whatever the cause, the prominent boomer ethic became the right of self-direction.

Perhaps as a reflection of the threat of nuclear war, the postwar boom economy, a war-stressed yet hopeful father, a frustrated work-at-home mother, and the boomers' sense of privilege, this group, for whatever reason, has gone on to obtain significant wealth. Representing 24 percent of the total U.S. population, boomers hold 80 percent of our country's wealth, account for 80 percent of all leisure travel and dole out 50 percent of consumer spending. There are approximately 76 million boomers in the U.S. representing a huge cultural demographic.[132]

Like a pig swallowed by a python, a phrase credited to American editor and author, Landon Jones,[133] this big boomer bump is moving through life and is now coming to retirement age. It's an urgent matter. This group of people, born just after WWII, are getting old, and there are lots of them. Never before in all of human history have people lived as long as we are living now. We are entering an unprecedented time, a time of a growing demand to fulfill the recreational and health-care needs of this very large retiring population. Imagine the fiscal repercussions coming from this demographic. With these numbers, it is reasonable to expect an expanding building boom for retirement homes and villages and an innovative and growing

---

131   http://www.wmfc.org/uploads/GenerationalDifferencesChart.pdf

132   https://www.cnn.com/2013/11/06/us/baby-boomer-generation-fast-facts/index.html

133   https://en.wiktionary.org/wiki/pig_in_the_python

travel industry. The growing entertainment industry will inflate even further. Winter migrations to warm climates will soar as will orthopedic businesses, which have already blossomed with the replacing of knees, shoulders, hips and vertebral discs.[134]

When those born after WWII age into their eighties, although potentially a demanding group, some will be able to tap into their ample fiscal resources. However, all are not well to do, and there will always be the elderly, poor and dependent. As boomers grow older and become very elderly, sick and disabled, there will be an expanding need for caregivers and care providers.

Caring for people with fractures related to falling and the associated complications will increase as will the growth and demands of assisted living and long-term care facilities. This begs the question: will boomers become a huge societal burden? This increasing population of retired elderly will put a strain on the health-care system. To avoid some of this, prevention and lifestyle changes should be paramount in our health-care agenda right now. (See **Chapter One.**)

Considering the "fight for social justice" nature of this group, one could hope that those who do not have the fiscal resources could be reasonably supported by resource-rich boomers, either by taxes or by fair-minded giving. What's more, many of these old codgers could still be active enough to physically help in providing care for those disabled with age. Boomers are expected to donate about $6.6 trillion in cash and $1.4 trillion in volunteer services

134   http://boston.cbslocal.com/guide/bidmc-fitness-2016-bommeritis -ailments-impact-baby-boomer-generation/

during the next 20 years as they retire.[135] Perhaps more relevant, they must learn how to help their spouse through this happy or difficult time of aging and end-of-life. Children of boomers (often millennials) will also be challenged in caring for their parents. We must find ways to provide for the elderly, whether those of advanced age are rich or poor, well or sick, alert or demented. Whatever the case, we should do it in a just and generous way.

The big challenge for boomers will be learning how to age with grace. Considering my generation's appreciation for self-direction, I am hopeful many of us will realize the value of having a living will (advance directive). (See **Chapter Five** for details on living wills.) It is important to note that **if boomers do not learn about living wills, there is great potential for tragedy.** Currently, two-thirds of American adults do NOT have an advance directive.[136] This will bypass futile efforts of resuscitation, breathing tubes, and feeding tubes. With wise and careful planning, boomers, and all Americans, can reduce their risk of a prolonged, expensive, and painful death. Worst case scenario: without preplanning or discussions with family about when to stop the aggressive medical care system, the result might be significant and unnecessary suffering. Best case scenario: those still in control and competent, who write an advance directive and talk about it with their families, will face dying without paralyzing fear but rather with peace and confidence that they will, most likely, achieve a comfortable and graceful death.

---

135   https://www.philanthropy.com/article/Baby-Boomers-Poised-to-Give-8

136   https://health.usnews.com/health-care/articles/2017-07-07/2-of-3-americans-dont-have-advance-directive-for-end-of-life

Indeed, it is this potential suffering that is partly responsible for this book. All of those aging and coming to retirement age need to see the writing on the wall. **Running away from the aging and dying process is to invite suffering.** Every elderly, or soon to be elderly person, needs to ask her or himself (preferably sometime before the need becomes obvious), "Do I want a comfortable death or a prolonged and suffering death?" You don't get to choose "no death." **Talk to your family TODAY about what your wishes would be if you would have a severe stroke or similar event and permanently lose your ability to recognize your family.**

It isn't hard to foresee a senior living community in the not too distant future in which elderly boomers hang together remembering common stories, demanding good service, expecting equal rights and fairness to all. There might be unresolved anger about the Vietnam war but there will still be dancing and laughing as the air is filled with the sounds of the Beach Boys, Joni Mitchell, Beatles and rock'n'roll! Finally, when one of those boomers is coming to his end and there is no reasonable treatment available, his family will know, will be there, and he will be comforted. If he did it right and spoke to his family, he will be allowed to die naturally, without a breathing and feeding tube, but with Joni Mitchell singing in the background.

DESIGN IN PREPARATION FOR AGING AND DISABILITY

It's estimated that about 33 percent of Americans over the age of sixty-five are disabled, yet only about 10 percent of all homes accommodate the needs of this growing population. When constructing or remodeling a home, it is only minimally more expensive to make it accessible to someone disabled. Despite the cost, I believe such changes are worth it. Having a home that allows accessibility, especially with an expanding elderly population, will only enhance resale value.

Having an accessible house, even for the fully physically capable, is both thoughtful and forward-thinking for those who might visit one day or for those who might experience physical changes in the future. Public buildings are required to provide for accessibility. Why not expect personal homes to follow suit in the near future?

The American Association of Retired People (AARP) provides an example of how to design a quality home that would be accessible to those who are frail or with physical limitations.[137] In these houses, all the flooring in bedrooms, bathrooms and kitchen is hard and noncarpeted; other living spaces are covered by short carpet; doorways are three feet wide; all doors, faucets and hand-held showers have lever handles rather than knobs; light switches are lowered and outlets are raised to more usable heights; nighttime lighting illuminates the passageways everywhere in the house but especially on the way to the bathroom; the dishwasher is at a higher height and the microwave at a lower height; closet rods, pull-out shelves and pantries are adjustable and reachable; there are grab bars everywhere in the bathroom including the tub and shower; the refrigerator and freezer are side by side; the washer and dryer are front loading; all thresholds are minimal and accessible; and there is a covered entry at all exterior doors with good lighting. Please explore the Internet for other excellent examples.[138]

---

137 https://www.slideshare.net/etapper/universal-design-tapper-kcdb

138 https://www.familyhomeplans.com/search_results.cfm?lowsqft=1&highsqft=1300&mc=38&plantype=1&bestselling=1&action=1&source=googleppc&ordercode=05WEB

Bottom line: When designing a new home, or redesigning an existing home, it is sensible to make your home accessible for all, ready for grandchildren, easygoing for guests with disabilities, and, should you become frail, elderly or disabled one day, your home will be accessible for you.

An essay:
Coming home

I HAVE INCLUDED the following essay which I wrote just before retiring from the clinic, in light of an increasing shortage of primary care providers (usually family practice or internal medicine). These are the specialties that are more attuned to the problems and special needs of the elderly and will be needed especially as boomers get older. I personally believe, as a general internist, that every individual in this country should have a defined, long-term care provider. This would both reduce the cost and improve the quality of health care for the elderly in this country by redirecting these people from the horrendously expensive emergency room to a primary care provider. Excessive overtesting would be reduced, preventive care would be provided, and, at the end of life, the defined care provider would know the patient's living will and would find it easier to respect the patient's wishes than would an unknown hospitalist or intensive care specialist from out of town.

While the geriatric needs of the elderly are increasing, why are there fewer people being trained in these fields? New plans, policies and efforts to increase the numbers of primary care providers should be made by state and national legislative groups, by health-care systems, by medical schools, physician assistant (PA) schools, nursing schools and by organized medical groups like the American Medical Association, the American Association of Family Physicians and the American College of Physicians (internal medicine).

Raised in the small prairie town of De Smet, South Dakota, it seemed natural, and affordable, to attend under-graduate and medical school in this state. I moved away to Georgia for eight years before once again returning to South Dakota where I have practiced more than 35 years of primary care internal medicine. My job has changed to part-time, and I've been referring my patients to other care providers. The exercise has been a melancholy experience filled with good-byes and lots of fond, glad, and sad memories.

This has highlighted, in my mind, the need for primary care providers in rural South Dakota and everywhere else. We simply don't have enough family physicians and internists in our country, and, as baby boomers are approaching old age and frailty, it's only going to get worse. A report from the Center for Health System Change notes, "Rural areas have 53 primary care doctors and 54 specialists for every 100,000 people who live there."[139] Experts say that's the right balance of equal parts primary care to specialist care, but the problem is in the low total numbers. "In contrast, urban areas have

---

139   http://www.hschange.org/CONTENT/725/?words=rural%20health%20needs%20for%20doctor

78 primary care physicians and 134 specialists for every 100,000 people." The numbers are better but the ratio is overloaded toward specialists.

What can be done to resolve this predicament? The usual answer to the rural dilemma seems one of salary. However, Maggie Maher, a financial journalist said, "It is not . . . about how much doctors make; it's about where they make it."[140] Rural South Dakota may not be where a physician's spouse can get a job or where either of them care to live. Maher explains that many physicians are drawn to city life for its anonymity and privacy, where patients know you professionally but not personally.

Just the opposite makes more sense to me. Rural care providers, like me, see our patients not only at the office but at the grocery store, football games, movies and church. It makes physicians more accountable, which is to everyone's advantage. It is a good thing that patients become friends, neighbors and peers. I find that this con-nectedness is important and rewarding for me. Medical students and residents making life plans need to realize the rewards of knowing your patients inside and outside of the office.

I've been blessed with, and am thankful for, a pro-fessional life jam-packed with wonderful and personal connections. I wouldn't have it any other way.

---

140   https://www.theguardian.com/commentisfree/2014/jan/28/obamacare -doctor-shortage-myth

---

THINGS YOU SHOULD KNOW

Questions and Answers about:
The Graying of America—Baby boomers:
great expectations and great danger

Question: You have defined the baby boomers, born 1946–
1964, as a large group of fiercely independent people.
How do they compare, by numbers, to other groups?

According to the 2016 U.S. Census Bureau data,
the Millennials (born 1981–1997) have just surpassed
boomers in numbers swelling to about 75 million and
growing with young immigrants.[141] Boomers are just
less than 75 million, and their numbers are shrinking as
deaths outpace the number of older immigrants arriving
in this country. Generation Xers (born 1965–1980) are
a smaller group mostly due to fewer births during that
shorter span of years. This group is caught between
two larger generations of boomers and millennials.

GENERATION	YEAR OF BIRTH
Greatest Generation	Born before 1928
Silent Generation	1928–1945
Baby Boomers	1946–1964
Generation X	1965–1980
Millennials	1981–1997
Plurals, iGens, or Gen Z	After 1997

---

141   http://www.pewresearch.org/fact-tank/2016/04/25/millennials
-overtake-baby-boomers/

As would be expected, when life expectancy increases, then large elderly populations will increase. It is estimated that the number of Americans sixty-five or older will jump from 41 to 71 million by 2029, a 73 percent increase.[142,143] Those born after 1997 are being called plurals (multiple races), iGens, or Gen Z.[144]

Question: Why is it so important to hear all this about the boomer generation?

The boomers are a huge group facing the demands of caring for very elderly parents or siblings, facing the aging process of a spouse/partner/friend, or confronting their own aging process. This is a group who would benefit from care providers (internists and family physicians) who have special knowledge in caring for the elderly (geriatrics). As stated earlier, it is especially urgent and important that boomers understand the value and power of an advance directive and speak to their families about those wishes.

---

142   https://www.census.gov/prod/cen2010/briefs/c2010br-09.pdf

143   http://www.wmfc.org/uploads/GenerationalDifferencesChart.pdf

144   http://www.washingtonpost.com/news/post-nation/wp/2018/02/24/mellinials-disrupted-the-system-gen-z-is-here-to-fix-the-mess/

Chapter Four

The Fountain of Giving

Valuing yourself, too

Case Study:
The case of the critical medical student

ONE EVENING, quite a few years back, a medical student was shadowing me, and we were called to see a failing elderly man in the emergency room. The patient's predicament taught us both about valuing every individual. During our evaluation, it became clear that the patient was in the ER because he was confused and emotionally upset, and, although these are important to address, he was not in the ER because of any acute or dangerous malady.

After we left the patient's side, my student made a negative comment about the distraught gentleman, "He isn't sick. He's just an incompetent, old guy wanting attention." I realized once again the certain, sad truth about how often very good people prejudge and discriminate against others in our society. The student had spoken disapprovingly of an individual not only because of the emotional nature of the problem but also partly because of the patient's dementia and age.

What is the value of any individual? It is not difficult to appreciate a young, talented musician with great potential for a creative and helpful life, a middle-life firefighter with the life-experience of rescuing many people from the jaws of a treacherous spot or even a mature college professor with a history of brilliant lectures who brought many of his students to enlightenment. More difficult is caring for an emotionally unstable, frail, elderly and dependent individual. An even greater challenge is to care for those who are abusive, bigoted, demanding, spiteful or just plain mean. The natural tendency is to give them back what we feel they deserve. Truly challenging is to care for the angry construction worker who blames everyone for his chronic back pain, the depressed and desperate cancer patient who is caught in a psychological maelstrom and strikes out at anyone who comes near or even the friendly, noncompliant, irresponsible, rehab-failing alcoholic who keeps on drinking while his body is malnourished.More pertinent to this case, how do we react and respond to an individual who is losing memory at the end of his life, whose very identity is lost along with the memory, who often becomes paranoid as his world becomes unorganized and who, at first, retains enough memory to be severely destructive to those trying to provide care?

What gives value to any person in our society? Would my student, or any care provider for that matter, feel different if she or he knew that the elderly gentleman was once a lovable baby, a promising young student, a hardworking farmer, a teacher or

20

even a care provider? How difficult is it to imagine that with some illness and over time, that elderly, failing and anxious person could be you or me?

It is easy to discriminate against people who are acting out and emotionally disturbed. I believe the desire to put down or ignore those who are different and less fortunate represents that lesser nature of our humanity. The challenge is to realize such bigotry and do battle against it. Caring for difficult people requires an uncommon kind of compassion which comes from a special part of our souls. During my professional life, there have been times that the challenging character of some patient has brought me to silently say to myself, "child of God . . . child of God." A good doctor should, and will, take care of defiant and angry patients just as well as the pleasant ones. Providing care for another is easy when that person is fun, clever, kind and appreciative.

Why should anyone want to take on the challenge of caring for a difficult person? Why should we reach for that uncommon kind of compassion? The answer comes from realizing the value of every individual no matter how offensive they may be. It is a care provider's ethical responsibility to provide care even to the despicable. (That's a good thing because we, too, can get a little despicable every once in a while.) All of us in health care take an oath to that effect. "We promise to diminish suffering and enhance health, look for evidence-based honest science, try not to do harm, and all the while respecting the rights of the individual for whom we are caring." Please note that the oath says nothing about giving less health-care if the patient is dispicable. If you endeavor to become a caregiver, whether you have had formal training or not, you have that same ethical responsibility.

There is another reason to value and care for the less fortunate and sometimes less friendly. "Doing good" rewards the giver.[145] This happens because altruistic actions not only come from, but also enhance our inner senses of value. What else could be more important? This humanistic characteristic is the inspiration that brings us to societal compassion and justice. When we value one person, we gain an inner ability to value many others, including ourselves, and that makes all the difference.

Of course, valuing individuals equally doesn't mean that treatment must be the same. The dying cancer patient with a life-threatening infection needs something different than the newborn with a life-threatening infection; the ninety-year-old with a cardiac arrest needs something different than the fifty-year-old with a cardiac arrest; the person with chronic (back) pain syndrome needs something different than the hospice patient with severe and unrelenting (cancer eroding into bone) pain.

Bottom line: There is no more important principle in the field of medicine than to realize how to value every individual no matter what medical or psychological problem, no matter what mean (or gracious) attitude, no matter what mental capacity and no matter what age or stage of life.

145   https://www.theodysseyonline.com/importance-of-golden-rule

THE HARVARD STUDY ON LONGEVITY, QUALITY AND HAPPINESS

Finding the capacity to love the other guy is a goal and a challenge of one's lifetime. I submit that taking good care of someone else results in realizing the value of others, and that learning to appreciate someone else brings the realization of the value of oneself. This, in turn, should bring one closer to self-fulfillment or, as some would say, the font of happiness. Sensing self-value, fulfillment and happiness ties in closely to the question about how to achieve healthy aging.

Have you ever noticed that bookstores seem to have a corner dedicated to books on how to be happy,[146] and, on the magazine shelves, you can almost always find at least one article with the same promise?[147,148] No question, every one of us would like to know the key to a good life. Books and magazines seem to sell because they claim they have the answer to that question.

Probably the most famous scientific study to define what predicts happiness and healthy aging began in 1938 and is still ongoing. The *Harvard Grant Study* started with 268 well-adjusted, male, sophomore college students and has followed their stories throughout the years.[149,150] Of course, these were Harvard

---

146   https://www.amazon.com/s/ref=nb_sb_ss_c_1_6?url=search-alias%3 Daps&field-keywords=happiness+is+a+choice+you+make&sprefix=happin% 2Caps%2C383&crid=1F9UX8JD1E385

147   https://www.gq.com/story/laurie-santos-how-to-be-happy-interview

148   https://www.psychologytoday.com/blog/click-here-happiness/201801/ how-be-happy-23-ways-be-happier

149   http://www.dailygood.org/pdf/dg.php?sid=573

150   http://hr1973.org/docs/Harvard35thReunion_Waldinger.pdf

boys. Many came from affluent families and were not your normal average Joes. Many achieved dramatic success: one was a best-selling novelist, four ran for U.S. Senate, one served on a U.S. president's cabinet, and one, JFK, was the 35th president of the United States. The study showed that one-third of these men experienced either significant mental illness, alcoholism,

or both, at some point in their lives. Indeed, they were perhaps not normal in accomplishments but certainly normal in experiencing misery.

John F. Kennedy[151]

There have been lessons gleaned from this research worth remembering. Cholesterol, IQ and childhood temperament had nothing to do with healthy aging while smoking, alcohol abuse and depression all had major negative effects. The most destructive characteristic appears to have been alcoholism.

Other findings included: 1) Financial success did not follow intelligence but rather followed friendship with others and a warm relationship with one's mother; 2) A warm relationship with one's father correlated with a sense of life satisfaction; 3) Getting a good education, striving for a stable marriage and developing

151   Official White House photo from https://commons.wikimedia.org/wiki/John_F._Kennedy

caring relationships (especially with siblings) correlated with a happy life; and 4) Regular exercise predicted mental health. Wise people should wrap themselves around these findings which emphasize these points: valuing others and oneself, while getting regular exercise, correlates with overall happiness and successful coping with life's troubles.

I read this happiness study to a few friends, asked for their thoughts and they casually came back with what I thought were scholarly responses. One suggested, "Pets sure help." Another advised, "You gotta have faith." Another said, "You need someone to love, enough to eat and work to keep you busy—that's it." Another said: "By giving of yourself, you exemplify the best kind of nature that humanity has to offer, and it turns around and rewards you."

Bottom line: Valuing others comes back to you. In caring for an ill spouse, parent or relative you can get as much or more than you give. Putting it another way, when you tap into the font of giving, the goodness spreads around and through you.

THE VALUE OF CREATIVE LISTENING

Valuing others and oneself might sound easy and doable, but it's not. For all of us, this goal is a lifelong quest. There is a tool available that makes "valuing others" easier to achieve. There are many references to a famous Dan Rather interview with Mother Teresa.[152] When Rather asked Mother Teresa. how she prayed to God, she answered, "I listen."

"And what does God say in response to your prayers?"

"He listens," was the answer.

---

152 http://www.l-i-t.org/listening-is-an-act-of-love-storycorps-on-being/

I assert that an effective method for learning and practicing the process of valuing others and oneself is to practice listening with heightened intensity. The talent of listening is not only the

key to being a good diagnostician in medicine, but it also enhances success in every field of work.

Mother Teresa[153]

Anthropologists suggest that very early in our evolution, humans were genetically built to be self-centered for survival purposes. Over the many thousands of years that have followed, our brains have developed to make us realize we need to socialize to assure protection. Combine the self-protection gene with the tribe-protection gene, and you have a human temperament for protecting the self and serving others. Whatever the source in our brains, many of the world's greatest philosophers and theologians throughout history have said that they found self-worth, meaning and self-fulfillment when they realized "it's not just about me". My wife Joanie, pediatric nurse practitioner, tells me that empathy and caring for another person occurs with the normal and natural development of a child; that is, unless this development

---

153   Personal picture taken in India by Evert Odekerken. From https://upload.wikimedia.org/wikipedia/commons/7/7f/Mother_Teresa.jpg

is arrested by trauma or a lack of social interaction. I agree that children can develop empathy naturally, but I believe as adults we can reach a higher plane of empathy which brings a higher level of self-fulfillment. How can we get there?

The other night a dear friend provided a popular aphorism on how to trick oneself into acting nice and doing good. She said, "Fake it 'till you make it. If you don't find the milk of human kindness welling up in your breast, then act like it's there. Then, over time, it will come." Practicing kindness will make it easier to find real compassion for the other person. I propose a good way to start begins with listening.

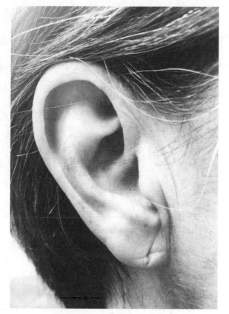

A listening ear[154]

Take it one step further. Years ago, I read a book by Joyce Brothers, *How to Get Whatever You Want Out of Life*,[155] which blatantly promised a simple and effective strategy to reach success in life. She advised that one can powerfully manipulate others by flattery. I should say that her counsel still seems repulsive to me, although I think honest flattery is sometimes acceptable. I think that when

---

154 Photo from private collection, 5/12/18

155 https://www.amazon.com/How-Get-Whatever-Want-Life/dp/B000HF1YJO

the motive for flattery is singularly to manipulate another for one's own profit, eventually the motive will be discovered, the manipulator will be found out as self-serving and he or she will become discredited. More importantly, the flatterer will not find the personal reward of unselfishly doing a good turn for another. I think that's a big deal.

What has this to do with listening and self-fulfillment? I believe the most powerful and beautiful form of flattery is to intensely listen to the other person with an honest motive to learn something. What a gift it is when someone is genuinely listening! Yes, perhaps it can be used, à la Joyce Brothers, to manipulate another; however, I believe that we should listen because it not only demonstrates the art of valuing the other guy but it is good practice. What's more, listening is how we learn something new. It can be the first step in a person's life-long quest to embrace valuing others and oneself as well as augmenting personal growth. Thus, one comes one step closer to self-fulfillment.

Of course, if there is careful listening, there can be a thoughtful response, and with that can begin a dialogue, an exchange, an enhancement of ideas, a conversation. The result may be that someone is influenced toward truth (rather than someone being manipulated to think the other person's way). Influence by an open conversation, when two people are listening, is entirely different than manipulation. Listening can promote an enlightened and virtuous circle of ideas. The opposite of clamor is not silence; it is real conversation.

I like to study, read and write all alone while in my favorite busy local breakfast café. I have done that all my professional life. This helps me concentrate for some reason. Still, sometimes I listen in on conversations going on with groups at different tables. Some folks go on and on without stopping or listening, and I see this as an imposition to the group of people who have gathered for an exchange not a lecture. This is not to criticize them, but only to say that the overtalkers are generally in need of something in the self-worth category and would receive more self-fulfillment if they listened more. Even when people do listen, they are often motivated by a wrong purpose. Stephen R. Covey, the author of *7 Habits of Highly Effective People: Powerful Lessons in Personal Change*,[156] said it effectively, "Most people do not listen with the intent to understand; they listen with the intent to reply."[157] His wonderful advice is to let go of the reply and, instead, to listen and understand first. Great interview techniques suggest that restating the original comment, before any other response, sets the stage for real exchange and interaction.

Sometimes if you listen very hard to a family member, to a friend, even to a very challenged patient, you can hear their cry for help, their hope to resolve a problem or their expression of caring and love. How does one listen for this delicate and refined resonance in a loud and cacophonous world? All the noise out there can make it difficult to hear. It simply takes an intense and careful effort at listening and sometimes even a thoughtful response. Consider how the improvisational jazz saxophone is noblest when playing in sync with the piano and base, not solo.

---

156   https://www.amazon.com/s/ref=nb_sb_ss_i_1_11?url=search-alias%3D-stripbooks&field-keywords=steven+covey.+7+habits+of+highly+effective+peo-ple&sprefix=steven+cove%2Cstripbooks%2C402&crid=2C0X0RQSX971L

157   http://www.quickmba.com/mgmt/7hab/

In the choir group I direct, we say, "Listen louder than you sing." (See **Chapter Eleven** Spirit Singing.)

Bottom line: I believe that a secret ingredient for a joyful life comes not with making more clamor but with very concentrated and intense listening. I think Mother Teresa would agree.

TEACHING BY EXAMPLE, SHOWING YOUR CHILDREN HOW TO CARE FOR THEIR AGING PARENT

While I was a medical student years ago, I was fortunate to have a cancer specialist (oncologist) teacher who taught us how to listen. He did it most powerfully by example. He would approach patients with ears wide open, listening with all concentration and with every sense on alert. He was known as the one who could perceive the nuance, the hidden pain, the color of the mood, the broken heart. He always said the best doctor is one that is open-minded and listens.

I had heard of his reputation as a true healer, and he didn't disappoint. He was one who found a way to bring the patient back to health relying not only on the knowledge of medicine but also on the knowledge of human nature. He had the capacity for intuition and the confidence to know when to cure; when to move to comfort; when to let go and sing a lullaby. Too many people stopped listening years ago, no longer taking advantage of learning by giving attention to another. Listening is like a super power thrusting us into warp speed. Whatever job or talents we possess, each of our lives could be more fully balanced if we learned to let go of unneeded preconceptions and fears, and opened our minds and creatively listened, truly listened, with all our might. My teacher, the oncologist, taught me that and did it by example.

Dorothy Law Nolte, psychologist and author of the poem, *Children Learn What They Live,* wrote, "If a child lives with acceptance, he learns to love . . . If a child lives with honesty and fairness, he learns what truth and justice are . . ."[158] The poem goes on, but Nolte's recurring lesson clarifies that children learn not by what we as parents say but by what we do.

What example do you provide, or have you provided, for your children regarding how you treat and support your parents? When the end of your parents' lives is near and time to help them move to comfort (to let go and sing a lullaby), how are you going to direct their care? How will your children support you when it's time at the end of YOUR life? What have they learned by example?

An essay:
A career in medicine

I REMEMBER THE MOMENT when I first thought about becoming a doctor. It was in a freshman biology class in De Smet High School when Ron Huisenga and I were dissecting a frog. The experience got me thinking about our family doctor and friend, Dr. G. Robert Bell. He used his intelligence to help his patients and his leadership qualities to help our community. He became a very well-respected person by providing caring, honest and evidence-based health care to our prairie community, 24/7, for many

---

158   https://www.psychologytoday.com/blog/overcoming-child-abuse/201112/children-learn-what-they-live

years. More importantly, he always appeared fascinated with life.

For two college summers, I worked as an orderly in big city hospitals. I spent hours washing patients, placing catheters into bladders, cleaning floors and listening to nurses. During that experience, I learned about humility, hard work, the value of the nurse's wisdom and, perhaps most importantly, how people die.

This fed my fire for getting into medical school. As I think back on it, there was nothing in my life I wanted more. (It is interesting that had I not been accepted into medical school, my alternative plan was to be a high school teacher.) Medical school and residency changed over time from "extensive schooling" to "learning on the job." Somewhere along the line, I realized that knowledge came not only from great teachers and mentors but also from fellow students. I also realized the best learning came when it was my turn to teach.

Now, after years of practice, I think the greatest lesson I have learned from medicine is the value of listening. Every single day is filled with listening to the nurse who senses the change in our patient, to the pharmacist who is watching for side effects, to the expert who knows the hottest and latest medical literature and to my partners who have had a case like this before. Most of all, I have learned to listen to the patient with all my senses, to see their movement of pain, to feel the fear in their eyes, to understand every beat of their heart, every breath of air, and every bead of sweat . . . always listening for a way to help.

It's a long way from dissecting a frog.

THINGS YOU SHOULD KNOW

Questions and Answers about Chapter Four:
The Fountain of Giving—Valuing yourself, too:

Question: You are saying that caring about another person should give me meaning and a reason to live. I am surrounded by selfish and angry people, and I have only enough energy to survive that anger, let alone to love them.

First, if you are being abused, find a way to escape safely. No one deserves mistreatment and trying to care for someone who is abusive is not rewarding and even dangerous. If you aren't being abused, that's a different story. This will not be easy, but I am convinced that, even in your situation, the rewards of caring can be fulfilling. Of course, loving an angry, nonloving sort of person is difficult, but that is also when there is the most potential for reward. If you are providing care to a nasty person, it is obvious that you are not providing care for the purpose of receiving any thanks. Knowing you are doing the right thing might have to be your only reward.

———— ⸎ ————

Question: The Harvard Study refers to rich males seventy years older than me. Nothing could be further from

my own life. I cannot believe there is any lesson I can benefit from that study.

I love the study, partly to realize how equally happy or unhappy we all are. Whether we are old or young, rich or poor, good and bad times strike all. The very rich and famous are not immune. People who are financially fortunate may not be fortunate in family or social ways. The truth is that we are all equally vulnerable to the same foibles and faults. We all have equal opportunity to achieve the rewards of giving.

Studies show that women may be advantaged as caregivers over men by their capacity for compassion and communication. Experience gives great advantage to anyone in the realm of communication, so advanced age might mean advanced understanding.

Bottom line: The lessons that come from this famous study can be good when one drops a conscious bias against people who are different.

Question: My son doesn't seem to be able to listen because he has ADHD. It is somewhat better when he is on medication, but he remains so distracted that listening seems beyond his ability. My husband doesn't seem to be able to listen because he, too, is stressed out by having a son who is dysfunctional from ADHD. What can I do to get them to listen to me?

It must be very frustrating to be in that environment. Tough situation! It is possible that your husband may also have some spectrum of ADHD himself. I would advise you to lean on the professionals to get help.

In this way, your family will sense your goodness.

———

Question: Don't you think you are overdoing the "listen" advice?

I think listening is important enough to warrant this discussion. So, you heard it a lot. You must have listened? (For more on listening to help face the fear of death, see **Chapter Twelve**.)

———

Chapter Five

The Golden Rule

An ancient and modern guide to making tough choices

Case Study:

The case of a woman after a brain injury left her in a permanent vegetative state

SEVERAL YEARS AGO, I was made aware of a young woman driven into a persistent vegetative state by a motor vehicle crash which induced severe brain injury. Sadly, she was still alive after years in a nursing home, and I became aware of her predicament when her mother had a change of heart after all those years. The mother requested the doctor stop artificial hydration and let her daughter die a natural death.

This change of plans came in conflict with the physician and the health system who were each reluctant to follow the mother's new directives due to family dynamics problems and the risk of a lawsuit. Despite all the expressed wishes on the mother's part, the patient is still unconscious on a feeding tube in the same nursing home.

UNDERSTANDING ETHICS

Each night my wife and I taught our kids a prayer that reflects a basic interpretation of medical ethics. "Dear Lord, help us to be kind, honest and respect other people's choices." These are basic principles, rules to help give us direction in daily life. **Kind** can be interpreted as "do good, and don't do harm." **Honest** can be interpreted as "Never lie, and base what you do on evidence-based (honest) science." **Respect other people's choices** can be interpreted as autonomy or "The right of self-direction, guaranteed by the U.S. Constitution." Caregivers, whether family or medical professionals, should realize these are ethical responsibilities that go with caring for someone who is vulnerable. The very nature of the vulnerability of an ill patient should clarify why medicine has required that physicians promise never to take advantage of someone who is in a compromised position. I believe understanding ethical principles and **medical ethics** is extremely important in this era when **business ethics** seems to dominate medical ethics.

The **business ethic** places the financial benefit of shareholders as the single, central and sole objective. Profit is the primary aim. The pharmaceutical practice of raising prices beyond reasonable levels is an example how those companies are marching to the rhythm of the **business ethic.** As CEO of General Electric, Jack Welch, once put it, "The ultimate measure of a company's success is the extent to which it enriches shareholders."[159] I submit that any professional AND any business who provides for vulnerably ill persons has an ethical responsibility not to take advantage of those people. To do so is unprofessional and unethical. We should hold all companies who provide medical services to ill people to the same ethical standards expected of physicians and caregivers.

In the same vein and in the recent past, physicians and hospitals acted independently, and the responsibility for providing ethical care for the patient was paramount with each independent party. Now, large health-care systems employ most physicians and care providers. Those of us trained in health care are no longer marching to our own drummer, but rather by the rhythm of the business health-care system that employs us. Do these large health-care businesses, run mostly by nonphysician executives, live by the same ethics as the physicians? All customers of the health-care system should expect them to do so and call them on it when they do not.

I am fortunate to be employed by a faith-based health-care system (Avera, of Sioux Falls, South Dakota) whose mission statement is patient-centric, an ethical map upon which the system leaders plan action. This should be the standard for all health-care corporations. An ethical foundation should be the base for the pharmaceutical industry, the health insurance industry and

---

159   https://books.google.com/books?id=fRbMAwAAQBAJ&pg=PT101&lp-g=PT101&dq=%E2%80%9CThe+ultimate+measure+of+a+company%27s +success+is+the+extent+to+which+it+enriches+shareholders.

the health systems industry, starting with the principles of medical ethics as their primary mission. If this isn't expected from business, it won't happen. Understanding ethics should help the care provider and the patient advocate as they do "business" with health-care providers.

WESTERN PHILOSOPHY AND BASIC PRINCIPLES OF ETHICS

There are many perspectives and distinct schools of thinking in the Western and Eastern philosophies of ethics. I like the sky-high view which divides Western Ethics into three groups. It is what I understand and what I have found to be most helpful when dealing with ethical challenges in my practice.

First, comes virtue ethics[160] which means making choices and taking actions based on specific virtues, such as doing good, not doing harm, telling the truth and respecting choices. A generally agreed upon definition of the word virtue is to "do the right thing" or to "act in a moral and correct way." It comes from an old Latin word meaning to act with integrity. I believe all health-care groups, organizations and providers should aspire to use virtue ethics.

Second, is an ethical principle based on German philosopher Immanuel Kant, who, in the late 1700s, developed what is referred to as Kantian moral autonomy. Those are fancy words for a simple philosophy based on self-direction and self-determination (like many eighteen-month-old children who scream, "I do it myself"). This means deciding for oneself the duties one should

---

160   https://plato.stanford.edu/entries/ethics-virtue/

fulfill.[161],[162] The U.S. Constitution defines the value of autonomy with words that speak to the right of self-direction as long as they do not reflect negatively on others. This Kantian principle has also become very important in virtue ethics and is described by the word AUTONOMY.

Immanuel Kant
18th century portrait[163]

Third, is the utilitarian ethical theory which places the focus of action solely on outcomes.[164] Utilitarian theory calls for "the greatest good for the greatest number of people" and does not relate to any virtue or any duty. It doesn't matter how you get there. The end justifies the means. The problem with utilitarian theory is: first, often it is difficult to foresee the long-term consequences of any action, and second, with this principle one can almost justify any action; no matter how unkind and cruel it may be, with some unprovable long-term goal (the end justifies the means). That said, utilitarian

---

161   http://www.csus.edu/indiv/g/gaskilld/ethics/kantian%20ethics.htm

162   http://www.iep.utm.edu/autonomy/

163   Painting by unknown artist, from https://commons.wikimedia.org/wiki/Category:18th-century_portrait_paintings_of_men,_artist_and_location_missing

164   http://www.csus.edu/indiv/g/gaskilld/ethics/kantian%20ethics.htm

theory makes one consider how virtues should result in long-term good and should make us question the virtue or action if it results in recurring long-term bad.

These schools of thought contain immense wisdom. My father hadn't studied these western philosophical principles but regularly promoted the Golden Rule as the grounding principle from which to answer hard questions. Almost every human religion has a variation of this common teaching: "Do unto others as you would have done unto you." In eastern religions, it is "Don't do unto others what you wouldn't want done unto you."[165] Either way, the Golden Rule begins with realizing the sacred value of every individual. Ethical choices are made easier when one truly values every individual, and that would include oneself.

Bottom line: I would amplify the lesson of the Golden Rule which appears to have been made especially for those of us who are, or will be, caregivers. We must first value the person for whom we care. This means we must value any individual, whether baby or octogenarian, woman or man, smart or demented, attractive or unattractive, mean or friendly. We need to see her or him as a child of God, of the universe, of nature. This is not to ignore the age of the patient, lifespan considerations, special needs and individual patient choices. As people providing for any compromised person, we need to care and value that person, and that should be the core of our ethics. Virtue ethics is better when we first sense the value of the individual, and, when there are confusing and difficult choices, virtue ethics help us sort out what to do next.

---

165   https://books.google.com/books?id=mPAmVYe-

VIRTUE ETHICS

Some would say the most important virtues or rules are the ten commandments from the Bible. I also like the single virtue described in the wonderful book *The Kite Runner* by Afghan-American Internist, Khaled Hosseini MD.[166] In the book, the wise father tells his son that there is only one virtue: "Do not steal." When the son asks about killing, he answers, "That is stealing another life." When asked about lying, he answers, "That is stealing the truth." I think there is something beautiful in concentrating and simplifying a broad list of ethical principles into a single virtue.

Ethical judgment requires balancing the scales[167]

When weighing in on heavy issues, I have turned to four specific virtues, and this has helped me in dealing with individual patients. 1. Do good (beneficence), 2. Don't do harm (nonmaleficence), 3. Tell the truth and trust science (veracity) and 4. Respect the other guy's right to choose (autonomy). Ethicists may speak of other principles, but I find these four most helpful in my dealings with the geriatric population.

Ethicists argue about which virtues are most important. Some would agree that each medical situation is different, and

---

166   https://www.amazon.com/Kite-Runner-Khaled-Hosseini/dp/159463193X

167   Illustration by Agradman, from https://commons.wikimedia.org/w/index.php?title=User:Agradman&action=edit&redlink=1

one should allow for balancing the virtues in each individual case. In other words, no specific virtue is more important than another. The following are some examples of how virtue ethics are applied in medicine and how they work when one moves from the classroom to the real world of health care.

Beneficence[168] means to do good, diminish suffering and enhance health. In short, it means to provide some benefit for the patient. Some would use the word kindness for this virtue. Meaning more than just providing medical care, beneficence may even be reflected by reducing medical care, providing support for the patient's family, referring the patient to another expert for more specific care or even allowing a natural death when the patient is dying. For example, while attending to a man with heart failure symptoms, I listened carefully as he talked about his wife who had recently passed away. Listening likely provided the elderly man more satisfaction, resolution and comfort than any of our best medicines. The principle of beneficence, for physicians and care providers, demands not only medical knowledge but also a lot of careful and compassionate listening.

Nonmaleficence[169] means to do no harm. In other words, it is to provide for the patient's maximum safety. One might consider this an unnecessary (even redundant) distinction, something that would be already obvious under the idea of beneficence. However, there are important reasons it exists as a virtue of its own. Certain known and tried medicines, devices or procedures

168 http://missinglink.ucsf.edu/lm/ethics/content%20pages/fast_fact_bene_nonmal.htm

169 http://web.mnstate.edu/gracyk/courses/phil%20115/Four_Basic_principles.htm

can be aggressive, invasive or painful and have the potential to cause more suffering than the malady they are aiming to treat. Also, the nonmaleficence principle becomes pertinent when any new medicines, devices, procedures or inventions are introduced. They each need to be carefully tested and proven safe before they are made available and prescribed for the public.

For example, before the surgeon takes the elderly and mildly demented patient to radical surgery, which may cause significant pain and weakness during rehabilitation, the surgeon should balance the potential benefit versus the potential pain and suffering that might occur. The goal is to do the best while limiting the amount of pain inflicted. Not long ago, I was one of a team that provided care for just such an elderly, mildly demented patient. With the family's direction and weighing all risks, we took that gentleman to surgery. Unfortunately, this resulted in a prolonged and failed rehabilitation, a fall and fractured hip and finally a gradual death with suffering. In retrospect, had we considered harder the significance of the dementia, the surgery might have been vetoed.

Another example of nonmaleficence in my practice is my effort to reduce medications. I tried to reduce the number of medications in every patient, at every juncture, in an effort to decrease the possibility of side effects or drug interactions. Through my life of practice, I became better at that virtue as I became more experienced in medicine.

Veracity[170] stands for the virtue of upholding truthfulness. Caring for the sick, injured or aging often entails dealing with

---

170   https://pocketsense.com/what-is-the-principle-of-veracity-12338205.html

many unpleasant truths and sometimes providing painful answers to difficult questions. Caregivers should not withhold these unpleasant truths, but, at the same time, they should try to avoid bluntly delivering them without considering how it might affect those involved. There should be room for compassion and some concern for speaking or communicating in a way that would allow for the best outcome. In other words, while caring for a person in need, one may need to combine the virtue of beneficence with veracity.

For example, I walked into the room of a patient who had recently been diagnosed with widely spread, metastatic terminal cancer, and I was the one who had the responsibility to tell her. I told her the exact truth and provided the statistics which can be frightening but I made clear to her that those are averages. Every person and every cancer is different. "We don't know what will happen or how soon. I know that you and I will both die one day, but nobody knows when. Every one of us should make the best of each day that we have left."

Veracity should also mean that caregivers AND care providers pledge to care for people using solid evidence-based science in deciding what to do while providing health care. **I like the definition of science as a search for truth.** It should be clear that what looks like good science is not always perfect and correct. What looks like evidence-based science can be wrong because of weakness in the experimental design (a poorly done experiment). In summary, veracity is two-pronged: first, tell the truth, and, second, base what you do on factual and good science. Factual and good science should be as good as you have, knowing that it may change in the future.

Some do not trust science or any standard means of health care because they have experienced a bad result or have watched as care providers betrayed the trust given to them. Unfortunately, bad results still happen, even with perfect care. I believe that the best chance for health-care success is by providing evidence-based care. A plan of any kind, when built on facts not falsehoods, will have the best chance of succeeding. Therefore, I liken science to a search for the facts: a never-ending, always skeptical search for the truth.

The more modern principle of **autonomy**[171] means providing for the patient's right to be reasonably informed about any care plan and providing no treatment without full and competent consent. The Living Will is a good example of the ethical principle of autonomy in action. I asked a very ill, very elderly woman, who was being admitted to the hospital, what she would want us to do if her heart stopped beating. "None of that resuscitation stuff," was her answer. "If you had a bad stroke would you want a feeding tube," I asked. Her answer was quick, "Only if I have a very good chance of coming back and knowing what's going on." I responded by writing on the chart, "Do not resuscitate (DNR)," and informed her family about her feeding tube wishes.

Essentially, the virtue of autonomy means that, as care providers, we must do our best to give our patients the tools necessary to make informed decisions regarding their care. If you are a person caring for another, then you have that responsibility. If you are

---

171 https://www.bma.org.uk/advice/employment/ethics/medical-students -ethics-toolkit/2-autonomy-or-self-determination

a person receiving care, you should expect to have the right to direct your own care as long as you are of sound mind and capable of doing so. The ethical challenge occurs when a person, whose competence is borderline, starts making unreasonable choices. In this situation, simple competency testing should be done, and, if indicated, there should be a consultation with a speech pathologist or a psychologist for more detailed testing. Sometimes an Ethics Committee needs to be asked to address difficulties and challenges that may occur. (More is said in **Chapter Six** about when one does or does not have the capacity to make decisions). It is so important to make a living will or advance directive and discuss them with your family BEFORE competence is lost. There are other medical virtues, too, such as justice, confidentiality, privacy and more, but for purposes of providing care or anticipating care for an elderly person, these four virtues work nicely: beneficence, nonmaleficence, veracity and autonomy. (Be kind, don't do harm, be honest and respect people's choice.)

Bottom line: There is not one perfect and most important virtue. We must take the four described virtues and balance them to make the right decision. We can try, even in a flawed way, to live ethically. We should live a life that is not selfish or harmful but helpful to others; not dishonest but truthful while considerate; not cruel and discriminating but respectful of the rights and choices of others. Then we should show our beliefs through actions as we teach by example.

TEACHING ETHICS BY EXAMPLE

Teaching someone the principles of ethics is as old as parenting. We try to teach our children how to live, to act, to make good choices. Through the ages, the storytellers have carried the burden of this responsibility, not only by entertaining the villagers as they gathered around the campfire but also by providing an example of a hero in the story. In this way, for many thousands of years, the storyteller has inspired young persons to become a hero by giving examples, metaphors and stories.

In a world of selfishness, dishonesty, political manipulation for power and discrimination, how do our children still find their way? Conventional and historical wisdom says that we learn by example. Just look at what examples abound these days: selfishness with criminals like Bernie Madoff, a Wall Street scoundrel; dishonesty with blatant false marketing by actors on TV; and discrimination by politicians and nonpoliticians against people of other religions, other races, other sexual orientation, other cultures, other anything. Indeed, if our children only learned by these kinds of examples, our society would be in big trouble.

Fortunately for all of us, there are many people who are good examples. Whether we know it or not, no matter the age, every one of us is on a quest for meaning. We find our way in life by choosing examples for living. I learned first from my parents how to treat children with kindness. There were many other examples for living: the farmer taught the work ethic, the football coach taught resilience, the debate coach taught intellectual curiosity, the college classmate taught kindness and the med school professor taught evidence-based science. I believe that we grow, especially, by example from the heroes around us. (Fortunately, the storyteller brings us metaphorical lessons not only from around the campfire but also through books, conferences, movies, TV shows, theater and even religions.)

The mythologist and religion expert, Joseph Campbell, often spoke about the hero's journey.[172] There is a similar story-metaphor coming from almost every culture which is meant to help the people find meaning by doing good deeds. The following classic hero story is from Greek mythology (note there are some similarities to the story of Jesus). It begins with an innocent baby, born from a mortal woman impregnated by a male god. The human-god baby becomes a young man and faces temptations from an evil menace and somehow escapes using wisdom. Maturing with the protection of the village, the young adult hero embarks on a quest for meaning during his earthly experience. The subsequent adventure commonly finds the hero facing challenges. The hero selflessly slays a dark angel, a fire-breathing dragon or some evil persona even though it puts himself in great danger. Often, he saves an innocent person while bringing compassion, truth, justice and equality to the nearby village.

Mythologist and religion expert Joseph Campbell in the 1950s[173]

172 https://en.wikipedia.org/wiki/Hero%27s_journey

173 Photo by Joan Halifax from https://commons.wikimedia.org/wiki/File:Joseph_Campbell_(cropped).png

The more modern hero story is different from the ancient hero's journey or Greek myth. The modern hero is an ordinary, significantly flawed person, someone with whom each of us can more closely relate, one who comes up out of the morass of our troubled society to represent something that gives direction and meaning to the lives of many. Huck Finn was a troubled character[174] raised by a drunken, child-beating father. Although Huck had little education and could be a scoundrel, he broke from his community's cultural bigotry to love and respect Jim, the runaway slave. The story brought understanding to the reader about the ugly nature of racism and discrimination and the value of simple honesty.

Another example of a modern hero comes with Johnny Depp's character, Don Juan DeMarco,[175] in the movie with the same name. The lead character, likely is schizophrenic or has some severe mental health ssue. He explains to the psychiatrist why he is Don Juan and why he has a life-long quest: "There are only four questions of value in life, Don Octavio. What is sacred? Of what is the spirit made? What is worth living for? And what is worth dying for? Of course, the answer to each is the same: only love." Don Juan is a flawed hero looking for the virtue of Love.

As a junior in medical school on the pediatric floor of Grady Hospital in Atlanta, Georgia, I first heard the age-old medical instruction from the intern above me: "See one, do one, teach one." Then I watched my instructor do a lumbar puncture on

---

174   https://mizzoumag.missouri.edu/2013/05/the-flawed-greatness
-of-huckleberry-finn/

175   https://en.wikipedia.org/wiki/Don_Juan_DeMarco

a baby who had a fever, in an effort to make sure there was no spinal meningitis. This procedure is also called a spinal tap. I saw several more before I did my first lumbar puncture under the instructor's watchful eye. After doing one or two more, and after reading all about it from the book, I taught another medical student how to perform a lumbar puncture on a baby. See one, do one, teach one.

Later that year I did numerous lumbar punctures on adults, and, two years later, as an intern on the neurology floor at Emory referral hospital, I presented a paper to fellow interns on the indications, techniques, complications and value of performing a lumbar puncture. Since then I have done many more lumbar punctures, always teaching my students nearby. I have realized how important learning and teaching by example is and, thus, have tried to be a good example at practicing medicine and at being a dad. Daniel Sulmasy, MD, PhD, a Catholic priest and ethicist, states that medical school teachers who are caring and trustworthy with their students, in turn, teach their students, by example, to be doctors who are caring and trustworthy with their patients.[176] "See one, do one, teach one."

Our modern hero is someone each of us could be. By finding and picking the right examples to follow, we can try, even in a flawed way, to live a life that is caring and trustworthy. In this way, people can discover a right path. Not only does our modern hero do the right thing, but she also helps others by being a good example.

---

176   JGIM, editorial pp. 514–515, July 2000.

An essay:
The Hippocratic oath and how it needed updating

THROUGH ANCIENT AND MODERN HISTORY, there is a tradition in the medical profession: each graduating medical student publicly takes an oath and promises to uphold high ethical standards. This hails back to ancient villages where clergy, lawyers and doctors would stand up in the town square and promise not to betray the trust of the public. It is a medical student's rite of passage which has been handed down for generations from our physician ancestors.

Historically, we recited the Hippocratic oath,[177] which is to swear by Apollo, the Physician, Asclepius, Hygiea, Panaceia and all the healing gods to preserve life and to care for all, regardless of rank, age or intellect. (This represented a shift in attitude in ancient Greece. Earlier, many had used the knowledge of medicines and herbs to poison others.) Also, the oath asks that the life of a slave, emperor, foreign man and child with a disability should be valued as equal in importance. (This was also a significant departure from the cultural biases and bigotry of the time.)

The traditional oath, however, is filled with outdated rules. For example, if the old oath is followed, the children of physicians would have preferential admission into medical school; surgeons could not cut out kidney or bladder stones or do any complex surgery except drain pus from

---

177   https://www.nlm.nih.gov/hmd/greek/greek_oath.html

abscesses; physicians could not take payment for providing care to patients except maybe room and board; and physicians would be conflicted in trying to provide enough pain medicines for suffering terminally ill patients. Indeed, the old oath was meant for another time.

Hippocrates[178]

I think it is safe to say that at every medical school in this country, graduating medical students still pledge to a contemporary version of the Hippocratic oath. Although there is some variation between schools, most versions promise to diminish suffering and enhance health; to do no harm; to speak truthfully and search for truth through science; and to respect the freedom of patient self-direction. Modern versions also are promising fair and just distribution of care when resources are limited, avoidance of overtreatment, avoidance of undertreatment, encouragement for physicians to ask for help when necessary and motivation to provide a warm, sympathetic and caring bedside manner.

---

178   Print of Aikin, John, 1747–1822 Enfield, William, 1741–1797, from https://commons.wikimedia.org/wiki/Category:Hippocrates

Bottom line: Caring for others less fortunate, requires an oath; this is more than tradition. It is a promise.

Questions and Answers about:
The Golden Rule:—An ancient and modern guide to making tough choices

Question: Regarding the case at the beginning of this chapter (about which a woman had endured severe brain injury and was in a permanent vegetative state:) Would stopping fluid feedings and allowing her a natural death be more merciful than keeping her alive for years in a vegetative state?

The answer is an unequivocal YES. The paradox of fluid replacement meant to sustain life is that it can also prolong pain and suffering. In this case, there is likely a significant burden of suffering from severe muscle spasms as well as the consequences of total bed rest and complete dependency. Even if she were alert and trapped in a dysfunctional body, consider the suffering due to an inability to move or speak. In addition, consider the persistent anguish of the family members who are repeatedly forced to consider the discomfort and suffering as well as the lost potential of this loved individual.

Question: Does withholding food and water cause suffering in end-of-life care?

The answer is an unequivocal NO. In fact, scientific data shows, during the dying process, brain endorphins, (natural pain relievers) kick in when respiratory function fails, oxygen levels get low, carbon dioxide levels climb and dehydration happens.[179] This allowed, a human being will slip away gently over an eight- to twelve-day period. This is how nature has done it for as long as humans have walked this earth; that is until we interrupted the natural process, less than a century ago, by learning how to provide artificial fluids in the form of feeding tubes or intravenous (IV) fluids. Of course, artificial fluids have rescued many lives, lives that needed to be saved, but the challenge is in understanding when rescuing is futile and causes undue suffering and harm.

As the end approaches, when people die in the old-fashioned way without tubes, they slip away easily and gently.[180] In contrast, people kept alive for prolonged periods with IV fluids or feeding tubes, without a chance of awakening, will likely suffer (as will their families). This is one of the most important questions to understand when caring for someone at the end of

---

179   https://www.curetoday.com/publications/cure/2012/summer2012/myths
-about-the-dying-process
180   https://www.ncbi.nlm.nih.gov/pmc/articles/PMC3083268/

their life. Paradoxically, providing fluids and feeding tube nutrition often does NOT relieve suffering but increases and prolongs it.[181]

Question: Is there a difference between not starting fluid feedings in the first place and stopping them?

The AMA Code of Medical Ethics, and the law of the land, both state that there is no ethical or legal difference between not starting treatment and stopping treatment. Any treatment started to enhance health and diminish suffering can be stopped, especially if treatment is no longer helping or is potentially causing harm.

Question: Do I, as an individual, or someone acting on my behalf, have the right to ask for tubes to be removed?

The American Medical Association's (AMA) Code of Medical Ethics states clearly, "Physicians are to sustain life but also to relieve suffering; and where one duty conflicts with the other, then the preference of the patient or his representative should prevail."[182] Like the

---

181 https://americanhospice.org/caregiving/artificial-nutrition-and-hydration -at-the-end-of-life-beneficial-or-harmful/

182 https://www.ama-assn.org/delivering-care/withholding-or-withdrawing -life-sustaining-treatment

CEO of a local hospital recently said, "The person, or the person's representative, should have the last say."

In this case, especially where sustaining life might cause suffering, the defined power of attorney (let's say it is the mother) has the right to ask to have life support and feedings discontinued. Further, the physician should honor those wishes unless this is not consistent with the physician's personal ethics. In the latter situation, the physician should transfer the patient to the care of another doctor. The same goes with the nursing home and their responsibility to find another facility to care for the patient if there is such a conflict.

Of course, if there are multiple people arguing over what is to be done or who has power of attorney (POA) over the individual, most often feeding tube nutrition would continue until the POA is defined or until the end. In an emergency room situation when the ER doctor detects indecision or has no clear direction from patient or family about resuscitation, everything will be done: breathing and feeding tubes will be inserted until the POA is assigned or until the patient finally escapes with death.

Question: What is the most practical lesson from this story of a woman in a permanent vegetative state?

You should talk to your family in advance about your wishes regarding a feeding tube when chances are futile for a return to reasonable function again. This is the most practical lesson: if your family members all know what your wishes are, they will more likely follow those wishes.[183] The family's wishes define the direction that the doctors and care providers will follow, even if you have an iron clad, lawyer-written, certified and notarized living will or power of attorney document. Talking to your family is most important when determining what you would and would not want, especially if recovery chances are poor. This conversation might prevent a lot of suffering.

The first point to take home is that you should define one power of attorney to make health-care choices for you and make a living will document with or without a lawyer. Following this, you should have a long talk with every member of your family explaining the one power of attorney and your health-care choices. Remember, an advance directive or living will doesn't outweigh the value of talking to your family. Second point, realize that sometimes, even when it appears you are absolutely doing the right thing, you may not be on the right track. Using ethical virtues in clarifying a direction can help you when you are struggling with tough choices.

Bottom line: Realize the value of comfort care when curative care is becoming futile and someone is approaching their dying time.

---

183   https://www.ama-assn.org/delivering-care/advance-directives

Question: You described primarily four ethical virtues. Is there one virtue that overshadows the others as most important?

The answer is no. I need to clarify this point once again. Experts say not one virtue is more important than another. Each case needs to be balanced according to the individual person and the individual situation.[184] Right to choose is NOT more important than honesty, doing good and not doing harm. Each one has its place and may be most important in a specific situation.

───※───

Question: Is it ever appropriate to lie to a patient?

The answer is yes. One's goal should always be to tell the truth to the patient, but there may come a time when balancing doing good, not doing harm and respecting choices, is accomplished better without telling the whole truth. An example is in dealing with an elderly newly demented person who becomes delusional and is convinced that his son is his long-deceased father. Experts suggest, now, that oftentimes it is best to simply go along with the delusion.[185] Another example might be in telling an untruth to avoid a severe emotional

---

184   https://www.scu.edu/ethics/ethics-resources/ethical-decision-making/ethics-and-virtue/

185   http://dailycaring.com/why-experts-recommend-lying-to-some-one-with-dementia/

trauma in a mild to moderately demented person. Of course, that deserves very careful consideration if the patient will eventually need to learn the truth. Again, it is important to realize that in trying to achieve balance, one virtue should not overshadow another.

<hr>

Question: Is it ever appropriate to deny a person's right to self-direct their care?

Self-directing care, which reflects valuing choice (autonomy), does not overshadow other virtues but is very important. For example, there may come a time when the choices of the patient are becoming progressively poorer and harm may be occurring to the patient or to others. Then the decision-making should be turned over to another person who should respectfully make the choices for the patient. That newly assigned patient advocate, or advocates (usually family), is obligated to balance virtues but mostly to respect the choices the patient would have made should she or he had normal capacity to choose.[186,187]

A physician or a judge can help the patient and family by making the determination when it is time to take away legal choices from the patient and also aid the family in making choices for the patient (substituted

186   https://www.ncbi.nlm.nih.gov/pmc/articles/PMC5109759/

187   https://www.mayoclinic.org/diseases-conditions/alzheimers-disease/expert-blog/dementia-and-independence/bgp-20128211

judgments). Sometimes the evidence of failing judgment becomes obvious because of fiscal issues. I had a very difficult case one time when a demented woman and her second husband were removing large amounts of cash from the demented woman's bank holdings, and the woman's son asked me what to do. I brought the adult children of the woman to meet with a judge and advised the judge of the situation. The judge stopped the removal of further money by the demented woman and her second husband.

Question: I am a caregiver of my father-in-law. Is it ever acceptable to put the person you are caring for accidentally at risk for harm?

It is virtually impossible to care for anyone without putting yourself and the person for whom you are caring at some risk. You have to live with that truth. The way to help someone is to take some risk and to put them at some risk, too. Helping them is worth the risk. For you to avoid any risk in providing care for someone is to not help anyone. Doing no harm is a goal but not always achievable. Use it to guide you, not rule you.

Question: Is it ever appropriate to care for someone in a way that you know will not benefit the patient or even do harm?

Yes. Balance the virtues. Sometimes telling the truth and respecting choices calls for withholding important care. Take, for example, caring for a person who is a Jehovah's Witness who is asking you to promise never to allow a blood transfusion. When asked, I have promised not to transfuse these patients, and I have always kept my promise even in times of great duress. A more challenging question occurs when a young child of Jehovah's Witness parents comes to a life-threatening situation requiring a transfusion. Should the ER physician follow the parental direction of no transfusion and face potential criminal prosecution, or should the transfusion be given to save the young life?[188] Another example occurs when the family wants the physician to do everything for their father who is dying from cancer. The physician should respect their choices and put in the feeding tube, or transfer the patient to someone who would.

Question: For a delirious dying patient, what is the most important therapy?

Delirium is a strange anxiety that sometimes overwhelms a newly confused person. It is amazing that common antianxiety medications fail for those in this condition. Benzodiazepams like lorazepam (Ativan) or

---

188   https://www.ncbi.nlm.nih.gov/pmc/articles/PMC4260316/

diazepam (Valium) are clearly ineffective for delirium and are NOT the first treatment. First line therapy for delirium is simply holding the patients' hand and providing personal reassurance. Second best is halo-peridol, a major tranquilizer.

Bottom line: The older I get, the more I am impressed that medicines are often second best to nonmedicinal ways to treat.[189]

Question: Is it ever appropriate to put to death (active euthanasia) a dying and suffering person?

This is a tough question and worthy of discussion. I believe that giving active euthanasia (providing a poison prescription or poisonous dose of medication with the INTENT to cause death) is never appropriate, even when someone is dying and suffering. Once physicians start on that path with the intent to cause death, the process becomes easier and more justified with every case. It becomes a slippery slope.[190]

I commonly prescribe aggressive sedation/pain medication for patients who are severely suffering and in the throes of dying. These medications are ordered with the INTENT to control pain, however, not to cause death. I realize this treatment likely brings

---

189   https://www.ncbi.nlm.nih.gov/pmc/articles/PMC3065676/

190   https://www.ama-assn.org/delivering-care/physician-assisted-suicide

these patients to an earlier death, but I do not believe it is wrong when the INTENT is for pain relief in a dying patient. It is not active euthanasia when the medicine is provided with the intention to treat pain. The word intent separates the act of providing enough pain medicine, even if it causes an earlier death, from the act of active euthanasia.

Question: What is passive euthanasia?

A better way of putting this is to "allow a natural death." Passive euthanasia means either to not start or to stop life sustaining therapy such as antibiotics, IV fluids, dialysis or respirator support when directed by the person dying or the family of the person dying.[191] There is some controversy with the term. There are those who say that withholding medical treatment (that likely would cause undue suffering) is not a passive decision.

Definition arguments can rage on, but I believe the intent to allow a natural death is an appropriate choice when the benefit of treatment is outweighed by the burden of the treatment. In cases of imminent death, despite all options, sometimes an inappropriate fear of death by the person dying, or by the family, prevents them

---

191   http://jme.bmj.com/content/31/2/64

from choosing this more comfortable option. I personally see this latter situation as tragic, and I'm concerned this kind of awful end is in the future of many who fail to face their own dying and are unwilling or unable to talk to their family about their wishes. (The fear of death is harmful to your health.)

———⁂———

Question: Would you please describe examples of patient dilemmas when virtues collide with one another?

1. Sometimes a medicine meant to "do good" also has a significant "do harm" side effect. For example, there is a dilemma when a person taking a baby aspirin daily to prevent a stroke, develops a long-term upset stomach and bleeding from the aspirin. When the choice to "take the medicine" versus "not to take it" is a draw, most often the best answer is drop the pill and to allow "do no harm" and Mother Nature win over the intervention. In this case: stop the aspirin. Of course, each individual situation needs to be considered. Sometimes, after some time, a lower dose of aspirin can be restarted.

2. Another example where the "do good" principle collides with the "do no harm" principle occurs when a stroke is severe enough to affect the ability to swallow, the prognosis is poor and family members start asking about a feeding tube early on. In my opinion, in the early hours and days

following a stroke, people often do better with less or no added fluids which allows for less edema of the brain. Usually I push for more time without starting a feeding tube. This allows us all to see how much recovery is going to occur. After a few days, it is easier to tell what is going to happen. Also, it should be evident by this time whether or not the ill person will be extremely compromised and require living her or his life out in a long-term care facility. At that point, I have found that the family is better able to decide and cope with their decision, whether it is to go full speed ahead with every intervention or not start IV fluids and not place a feeding tube.

3. Another example where the "do good" and "don't do harm" collide is when a long-standing stroke patient has, over time, lost the ability to protect his airway, inhales his food (aspiration), and develops pneumonia for the umpteenth time. An ethical problem arises when the family is split between a full-court press and letting him or her go. In this scenario, I spend time daily with the family trying to bring THEM to healing, to help THEM find unity and to understand their duty is to **respect what that patient would have wanted were he or she able to make the decision.**

4. Sometimes "freedom to choose" collides with the "do good" principle. For example, this dilemma occurs when a person of the Jehovah

Witness or Christian Scientist faith is bleeding and says, "no" to transfusion or any other standard form of treatment. Once a physician has met and agreed to care for a person of that faith and promises to respect their choice of no transfusion, then I believe the physician should fulfill the promise and NOT transfuse or NOT provide the treatment in accord with the verbal contract. I also respect a doctor's right to say "no" to being this patient's doctor, but that decision should be made at the first meeting when asked about transfusions.

5. Sometimes "truth telling" collides with the "do good" principle. An example would be when an ill person has cancer and the family asks the physician not to tell the patient. **If the patient is competent**, the family does not have the right to withhold information from that person. In fact, I first ask permission of the competent ill person if I can talk to that person's family about her or his illness. If the ill person does not have the capacity to understand the situation, then, and only then, do I go to the family first. If the patient has borderline dementia, I simultaneously inform the patient and the family. The family will be educated that, as the dementia progresses, they should still involve the ill person in decision making as much as possible. If I am caring for an incompetent or even unconscious ill person, I try

to have most conversations with the family or the nurse **in the room with the incompetent ill person**, making the discussion about the patient audible to her or him, especially if the person is close to death. Why not? The words the family and I would be having are always caring and considerate even if the conversation is frankly about dying.

6. Sometimes "truth telling" and "freedom to choose" collide with the "do good" principle. Years ago, I was called by a social worker to see a person with a progressively paralyzing condition. The social worker noted that the patient's family was protecting her from the news of the severity of her condition. Decisions for aggressive therapy were being made by the family even though the patient had the capacity (was competent) to make her own decisions. (Capacity is like driving safely and competent is like having a license to drive.) An aware social worker thought this was not fair to the patient and wanted me to talk to her. I came to the bedside, and, with the family present, I spoke honestly to the person about her terrible, deteriorating neurological condition and informed her that she had the right to refuse treatment if that was her desire. I spoke with compassion, trying to be supportive, and did not strip her of all hope. She was obviously upset by the bad news, and the family reacted angrily, ordering me to go away and

to never come back. I felt very sad yet justified in doing what I did, and I think the person with the illness subsequently made some tough choices. I was surprised that she died a few weeks later. The important point is that **a competent patient's choice overrules the family's choice.**

7. More examples when one virtue collides with another happens when someone asks:

    A. . . . for more pain medicines than you, as a care provider, are comfortable providing. Care providers also have the right to choose. When appropriate, care providers should say "no."

    B. . . . for patient-directed, physician-assisted suicide, when the patient is suffering with very terminal illness. I struggle with a patient's intent to commit suicide (especially if there is ANY possibility of depression) or the physician's intent to cause death. On the other hand, I do not struggle with the intent to relieve suffering, so the physician or care provider should do their level best to provide more pain relief for the patient when apropos.

Bottom line: The care provider and care giver should start with valuing the individual. This is the core of medical ethics. Also, they should be having open communication, listening as well as talking with the patient and family during tough times and good times. I think it is also especially important that the care provider and care giver is aware of the heightened risk of depression during any illness and that goes double during the dying process.

These are ethical responsibilities for all care providers, care-givers and families trying to help any individual with any medical problem but especially one who is dying.

Chapter Six

Memory Lapse

Alzheimer's, Parkinson's and other causes for dementia

Case Study:
Two women diagnosed with dementia, a study in comparison

IN THE SAME NURSING HOME, two patients live with the same diagnosis of dementia but with very different demeanors. Both had full lives and were productive and creative members of society. Both were loved by their families before and with their dementia. Both were diagnosed with the same disease, yet the condition varied dramatically from one patient to the other. Now, years after their dementia began, Mrs. A holds a doll in her arms most of the time, seems to always have a beautiful smile and is agreeable to the nursing staff as they guide her through the day. Mrs. B lies in her darkened room, cocooned in her covers, scowling at any who approach. She appears afraid, suspicious and angry even to her beloved daughter, who has always been the apple of her eye. Both Mrs. A and Mrs. B have dementia, and, yet, each is so very different. The daughters of Mrs. A and Mrs. B visit at least once every day to feed their mothers over their lunch breaks. Both daughters are extremely supportive. What drives the daughters to be so attentive, especially the daughter of Mrs. B who is almost punished when she comes to see her mom? This story of comparisons simultaneously shows how different dementia may present and how loyal and consistent caregivers can be despite that difference.

Loving one-hundred-year-old woman with doll[192]

GENERALIZED DEMENTIA, DEFINING AND TESTING

Dementia is a broad term describing memory loss, thinking changes and deterioration of social ability, all of which interfere with daily acts of normal living. The American Academy of Neurology defines people with generalized dementia as having

---

192   Photo from private collection, with permission by family

"impaired intellectual functioning that interferes with normal activities and relationships."[193] Dementia is not a simple topic. It is not a specific disease but rather a broad category of conditions caused by several different brain disorders. Dementia can evolve with a myriad of symptoms, affecting individuals in many ways and requiring varying kinds of treatment. While the word dementia can mean many things, dementia is NEVER a derogatory or negative term. It is a debilitating condition but NOT a pejorative descriptor.

From a physician's standpoint, dementia is a huge diagnostic and therapeutic challenge. From a personal standpoint, it is a terrible and dreaded condition that, if not handled with care, can tear families apart. The list of causes for dementia, noted on the graph found later in this chapter, indicates that only a few causes are reversible, and, although there are some treatments to lessen symptoms for a few months, most causes are progressive and devastating, despite medicine. That means the diagnosis and work-up is very important so that treatable causes can be defined and treatment can be initiated. Almost 6.8 million people in the U.S. have some form of dementia, and one-half of all people older than eighty-five will be diagnosed with the condition.[194] (Not to be so discouraging, another way of looking at it is that almost one-half of those older than eighty-five have NO significant memory loss and are NOT demented.)

193 http://tools.aan.com/apps/disorders/index.cfm?event=database:disorder.view&disorder_id=903

194 https://www.ninds.nih.gov/Disorders/All-Disorders/Dementia-Information-Page#disorders-r1

The cardinal sign for dementia is the loss of antegrade memory, more commonly called **short-term memory loss**, which means losing the ability to learn a new thought and to retain that new memory. Short-term memory loss is a going-forward process. A simple test for **short-term memory loss** is to ask the person to remember three named places or objects, and several minutes later, ask her or him to recall those places or objects. (I usually change it up by picking some state in the U.S., then a fruit or vegetable, and finally a tool or auto of some kind.) Sometimes people with significant dementia can still remember much of their distant past, but what is most significant and debilitating is that they cannot learn a new thing. Note that, although important in the work-up, no laboratory or imaging test is as crucial to the diagnosis as this simple test. Also, note that the condition can range from mild to severe, the onset gradual or rapid (although usually it is subtle and the decline is slow), and the cause is spontaneous or genetic. Generalized dementia is a very broad category, indeed! (More on this test later in this chapter.)

Besides **short-term memory loss**, other signs for generalized dementia include changes in muscle function (especially with walking gait), disorientation, personality and behavioral changes, suspicion of those around them, difficulty with planning and organization (executive function), agitation and frustration, hallucinations and delusions that can be visual or auditory, inappropriate and aggressive sexual behaviors and decreased ability to make reasonable decisions.

DIAGNOSTIC CLUES AND MEDICAL EVALUATION
OF DEMENTIA:

The multiple causes of dementia[195] include: Alzheimer's dementia, which is gradual and with no or minimal walking-rhythm (gait) abnormality until very late; vascular dementia, which can happen in an abrupt manner and can suddenly and repeatedly worsen in a step-like worsening character; Lewy body dementia, which acts like, or is associated with, Parkinson's disease; Frontotemporal dementia, which can cause huge personality changes; dementia associated with acute and chronic thiamine deficiency most often related to alcohol excess; and Chronic Traumatic Encephalopathy (CTE), which follows repeated head trauma such as found in bicyclists, football players, boxers and soldiers.

When there is more than one cause of dementia, it is called mixed dementia. For example, Alzheimer's and vascular dementia often run together. In fact, some suggest that for Alzheimer's disease to occur, there needs to be at least some vascular disease. To support that, there are cases where autopsy findings show in the brain the pathological and microscopic (plaques and tangles) of Alzheimer's in people who had NOT been demented. There is evidence that lifestyle changes aimed at preventing vascular disease also prevents Alzheimer's, supporting the theory that the two are related.

The different conditions to consider when evaluating someone with dementia also include memory loss from thyroid deficiency, B12 deficiency, brain tumors, depression and overall weakness from medical problems like heart failure,

---

195 http://www.alz.org/dementia/types-of-dementia.asp

emphysema (COPD), infection, kidney failure and other complex chronic medical problems. Proper medical evaluation should occur if a loved one starts excessive repetition of stories or requests, loses the ability to hold on to a new thought or if there are any significant and unexplained changes in her or his mental capacity.

Unfortunately, those persons experiencing the condition of dementia don't usually seek out medical care and may try to cover up their problem. It becomes an important responsibility of the spouse, child, sibling or friend to get the patient to a care provider and to explain to the doctor their observations. (Everyone should have a good general exam once a year, so this is a good excuse to get them to the doctor if the person with possible problems is reluctant.) Most care providers appreciate having the spouse or a knowledgeable adult child in the room with the one being examined to make sure everything is said that needs to be said, especially if there is concern about dementia. If you can't attend the appointment with your loved one, speak with the doctor or leave her or him a message with your concerns prior to the appointment. Please don't give up if the doctor doesn't catch early dementia the first time. In my experience, the spouse, or the adult children, often provide the most important clues to the diagnosis of dementia.

A general medical exam is important in evaluating anyone with possible dementia and should include a careful questioning about each of the organ systems (medical people define this as "the review of systems") and a careful top-to-bottom physical exam. Laboratory tests should include a complete chemical panel, complete blood count, thyroid tests (TSH and Free T4), a vitamin B12 level, and even a syphilis test (VDRL or RPR) if there is any possibility for exposure in a lifetime. Finally, in those with a significant change in memory, either a CT scan (computerized sliced X-ray pictures) or an MRI (magnetic resonance imaging) of the brain should be done, at least once, to rule out tumors. The CT is most helpful for defining when there is bleeding and, in general, is best when the neurological changes occurred in the recent past (days to a few months). The MRI is most helpful for defining when there are tumors and the subtle changes of multiple sclerosis (MS) or similar structural brain lesions and is best when the neurological changes range from months to years. This will be decided by your physician or neurologist. Most of the time when I have ordered a CT or MRI for evaluation of dementia, these imaging tests were normal. Don't expect an answer from these imaging tests, but one or the other should be done to make sure no tumor, blood clot, dilation of the brain ventricles (fluid lakes normally found in the brain) or brain mass is growing within the skull. Alzheimer's disease is the likely diagnosis when these tests are normal or negative, short-term (antegrade) memory continues to deteriorate and gait is relatively preserved.

THE MINI-MENTAL EXAM AND OTHER TESTS TO DEFINE DEMENTIA

The most well-known and simple test for brain power, or capacity to think, is the Mini-Mental State Examination (MMSE),[196] which has been patented, and the patent owner requires payment

---

196 http://www.geripal.org/2011/12/copyrights-and-copylefts-in-medicine.html

to use the test. The MMSE has been shown to be less sensitive for early dementia than the less-well-known Montreal Cognitive Assessment (MoCA) which is free to be used by anyone.[197,198] Also free, and helpful, is the St. Louis Mental Status (SLUMS) test.[199] While all three are good tests, I prefer the MoCA and the SLUMS, as they are freely available to anyone and may be better tests. However, many care providers are most familiar with and prefer to use the MMSE, so this discussion will refer primarily to the MMSE. There is also a three-minute test called the Mini-Cog which involves a three-item recall test for short-term memory problems and a simply scored clock drawing test which acts as a similar memory screen.[200]

I often ask speech pathologists to help make decisions about competence. They usually use multiple tests including the MMSE. The diagnosis remains a very complicated issue, and a team approach for diagnosis is best. Attempts at treatment and reha-bilitation are important for the person affected as well as for their family. Consulting a neurologist can be very helpful in reassuring the family. Discuss the need for a neurology consult with the primary care doctor as often there is nothing more to be gained with a consultation, and too many opinions may cause distraction, confusion and misdirection for the patient and the

197   http://onlinelibrary.wiley.com/doi/10.1111/j.1532–5415.2005.53221.x/full

198   Nasreddine, Phillips, Bédirian, Charbonneau, Whitehead, Collin, Cummings, Chertkow: The Montreal Cognitive Assessment, MoCA: A Brief Screening Tool for Mild Cognitive Impairment, J Am Ger Soc. 30 March 2005.

199   http://medschool.slu.edu/agingsuccessfully/pdfsurveys/slumsexam_05.pdf

200   https://mini-cog.com/

family. Sometimes a phone call by the primary care physician to a neurologist is all that is needed for everyone's reassurance.

I had a patient, about eighty years of age, who came in with mild pneumonia and was quite dehydrated and malnourished. I presumed that much of this acute illness was the result of the side effects of several medicines he was taking for his multiple medical problems. On arrival, his MMSE score was 16. (Twenty-four to 30 is scored as normal, 19–23 is mild dementia, 18 or less is moderate to severe dementia. In general, the cut-off for competency to make legal decisions is somewhere around 20.) After two days of careful treatment in the hospital, with removal of some unnecessary medications and with improvement of his pneumonia after effective antibiotics, his MMSE gradually improved and, before sending him home, it was 25, which is within normal limits. This case illustrates how there is often variability in the brain function in the same patient over time, how medicines can affect thinking and how important general health is to brain function. When intellectual loss as defined by one of these tests is of acute onset (happened quickly) and is reversible, then it is not likely dementia but rather is better defined as delirium. The MMSE is up for interpretation in each individual case depending on the whole health picture of that individual.

Several years ago, I used a different, simpler, three question test. First, how does the patient function at home over time? (I call it the "Tupperware in the oven question" because one of my patients, years ago, perfectly illustrated her judgmental dysfunction by her dangerous cooking choices.) Second, how well does the patient do in remembering three places or objects? (Remembering three objects is expected with normal function; remembering only two indicates mild to moderately compromised memory; and remembering one or less indicates seriously compromised memory function.) Third, how well does the patient do with all the other typical tests for dementia? (These tests include asking the patient to: count backward, explain orientation to time, to place, to situation, draw a clock and repeat and explain a phrase such as, "A stitch in time saves nine," or "An apple a day keeps the doctor away?") (For the third part, I usually just ask the "explain a phrase" question.)

I conducted a study of **all the patients** in two different nursing homes using the aforementioned three-question test. Using this test, I compared my results to the simple yes or no opinion of the head nurse when she was asked, "Is this patient demented or not?" (At that time, medical records often did NOT point out the patient's diagnosis of dementia.) It was interesting to find that the nurse's opinion matched perfectly with our three-part test method. I first conducted this study in the mid-1980s and then again in the mid-1990s, and, both times, the results of this test matched the head nurse's opinion. This finding speaks to the value of a common-sense opinion, especially of a trained nurse, or even of those who know the person well.

Pertinent to this discussion of diagnosing dementia, I also discovered a higher percentage of nursing home patients were demented in the 1990s as compared to the 1980s. The first study in the 1980s found that about 50 percent of those living in the nursing homes I studied were affected by mild or worse dementia, while ten years later, the percentage had climbed to about 75 percent. Most of these patients had dementia along with other medical illnesses.

I think that the increasing percentage of dementia in nursing homes, over those ten years, was due to the reduction in how our society paid for nursing home care. In addition, those who were high functioning elderly and who needed only a minimal amount of help, moved from long-term care to newly developed assisted living centers. Now, if people need some help, they can first go to a less expensive independent living community, then to an assisted living facility before finally needing a more expensive skilled nursing home. When these step-up types of care became available, it raised the percentages of people with more severe disabilities and with moderate to severe dementia receiving care in a skilled nursing home. I mention this because it reflects an important change over my professional lifetime in caring for people with dementia. Most importantly this trend has allowed those with minimal disability or mild dementia to keep their independence much longer and even delay the need for the diagnosis and label of dementia.

AT HOME WITH DEMENTIA

In the U.S., there are almost five million people with mild to moderate dementia, and studies show that about 70 percent are at home, either alone or with a caregiver (often a spouse). If people with mild to moderate dementia can stay home safely, this saves Medicare and Medicaid a great deal of taxpayer money. More importantly, this provides those people affected with dementia their preferred environment. Indeed, it is important to allow all people the chance to stay at home whenever possible.

Recent Johns Hopkins research studied more than 250 people with dementia who were living at home[201] and found that 99 percent of those with dementia and 97 percent of their caregivers had at least one "unmet need." Safety issues, such as poor lighting in nighttime walkways, were the greatest unmet need, and unmet needs resulted in a higher risk of falling. Other unmet needs included inadequate exercise, poor follow-up with health-care providers, not having prepared legal and estate planning and not receiving needed help with medications and the activities of daily living. Researchers found that those with lower income, with depression and with borderline, rather than severe dysfunction, had significantly more unmet needs.

When there were at-home caregivers for folks with early dementia, the caregivers were often not aware of these deficiencies. The study also pointed out that the needs of the caregivers were often ignored or unrecognized. Remarkably, at-home caregiver stress and depression were of the strongest predictors for an earlier move of the compromised patient to a long-term care facility (nursing home).

Methods to enhance a person's ability to stay at home are not difficult. Preparation for legal issues and estate planning should be done early and BEFORE memory loss. Other methods include providing raised toilet seats, grab bars in the bath and bedroom, properly tacked-down carpets, good nighttime lighting and proper day- and nighttime footwear. Researchers also strongly advise

---

201 http://www.hopkinsmedicine.org/news/media/releases/living_at_home _with_dementia

providing enhanced support for caregivers such as educating them about support services available (social services, occupational therapy and caregiver support groups). In addition, screening for **depression in the caregiver** should be provided, and, if present, treatment should be provided. Helping the caregiver would go a long way in helping people stay at home as they age.

Adult Day Care (ADC), when available, could be another resource for those caregivers. An ADC can provide care for a person living with dementia while family members are at work or school. Unfortunately, this resource is not available everywhere, primarily because it is underfunded.

Bottom line: Most of us (and our families) are not prepared for the possibility of dementia in our aging family. If we prepare, we greatly improve the chances for those being affected with dementia to stay at home.

My friend, microbiologist and researcher, Kyle Hain, provided the following in a personal story which I found profoundly moving and appropriate to share here:

"I watched as my grandmother slowly slipped into dementia. What's worse, she knew she was becoming demented and was so incredibly depressed by it. It was terrible for my family, most especially for my mother who took care of her daily. To this day, I still don't understand how my mother did it, but it was incredibly hard for all of us. I know Mom made a lot of right steps: got my grandma into a good long-term care facility with good people when the time was right; she kept an amazing support network around; she visited regularly yet made sure it didn't become her life; and she kept a positive attitude filled with humor, always reflecting on the good times and making the best of her situation. I don't know the fullest extent, but, perhaps, she was talking to someone as well, a counselor or someone who could help her understand her feelings. If she wasn't, she should have. My father, who was supportive, but not entirely active in the process, told me how much of a godsend Mom was; how he's so happy to have her because he wouldn't be able to handle it emotionally if his parents ever ended up the same way."

(For more on this topic of caring for the caregiver, see **Chapter Seven.**)

THE DIFFERENCE BETWEEN CAPACITY AND COMPETENCE

Capacity is a functional term while competence is a legal term. Capacity describes the capabilities of the individual. Is the person in question capable of learning a new thing? Is she or he capable of living and functioning independently? Competence, by comparison, is defined by a duly qualified medical-mental health professional or a judge. A competent person has the necessary mental capacity to make reasonable legal choices. An incompetent person does not. Examples of legal choices that could be taken away from an incompetent person would include writing a check, making a will and writing a living will.[202] Capacity is a descriptor. Competence has legal consequences.

202   https://lifeinthefastlane.com/ccc/capacity-and-competence

The legal definition of a competent individual (one who can make legal choices) is one who can demonstrate four elements: 1. Understand the choices and alternatives available, 2. Realize the consequences of those choices, 3. Communicate the choices and 4. Bring action to the choices in a rational fashion. In my opinion, **competence can roughly be determined with the three-question memory test described earlier.** When there is no clear-cut definable dementia but there is concern, then it might be good to have the primary care provider, a neurologist, a speech pathologist, an ethics committee or a judge be part of this process. Another component to the definition of competence comes into play when the individual may have a normal memory but is psychologically disconnected from reality. When I need to determine if someone is psychologically competent or not, I generally refer them to either a psychologist, a psychiatrist or a judge.

ALZHEIMER'S DEMENTIA

Alzheimer's disease causes more than 60 percent of all dementias. This condition is characterized by a gradual, unrelenting short-term (antegrade) memory loss. Again, short-term memory loss occurs when one can't learn a new thing. This usually is associated with a subtle personality change along with a steady, general and nonreversible deterioration of memory over time.[203] Often, but not always, Alzheimer's disease is age related, and there is preservation of the walking rhythm (gait) until the later stages of the disease. This characteristic helps differentiate Alzheimer's

---

203 https://www.ninds.nih.gov/Disorders/All-Disorders/Alzheimers-Disease-Information-Page

disease from stroke-induced dementia and most other forms of dementia since they generally cause gait dysfunction. Ninety percent of Alzheimer's disease occurs in those older than sixty-five-years old (late onset Alzheimer's disease) leaving ten percent in those younger than sixty-five (early onset).

There are two great challenges in dealing with people who have Alzheimer's disease. First, this can develop so gradually that the changes are not noticed and definable or are just blamed on getting older. Second, sometimes the earliest sign of the condition is paranoia or other emotional changes in the patient. For close family members or friends seeing and living with these heartbreaking changes, the condition of Alzheimer's can be cataclysmic, making it very difficult to deal with the person losing her or his memory.

Complicated microscopic findings on autopsy are usually found in people who were affected with this disease (amyloid plaques, neurofibrillary tangles, loss of connections between neurons, and neuronal death with shrinking of the brain). I mention these after-death pathological findings only to make the point that, in general, these are found in people with the clinical diagnosis of Alzheimer's disease (memory loss, dysfunction of the activities of daily living, and emotional changes) or mixed Alzheimer's with vascular dementia.

VASCULAR OR STROKE-INDUCED DEMENTIA

Vascular dementia is typically caused by a single large stroke or a series of abrupt minor strokes with repeated events in a step-by-step (the experts call this saltitory) overlapping way with improvement between events. Vascular dementia also can result from subtle multiple tiny strokes (multi-infarcts) that affect both sides of the brain and causes generalized dementia.[204] The abrupt or more sporadic nature of vascular dementia generally helps differentiate it from Alzheimer's disease, although multi-infarct dementia (MID) may look much like Alzheimer's. MID is different from Alzheimer's because patients with multi-infarct dementia often have a slow and short shuffling gait, urinary incontinence, and some swallowing difficulties (findings somewhat different from those with Alzheimer's alone).

By comparison to larger strokes, Alzheimer's is a relentless, gradually worsening process usually without gait abnormality. It is fascinating to me that vascular dementia causes 50 percent of all dementia in Japan but causes only 20 to 40 percent of dementia in Europe and the U.S. Although we don't know why ratios are different in two countries, it must be that Japan has either less Alzheimer's disease or more vascular disease. I would speculate that they have less Alzheimer's considering their diet, relative lack of obesity, and higher activity levels.

A stroke is defined by a blockage of blood flow to brain tissue. This can happen from a clot that starts in a brain artery, from a clot that travels from somewhere else and lodges in a brain artery or from a brain-bleeding event from a leaky or ruptured artery which, in turn, eventually blocks blood flow to brain tissue. These interruptions of the oxygen and nutrients supplied by the blood result in various degrees of sudden brain damage. In contrast to Alzheimer's, vascular disease may or may not progress over time.

---

204 https://www.ninds.nih.gov/Disorders/All-Disorders/Multi-Infarct-Dementia-Information-Page

The patient with vascular dementia has a history of high blood pressure (HBP), diabetes or heart disease about 80 percent of the time. Prevention of vascular dementia is clearly related to preventing or controlling one or more of these deadly conditions. Aside from living a good lifestyle and preventing or treating sleep apnea, commonly physicians and care providers promote statin or cholesterol treatments in an attempt to prevent vascular disease. (See **Chapter Two** for a discussion of the minimal help these medicines provide in preventing vascular disease. **I believe that statin or cholesterol-lowering medications do not even come close when comparing statins to a healthy lifestyle in preventing vascular disease.**) Probably the most important medication to prevent more brain-clotting caused strokes is 81mg to 365mg of simple aspirin or a similar antiplatelet drug. These antiplatelet medications (these thin the blood by removing platelets that help with clotting) should not be started if there is evidence of bleeding into or around the brain which is another cause for stroke symptoms. When anyone appears in the ER with a new stroke, along with a careful history and examination, the CT scan defines whether the stroke is due to a clot or a bleed and what treatment is best and safest. Please establish a relationship with a knowledgeable and trustworthy physician or care provider in managing this complex disorder.

People with vascular dementia commonly have an unusually slow and short marching gait, urinary incontinent, swallowing difficulties and some alteration in speech. Vascular dementia may cause less memory loss and more personality change, but those findings are highly variable. Also, in contrast to the smooth,

gradual deterioration of Alzheimer's disease, vascular dementia
usually progresses in a step-like, jerky (on-again, off-again) manner
of deterioration, like going down steps. Although every case is
different, vascular dementia may run together with Alzheimer's
disease in a way which is called a mixed dementia.

PARKINSON'S LEWY BODY DEMENTIA

Another cause of cognitive deterioration and memory loss is
Lewy body dementia (LBD) which acts like, or is associated with,
Parkinson's disease.[205] Along with worsening memory issues
(progressive cognitive decline), there are hallucinations, loss of
abstract thinking, greatly fluctuating attention and alertness
and depression. Although the cause of LBD is not known, this
condition is characterized by Lewy bodies (which are abnormal
brain protein deposits) found in the nuclei of the nerve cells that
control memory and muscle control. Although some people with
Parkinson's disease have Lewy bodies and are burdened with
dementia, some are without Lewy bodies and without dementia. (Just to make it even more confusing, some people with
Alzheimer's disease and no Parkinson's disease also have Lewy
bodies.) When a patient with Parkinson's disease develops this
type of dementia, some would label it separately from Parkinson's
disease, calling it "dementia with Lewy bodies." Usually Lewy
body dementia causes a more rapidly progressive dementia than
Alzheimer's; however, the treatment options are just as poor as

205   https://www.mayoclinic.org/diseases-conditions/lewy-body-dementia/
symptoms-causes/syc-20352025

for Alzheimer's[206] which are only symptomatic, temporary and, presently, disappointing.

FRONTOTEMPORAL DEMENTIA

Frontotemporal dementia (FTD), which commonly affects fifty to sixty-five-year-old people, can cause huge personality changes and was originally called Pick's disease.[207] This is a diverse group of uncommon disorders (the causes of which are poorly understood) that involve neuronal loss in the frontal and temporal lobes of the brain. FTD accounts for 20 percent of young onset dementia. In 40 to 75 percent of the time, FTD is misdiagnosed as early onset Alzheimer's disease. People with frontotemporal dementia can be classified into three groups: 1. Those with changes in social and personal behavior indicated by a loss of social awareness, poor impulse control, a lack of tact, agitated or blunted emotions, listlessness, overly compulsive behavior, increased sexual interest, changes in food preference, neglect of personal hygiene and decreased energy; 2. Those with impaired word comprehension even when her or his speech flows normally; and 3. Those who are nonspeaking. The latter two groups may or may not experience behavioral changes.

Along with deficits in language skills such as expressive difficulty (speaking) and receptive difficulty (understanding what others are saying), sometimes there are movement problems with FTD that look like Parkinson's disease or amyotrophic lateral sclerosis (ALS or Lou Gehrig's disease.) With FTD, there can be

206   https://www.ninds.nih.gov/Disorders/All-Disorders/Dementia-Lewy
-Bodies-Information-Page

207   https://www.ninds.nih.gov/Disorders/All-Disorders/Frontotemporal
-Dementia-Information-Page

tremor, rigidity, spasm, poor coordination, swallowing problems and weakness. It is also interesting that half of those with FTD have a family history of depression.

ACUTE AND CHRONIC THIAMINE DEFICIENCY AND ASSOCIATED DEMENTIA (WERNICKE'S ENCEPHALOPATHY AND KORSAKOFF'S AMNESIA SYNDROME), MOST OFTEN DUE TO ALCOHOL EXCESS

Wernicke's encephalopathy is a fancy name for an acute phase of thiamine deficiency (thiamine is also called vitamin B1).[208] Thiamine deficiency can happen as the result of malnourishment from eating disorders, unusual diets, chemotherapy, prolonged vomiting and, most commonly, from alcohol abuse. Symptoms of Wernicke's encephalopathy include the loss of muscle coordination, balance problems, vision issues, confusion, low temperature, low blood pressure and coma. Treatment is intravenous or intramuscular thiamine supplementation during recovery and, later, oral supplementation or, better yet, a balanced diet to include plenty of nonstarchy vegetables, fruit and the avoidance of alcohol.

Dry Martini[209]

208   https://pubs.niaaa.nih.gov/publications/arh27-2/134–142.htm

209   Photo by Cdeverist at English Wikipedia from https://commons.wikimedia.org/wiki/File:Martini_2.jpg

Korsakoff's amnesia syndrome is a chronic phase of thiamine deficiency that occurs over a prolonged time period, or repeated acute episodes, resulting in permanent damage to nerves, spinal cord and brain. The major symptom is permanent short-term (antegrade) memory loss. Along with this devastating effect, there can also be disorientation, vision problems, tremor and coma. Many believe that Korsakoff's syndrome is Wernicke's thiamine deficiency syndrome but reoccurring until the memory loss becomes permanent. (For more on alcohol see **Chapter Two.**)

CHRONIC TRAUMATIC ENCEPHALOPATHY (CTE)

Chronic traumatic encephalopathy (CTE, also called traumatic brain injury or dementia pugilistica) represents a progressive, degenerative, permanent dementia found in people who have experienced multiple, blunt, traumatic injuries to the head and brain.[210] Initially recognized in boxers, CTE has been recognized in those who have participated in bicycling, football, baseball, softball, basketball, skateboarding, soccer, watersports, rugby, ice hockey, wrestling, cheerleading, rodeo (especially bull riding) and other sports.[211] It is also noted to occur more often in people who have experienced repeated concussions from domestic violence or military combat experience.

Timing of a second brain injury seems to be a major factor for making the brain injury permanent with more long-term problems

210   https://www.ninds.nih.gov/Disorders/All-Disorders/Traumatic-Brain -Injury-Information-Page

211   http://www.aans.org/en/Patients/Neurosurgical-Conditions-and -Treatments/Sports-related-Head-Injury

when the second is shortly after the first. This explains why those with concussions should NOT go back in the game. The rule is to stay out of play for a period of time, such as two weeks after symptoms resolve, when the concussion is severe (loss of consciousness).

Army-Navy game
December, 2000[212]

Symptoms often begin years after the trauma even if it were a repeated mild trauma. Early on, those affected experience confusion, disorientation, dizziness (vertigo) and headaches. Progression usually occurs with memory loss, paranoid behavior, aggression, depression, judgmental changes and, eventually, speech, visual and swallowing difficulties. On autopsy, there is characteristic brain shrinkage and an enlargement of the fluid-filled pockets or the lakes (ventricles) within the brain. Pathological changes of CTE, which can be seen on the microscope, include the loss of neurons, protein-amyloid deposits (tau protein) and certain tangles of nerve insulation cells.[213,214]

---

212   U.S. Navy photo by Photographer's Mate Airman Saul Ingle from https://commons.wikimedia.org/wiki/File:001202-N-1539I-002_Navy_Football_Game.jpg

213   http://concussionfoundation.org/learning-center/what-is-cte?gclid=C-jOKEQjwt6fHBRDtm9O8xPPHq4gBEiQAdxotvDIffM9f2umsKWL25sjWn-NzF49aj9WfFnOpFsOecKcgaAIxZ8P8HAQ

214   2017 Concussion in Sport Group concussion, British Journal of Sports Medicine. Oct. 2016.

DEMENTIA TYPE	ONSET AND TIME ISSUES	CAUSE(S)	FINDINGS ON EXAM	DIAGNOSTIC CLUES	TESTS AND TREATMENT
Generalized Dementia: rule out: B12 deficit, Low Thyroid, Syphilis, Brain tumor, Depressed, Gen. Med. problems, Drugs, B1 deficiency	Mixed	Listed on Dementia type column to the far left	Mixed	Mixed	B12, Thyroid tests, syphilis test, careful general Hx* and Exam, CT* or MRI*, maybe LP*, B1 (thiamine) supplement
Alzheimer's	Slow and gradual	Unknown	cover-up on Hx.	Gradual onset, normal gait, paranoia	MRI & LP may find clue, absent other abnormalities, Supportive Rx* only
Vascular (stroke) Thrombus in artery, Clot flipped from carotid or heart, Subdural hematoma, Bleed into brain	Sudden and step-like progression	Single or multiple, small or large clots form within brain vessels, flip from carotids or heart, or bleeding on outside or into the brain	Hx. of DM*, CAHD*, HBP*, sometimes asymmetrical neural findings	Slow, tiny steps & marching gait, one-sided weakness, swallowing difficulty	CT scan better than MRI, EKG*, echo of carotids and of heart indicated. Start aspirin, clopidogrel (Plavix), or aspirin/dipyridamole (Aggrenox), or warfarin if atrial fib*
Parkinson's Lewy Body dementia	More rapid onset than Alzheimer's	Unknown, why often associated with Parkinson's	Rigidity, slow to initiate movement, tremor that reduces with movement	Hallucinations, fluctuating attention	Medication for Parkinson's (which is only symptomatic and not great) and supportive Rx
Frontotemporal dementia	Several types and variable nature	Unknown, frontal neural loss from unknown cause	Huge personality changes, loss impulse control, compulsive, poor hygiene	Like Alzheimer's but in younger person with severe loss of social awareness	Supportive Rx

DEMENTIA TYPE	ONSET AND TIME ISSUES	CAUSE(S)	FINDINGS ON EXAM	DIAGNOSTIC CLUES	TESTS AND TREATMENT
Alcohol induced (acute: Wernicke's, chronic: Korsakoff's)	Variable depending on alcohol and nutrition	Some think acute and repeated vitamin B1 (thiamine) deficiency	Marked antegrade memory loss, can't find own room in hospital	Poor balance, falling, confusion, low temperature, low blood pressure, coma	Stop drinking, thiamin supplement, improve nutrition, (best thiamin foods: yeast, cereal, beans, nuts, and meat)
Chronic Traumatic Encephalopathy	May come on years later	Repeated head trauma	Early: HAs*, confusion Late: memory loss, paranoia, aggression, depression, speech and swallowing	Hx. of head trauma	Prevent problems by avoiding head trauma, after first concussion, no more sports for 2 weeks, concussion defined as any stars, neuro happening, or loss of awareness
Condition caused by Generalized Medical Illness or one of many medications	More likely quicker onset	Underlying generalized illness that could involve any organ system, or one of many medications such as cold medications or tranquilizers, bladder pills, lipid drugs, etc.	Very dependent on the kind of illness	Dementia associated with another illness and or multiple medications	Defined by a careful clinician who spends the time to take a careful Hx and thorough examination Consider trial off all unnecessary drugs

*: Hx: history, CT: computer tomography X-ray, MRI: magnetic resonance imaging, LP: lumbar puncture, Rx: treatment, EKG: electrocardiogram, DM: diabetes mellitus (diabetes), CAHD: coronary atherosclerotic heart disease, HBP: high blood pressure, atrial fib: atrial fibrillation, HA: headache

MEDICINES FOR DEMENTIA

Deficiencies of Vitamin B12 and thyroid hormone can cause dementia. Periodic blood work to test for these deficiencies are recommended for those with memory issues or for anyone over the age of sixty-five. If deficiencies are found, supplementation is recommended. Except for a B12 supplement or thyroid replacement, there is no scientific support to say that any herbal or hormonal supplement will prevent or treat dementia. See the previous chart to define specific therapies for specific conditions, but, in general, BEWARE of anyone promoting the sale of a product for dementia, no matter what false promises they give. (See **Chapter One** which shows that the best preventive for dementia is walking 30–60 minutes a day, eating a balanced diet of fewer calories, and developing friendships.) For vascular dementias, in general, 81mg of aspirin or another antiplatelet medicine helps prevent clotting. For atrial fibrillation (irregular heart rhythm), full anticoagulation with warfarin or a newer warfarin-like agent is indicated (this is a complex rhythm problem with medication that requires careful monitoring). For dementia associated with other medical illness, look at improving the medical condition and reducing medicines when possible.

The best medicines we have for all the other types of dementias will only allow some return of function, while the process of deterioration continues. This disease is like slowly sliding down a hill. The medicines can bring you only partially back up the hill, but then you will still continue sliding down the hill. Most discouraging is that, despite these medicines, the deterioration of memory is relentless.

There are only two groups of drugs used typically for Alzheimer's and generalized dementia, and several options are available from each group. I usually prescribe donepezil (Aricept) from the first category and memantine (Namenda) from the second. Each works differently in the brain. The donepezil dose I usually prescribe is 5mg unless the patient is a big person. The original studies showed only a very small improvement by increasing from 5mg to 10mg, so I rarely go to 10mg, although the pharmaceutical company pushes for 10. If the patient is doing well with donepezil alone, I usually will not add memantine until the condition significantly worsens. I make sure family members realize that they are to help me choose when, or whether, to use these medicines and when to stop them. This is especially pertinent because these medicines are expensive, not always covered by insurance or Medicare and don't always make a lot of difference when the problem is severe.

I usually encourage the family to direct me to stop the dementia medicines when the patient has minimal social response to family visits. I explain to the family that they will likely see a reduction of mental function in the patient at that time; however, at this level of severity of dementia, families usually are okay with stopping the medication. I did have one patient's husband want me to try the medicines again despite her severe dementia. He was very attentive to his wife even though she was completely nonverbal and almost catatonic (a frozen psychological and neurological condition). The medicine had been tried and discontinued years earlier as her condition was so severe. Things were different now as she was now in the long term care center and the two of them had a regular routine. I restarted the donepezil and memantine as he asked, and, after a number of weeks back on the medications, although still extremely compromised, she seemed to almost recognize him again. To our surprise and delight, she even began singing when prompted by her husband. He was delighted and the medications were continued for another year or so. The use of medication for dementia is quite dependent on each situation and especially on the family's direction.

An Essay:
The privilege of driving when young and when old

As a teenager, like many others, I yearned for independence and resisted my parent's rules and restrictions. Now, 55 years later, I realize my parents struggled with how much freedom to allow me while best guiding me into adulthood. It's an old story: kids want freedom, parents are reluctant to give up control. Think back when you first obtained a driver's license and borrowed the family car. Remember, after some error in judgement or indiscretion, how the car-privilege was taken away, and, even when justified, how devastating that was?

The tables turn when an aging parent is threatened or devastated by losing the car-privilege after some error in judgment or just because of advancing age. As a geriatrician, I have heard too many adult children ask me, as the doctor, to tell their parents to stop driving. To the adult child, this is protecting dad. To the elderly dad, this is a double blow, losing the feeling of independence that comes with driving AND the freedom to be mobile. Think about it, who's more dangerous on the road: an eighteen- to twenty-year-old male driving a muscle car, a sixteen-year-old female driving while messaging on a cellphone, or grandma driving her Buick only during the day and only in town?

A warning: parents who are stingy in allowing their children enough freedoms, like driving privileges, may find, later, that their children lack the general experiential training to make good choices when becoming young adults.

Much later, almost tit for tat, some of those same aging parents may find that their adult children may aggressively want to take away their driving privileges.

Elder driver[215]

There are three lessons here. First, elderly persons who are competent should be allowed to make their own choice about when to stop driving. In my years of practice, I have advised many competent, elderly people: "If you think you might be putting others or yourself at risk, then YOU decide when to stop or cut back on driving." When night vision is poor, neck flexibility is reduced, reflexes are slowed, hearing is poor, posture reduces view . . . then think about it. If you can't decide, or if this is a borderline question, consider a "Driver Improvement Course for Seniors" through the American Automobile Association (AAA) and see what they advise. Then make that choice.

---

215   Photograph by **Terceira Idade** from https://www.flickr.com/photos/

(Again, many of the compromises of aging could be prevented, or at least temporized, with a lifetime of regular exercise and a walking program.)

The second lesson, is that elderly persons who are NOT competent should not drive. This should occur when their short-term memory (cannot learn a new thing) is poor or when accidents start piling up. That may be the time for someone to step in. If there is an uncooperative person who is unwilling to be evaluated, I have seen families notify the police of the situation. Especially, after an accident of any kind, the authorities can do the heavy-lifting and remove a driver's license.

The elderly person first needs to see the doctor for an evaluation. Vitamin B12 deficiency, thyroid deficiency, brain tumor or any significant medical condition needs to be considered in every person with newly diagnosed dementia. Afterward, if declared incompetent, it means no driving, will-making, check-writing or consenting to an operation. At this point, a previously defined durable power of attorney (DPA), or one appointed by the court, should begin making decisions for that person.

An "incompetent individual" is one who is 1. Underage, 2. Mentally compromised from birth and never been competent, 3. Incompetent due to emotional illness or 4. Has developed dementia from one of several conditions. These incompetent individuals should have a family member, or members, or an assigned DPA make substituted decisions for them. Medical decisions should

NOT be made by the doctor or the medical facility but rather by a representative of the incompetent person. The medical doctor and facility still has the duty to inform the DPA about the treatment planned and to obtain consent from the DPA to go forward. This is called "informed consent" and no treatment, whether medical, medicinal or surgical, can happen without it. To put it in another way, the DPA becomes the one who will make substituted decisions on behalf of the incompetent person. In every case, those making substituted decisions should make decisions that benefit the patient, do not cause harm, are made based on honest communication and honest science and respect the choices of the patient.

It is important that the DPA should involve the demented or incompetent individual in decision-making as much as reasonably possible. In addition, any substituted decision made for a patient, who once was competent, should be a decision in line with what the patient would have wanted should she or he still be competent. The DPA does NOT have the freedom to choose outside this rule.

The third lesson is for everyone and every family to realize the importance of the freedom to drive. This goes for youth trying to grow up and discover their independence as well as for the elderly trying to age with dignity. We should all appreciate what a precious freedom it is to drive.[216]

---

216   https://www.cdc.gov/motorvehiclesafety/older_adult_drivers/

Questions and Answers about:
*Memory Lapse? Alzheimer's, Parkinson's
and other causes of dementia*

Question: We used to hear the cause of dementia was "hardening of the arteries." Is there any truth to that old saw?

Vascular disease is usually from atherosclerosis which might be another way of saying "hardening of the arteries." As stated earlier, most dementia in the U.S. and Europe is from Alzheimer's, which is not, by definition, caused from vascular disease or "hardening of the arteries," but it might be related. Most experts will advise that we don't know how to prevent Alzheimer's disease, but it seems to occur more often in those who are predisposed to vascular disease and vascular dementia. Therefore, there is truth to that old saying and belief. At this time, our best recommendations to prevent Alzheimer's disease is to do what you can to prevent hardening of the arteries and eat a balanced diet without too many calories or carbohydrates, exercise or walk 30 minutes a day, avoid smoking, and stay connected to family, friends and community.

———～～～———

Question: I'm in my forties and lately I've been noticing I can't remember names as well as I used to. Does this mean I'm becoming demented?

Join the club. Remembering the name of that movie you went to last month, or the name of that song you used to sing, are commonly not as easy to recall as they were when you were twenty. It doesn't get any better as you age. This doesn't mean you have Alzheimer's disease. Not remembering everything we would like to remember is a common occurrence for all of us as we age. Some say, as we get older, we automatically dump a lot of that stuff we don't need to remember to save room for the more important memories. Still, loss of the ability to learn a new thing can mean there is dementia. Realize that it is the whole picture that matters, not just forgetting names. (For more details of Alzheimer's disease, please review the summary presented earlier in this chapter.)

Question: Our son was playing football, and, after his head was hit hard by another helmeted player, he had a few seconds of confusion. That passed quickly, and the coach sent him back into the game. Was this a concussion? Should he have gone back to play football so soon?

A few seconds of confusion is, by definition, a concussion. No, he should not have returned to the game. There is scientific evidence that the brain is especially vulnerable for long-term and more permanent damage if a second concussion happens within a particular time frame after the first. Experts advise that after a severe concussion (loss of consciousness), coaches should wait until all signs of the concussion have been resolved and then wait two additional weeks before returning the player onto the football field. For a few seconds of confusion, the time out of play could be reduced, but coaches and parents should review the rules as defined by the Concussion Foundation. (See the discussion presented earlier in this chapter on Chronic Traumatic Encephalopathy.)

I have struggled to find simplified rules with this type of issue, and the more I consider this topic, the more I realize how complicated it seems to be. If a concussion is suspected, pull the player from the game. There should be no return to play until the player is symptom-free, and the neurologic exam-ination is normal. In general, the typical time off, after loss of consciousness, is two weeks for adults and up to four weeks for kids.

～～

Question: My mother is in her nineties, and I am afraid her reactions are slower than they should be to drive. She only drives her friends around town to club meetings during the day. She doesn't drive long distances on the highway, and she doesn't drive at night. Should I find a way to stop her from driving?

I presume, by the tenor of the question, that your mother is competent, capable of writing checks, doing her business, and living on her own. Unless she is having problems bad enough to bring you to take all those privileges away, please let her make her own decision to drive or not to drive. You could encourage her to make the choice to avoid driving when she thinks she might be putting people at risk. Those at risk would include herself, the people in her car, the people meeting her on the road, or the children running out into the road. Let her take herself seriously as an ethical person. Be reassured that the risk of her causing a significant injury, statistically, at her age, never reaches that of an under twenty-year-old woman. (Men reach that level of risk at eighty-five and women never reach that level of risk.) Finally, if this is a borderline functioning question, I would advise the AAA "Driver Improvement Course for Seniors," and let her decide.

Chapter Seven

In Sickness as in Health

On sustaining oneself while providing care for another

Case Study:
The case of the watchful family and the reluctant physician

NOT LONG AGO THE FAMILY OF AN ELDERLY, long-term care patient called me to help with their mother. The nurses in the long-term care facility and I had missed the patient's recent deterioration. After examination, I admitted the elderly patient to our hospital for a change in status with worsening mental confusion, severe back pain and failing kidneys. Her family was fit to be tied. They thought the changes were possibly the result of too much pain medicine which, I might add, was provided under my direction by the nursing home nurses. It turned out that the family was partially right. During the hospitalization, I realized that the watchful family saved the life of this patient. Indeed, I discovered some of the patient's confusion was the result of an infection and dehydration all made worse by her pain medicine. The patient's deterioration reversed after intensive evaluation and treatment. The nurses at the long-term care facility hadn't realized these problems were occurring partly due to the cover-up by pain medicines. It was the family alert that saved the day.

After a few days in the hospital, the back pain was less and pain medicines were able to be reduced. The patient was rehydrated and kidney failure improved. Her infection was treated, she was more alert and she was reasonably comfortable. She returned to her care facility with her overall condition remarkably improved. The family had been stressed and a little angry. They appeared relieved after I gave them some daily time, listened to their concerns and recognized the value of their input. Despite my sense that I am part of a team that provides some of the best health care around, we, the team, must admit that we need all the help we can get, especially from a watchful family.

A beautiful one-hundred-year-old woman with a watchful family 2014[217]

Bottom line: We should all appreciate the value of the watchful family. The human component is what puts the word "care" in the health-care business. In fact, it is the caring that makes it all work. It is also the human component which accounts for the possibility of mistakes. I repeat: all providers, in this very complex world of health care, are human. We can, and will, make mistakes.

SIMILARITIES IN CARING FOR THE YOUNG AND OLD

There are some strong similarities with raising children and providing care for an aging and dependent parent. Raising our four children was, and continues to be, a very rewarding experience even though they are now all grown up. Once my wife, Joanie, and I made the leap of having children, we have never landed. We are still worried about them and fuss about each of their life troubles. Still, it was a fabulous thing to raise kids as the more one cares about someone, the more it seems to give meaning to life. I dare say it is the same with providing support for an elderly person. Joy follows when caring for someone. My heart warms as I recall how we both cared for our parents during the last season of their lives.

Raising our children was, and continues to be, a shared responsibility of love, and my spouse and I both brought different talents to this endeavor of raising young children. So, it was with the caring of her parents and my parents. Joanie looked at my mother's feminine side and provided needs that I didn't see, such as hair care and makeup needs. I could be a male confidant to Joanie's father. Each of us took a larger role in the care for our own parents as they progressed through the process, and each gave support to the other while we were stressed by the failing situation. We each had our strengths in caring for our young children and our elderly parents. We both appreciated the support given by the other during the stressful times. In our case, caring for elderly parents was very much like caring for our children.

Preston, Carter, Julia, the author, Joanie and Eric Holm
September 2016[218]

I think, in retrospect, the most powerful teaching tool we used with our children was to show them how we interacted with each other with kindness and respect. One book I read on raising children advised to speak positively about the other parent and treat her or him well. Then the kids will be all right. This point is summarized with the quote, "The most important

---

218   Photo from private collection

thing a father can do for his children is to love their mother."[219] This is not to criticize or disparage, in any way, a single parent raising children alone or lesbian/gay/bisexual/transsexual/queer (LGBTQ) families raising children. The statement is basically saying that the best way to raise children and teach love is by example. This is similar in caring for an elderly and dependent person. Care providers teach others about the value of the elderly by showing compassion to the elderly.

In caring for others, I believe it is important to let your heart speak to you, walk in the other guy's shoes, search for resources when needed and learn from the experience (the best teacher). This is more important than any training although it is important to seek help or resources in order to do the best job. As in caring for a young child, if the challenge of providing care to a dependent elderly person becomes more than you can handle, get help and get training.

Most people of experience would probably agree that the joy of parenting and the joy of caring for an elderly family member are both worth the risk of pain. Both experiences provide huge challenges and huge rewards. The words from Garth Brooks's song, *The Dance,* written by Tony Arata, function the same for children or elderly loved ones, "I could have missed the pain, but I'd of had to miss the dance."[220]

In contrast, it is okay NOT to be a parent, and NOT to be a caregiver if it isn't in your bones. People have different talents, and caregiving may not be for you. Do not feel guilty. If you

---

219   https://www.mamanatural.com/most-important-thing-a-father-can-do/

220   https://en.wikipedia.org/wiki/The_Dance_(song)

don't like doing it, you may not be a good provider. If finances allow, hire someone else to do this job.

On the other hand, if the elderly person in need is NOT your relative, but you are compelled to help, consider lending your hand. Just be sure that every relative of the patient is accepting of your help for their loved one, and be careful not to put yourself in a legal spot. Again, it is important to call for help when needed, frequently connect with others about what is going on and keep a twice daily written record of what you are doing or problems that you are encountering. Finally, there are people out there who need the help, and, if you have a mind to, this may be a field of interest that you should explore.

Virginia Smith and her daughter Joanie Holm, December 2006[221]

221   Photo from private collection

I believe the adage, "It takes a village," is as true in caring for the aging as in raising children. We had the help of a community of relatives, friends, neighbors, teachers, coaches, church advisors, doctors and more while raising our children. Why did it surprise me to discover that caring for our parents at the end of their lives was also a community experience? Our parents and family members are clearly worth our help but, commonly, require more than a single person or a couple can handle. There are community resources that are available to prop us up as we care for others. We live in a community of helpers, as listed above. For the elderly there are also social services, health systems, assisted living centers and long-term care facilities. We should not be reluctant to tap any of them for help when needed.

ANOTHER PRACTICAL BOOK ON HELPING YOUR MOM AND DAD THROUGH AGING BARRIERS

In a search for information for those who become caregivers for one's parents, I read a book by a retired Mayo Clinic eldercare specialist, Dick Edwards. He wrote the book with the help of Mike Ransom and Ruth Weispfenning, and it is entitled *Mom, Dad . . . Can We Talk? Insights and Perspectives to Help Us Do What's Best for Our Aging Parents*.

In it, they speak to the value of having important and caring conversations with your parents about end-of-life choices. In caring for parents, they advise making and distributing responsibilities of support among the children including finances, healthcare decisions, home maintenance, transportation and so on. They give practical advice on reducing the "stuff" of a lifetime and suggest dividing this up into things to sell, things that are heirlooms, things that are just of sentimental value as well as how to settle with all of the family members about distributing them. The book is chock full of sensible and levelheaded advice with stories to illustrate their points. It is a short and readable book that provides for ways to help children of failing parents, and I strongly recommend it. Go to their website listed below if you are interested.[222]

PROMISING INSTEAD TO ALWAYS CARE FOR THEM

Despite the resistance to living in a long-term care facility, 1.4 million older Americans reside in such a place. Though different from living in one's home, assisted living facilities or long-term care facilities can be wonderful places for aging adults to find companionship and excellent care. Prior to selecting a facility, the patient or the family should check licensing, certifications and qualifications. Experts suggest getting to know the staff; evaluating the facility for cleanliness and safety; ensuring that residents are well nourished (especially those that have special nutritional needs); watching for activities and routines; and looking for signs of neglect or abuse. (For more on abuse, see **Chapter Nine**.) Once your loved one is settled into their new environment, it is ideal if a caring family can make frequent visits and monitor the care provided.

In 2001, California Representative Henry Waxman presented a report indicating that 9,000 abuse violations occurred over a two-year period across the nation.[223] Waxman reported that

222 www.momdadcanwetalk.com

223 https://www.cbsnews.com/news/nursing-home-abuse-increasing/

nine out of ten long-term care centers were excellent, but one in ten had citations of serious incidents. In 2017, a National Public Radio (NPR) journalist reported on an alert from the Office of Inspector General that 25 percent of serious cases of long-term care abuse are not reported to the police. However, records from 2015–2016 revealed 134 cases of abuse of long-term care facility residents from 33 states which required emergency room evaluation.[224] Any abuse of people unable to defend themselves is unconscionable, but 134 cases in 33 states means significantly fewer incidents of abuse in 2015 and 2016 than reported by Waxman in 2001.

In my 36 years of experience caring for people in three long-term care facilities in two communities of South Dakota, I have seen that most people fall into the rhythm of their new life. They enjoy the morning group breakfast, share in the activities and music, relish their afternoon nap, establish routines and friendships and enjoy their lives like they did before moving into a long-term care facility. Overall, I see long-term care facilities as full-service hotels with extra care and service.[225]

It is not uncommon to see people move from the home where they raised their families, to, sequentially, an apartment, a senior-living apartment complex with shared meals, an assisted living community and, eventually, a long-term care center. Each move allows for maximum independence without requiring people to depend so much on their family. I

224   https://www.npr.org/2017/08/28/546460187/serious-nursing-home-abuse-often-not-reported-to-police-federal-investigators-fi

225   https://www.ncbi.nlm.nih.gov/pubmed/22642199

have seen, time and time again, when a failing elderly person moves into an assisted living center and is given just the right amount of help, the result is that the elderly person finds new friends, social rhythms, and her or his independence is preserved much longer than what would have occurred without the assisted living center.

If life transitions are getting you down, do not let fear make your life miserable. If you are a caregiver, and your loved ones ask you to promise you will never send them to a nursing home, promise, instead, to always care and provide for them in the best way possible, including a long-term care facility when needed. Do this without guilt. We should all make the most of every day, and eventually we must let go of stuff. We should all know this by now: it is our friends and family and enjoying the journey that matters, not stuff. Death is a natural ending and only an abbreviation at the end of a marvelous poem.

FINDING THE RIGHT PLACE AND THE RIGHT DOCTOR

First, a few words about choosing a physician or care provider. Of course, we all want a doctor who cares. If you have found one, realize that when they are caring, competent, and knowledgeable, then they are going to be busy. People hunt them down and latch on. You want a busy doctor, physician assistant (PA), or nurse practitioner (NP). A humble and compassionate care provider is one thing, but she or he also needs to be competent and knowledgeable, too.[226] Find the balance and make no apologies for switching when appropriate. When

---

226   https://www.ncbi.nlm.nih.gov/pmc/articles/PMC1124230/

you've found one, you may have to sit in the waiting room, so bring a good book and be patient.

We all know people who treat others poorly, especially those who are less advantaged or on a lower level of some hierarchy. Shame on the employer who deals with an employee badly, a prison guard who harasses a prisoner hatefully, a teacher or parent who supervises a student or child unjustly, or, to make the point, a doctor who treats a nurse or patient poorly. Do not accept or endure this kind of care. Report them and find another care provider.

Finding the right assisted living (AL) or long-term care facility (LTCF or nursing home) for yourself or for your family member is also a matter of choice that requires no apology but may require patience. Like picking the right doctor, careful research should go into finding the right place. If you have problems with some aspect of an existing LTCF, communicate your concerns with the staff and administrator. If you are not satisfied after negotiating the situation, consider a change in location. Although making a change will require significant effort, do so when it will improve the situation for yourself or your loved one. When a possible change is looming, I would suggest having a conversation with the administration of the place you are leaving to explain why it is happening. Do this without emotion but rather as a gesture of kindness. Do this as a favor so the AL or LTCF you are leaving may discover how they may improve, and the remaining patients may benefit from those improvements. If the administrative person reacts negatively, chalk it up to human nature, do not be emotionally dragged into a battle, realize it is their problem not yours and move on.

An Essay:
Women often carry the burden for all

Why has the health-care industry directed so much marketing attention to women? Statistically, women seek out medical care for themselves more often than men. Some would suggest this is due to the role women play in having babies and the medical relationships that are established providing that wonderful reproductive role. Therefore, it is no surprise that her medical connections with a health-care provider continue through a woman's lifetime.

There are more reasons than having babies that draw middle-aged women to a health-care provider. In 2004 the Kaiser Women's Health Survey interviewed 2,800 women and found that while 10 percent of women who are in the age of reproduction (eighteen to forty-four) say they have arthritis, hypertension, asthma or another medical condition, 30 percent have those problems after reaching their middle years (forty-five to sixty-four) and 60 percent after reaching sixty-five. The U.S. Department of Labor states that women utilize more health care than men, accounting for 60 percent of all expenses incurred at doctors' offices.[227]

However, there are more issues than her own health problems to impact her life. We also know that, about

---

227   https://kaiserfamilyfoundation.files.wordpress.com/2013/01/women-and-health-care-a-national-profile-key-findings-from-the-kaiser-women-s-health-survey-conclusion.

80 percent of the time, women are the family health care decision-makers and are more likely to be the caregivers when a family member falls ill. More often than the father, the mother chooses the child's doctor or provider, makes the appointment, brings the child to the clinic or hospital and makes sure follow-up care happens.

Very often she not only coordinates this for her children but also for her husband, and for her and his elderly and frail parents. The Kaiser study found 12 percent of women, compared to 8 percent of men, care for a sick or aging relative. She not only provides for the family member's housework, transportation and financial decisions but also administers pills, shots, baths and dressing changes. She often gives up many hours a week to bring health care to others.

No wonder health-care companies are marketing to women in their middle years! We must be thankful and give them support in return.

THINGS YOU SHOULD KNOW, Q & A

Questions and Answers about:
In Sickness as in Health—On sustaining oneself while providing care for another

Question: Who is this book written for since you have written this whole chapter on caregivers? (Author's note: Again, in this text, the word caregiver refers to family members caring for a loved one. The word care provider refers to the physician, nurse practitioner, physician assistant or nurse.)

Originally the book was all about caring for aging parents. One of the younger doctors in our hospital/clinic jumped up and stopped me as I was leaving the hospital floor one morning and said to me, "Rick, you have to write a book on how to care for aging parents. We need something like that, and you should do it."[228] I looked for a book that did just that, and, although there are books out there that touch on the topic, none fulfilled the needs of a caregiver learning the ropes. After I was a third into writing this book, I realized that, perhaps more importantly, the book may be read and may truly benefit the aging person. I'm one of them. We should have a way to learn how to avoid the perils of aging and how to face dying without panic. However, this chapter is written especially for the caregiver.

Question: I am a caregiver for my elderly, frail and mildly demented father-in-law, and I am not happy doing it. We are working his farm, and I have no choice but to be the one to provide for this confused and somewhat angry old man. Help!

First, if you aren't enjoying caring for him, and, indeed, you do describe a challenging case, you probably should NOT be the caregiver. If you're not happy,

---

it is unlikely you will do a good job. Second, doing this work will make you resent your husband, and that relationship is very important for your overall well-being. I would find another job and hire out the caregiver job or move the patient to an assisted living center. If the demented father-in-law is documented as being demented, then the durable power of attorney makes the decision, not the patient. In that case, likely your husband will make the decision, and even if the elderly gentleman is angry or resistant, this move likely would be the best thing to do. In the long run, the father-in-law will likely be happier in an assisted living center or a long-term care facility, and the move would benefit the family as well.

Question: How does one know when it is time to quit home care and send my severely demented wife to the long-term care facility?

When your wife can no longer do the activities of daily living, which includes no longer being able to feed herself, then it certainly would be apropos. A more important measure for this move might be the level of your tolerance and happiness in caring for her. You obviously have gone way past what most people would do in fulfilling the promise, "in sickness and in health," and should feel no guilt in directing her to an AL center or LTCF that has evolved to care for just such people.

If you feel anger or frustration in providing her care, it is a strong sign that it is time.

————ᨆᨆ————

Question: Is it important we find a nursing home with a memory unit for my grandfather with dementia, or will any nursing home do?

I have watched how some long-term care facilities and even assisted living centers advertise that they have memory units for those with dementia. Initially, I was skeptical because 50 to 75 percent of the patients living in a LTCF have dementia. All LTCFs must be ready to deal with dementia. That said, there are places that have special areas of their AL or LTCF allocated for people with dementia, and the staff has had training to address the special needs required by such patients. I would interview and visit all the reasonably close AL centers or LTCF. If the dementia is severe, the best placement will be a LTCF. Evaluate the facility and ask about the staff training to see if this is the best place for your loved one.

————ᨆᨆ————

Question: I am starting home care for my husband who is struggling with some vascular complications of diabetes. He has neuropathy, blindness, a previous heart attack and mild dementia from a stroke early last year.

I want to try to take care of him, but I would like some training. What do you recommend?

I would suggest discussing this with one or more of the following: a home health agency, an AL center, a LTCF or a training center for becoming a certified nursing assistant. These people will give you good recommendations. Taking a course on being a certified nursing assistant may be very helpful to you. (See these references.[229,230,231,232])

---

229   http://www.battleofsaipan.com/homecare/HomeCare_041230

230   http://www.huffingtonpost.com/john-shore/elderly-parent-caregivers_b_823443.html

231   https://money.usnews.com/money/blogs/the-best-life/2011/07/18/10-tips-for-caring-for-aging-parents

232   http://www.aarp.org/home-family/caregiving/info-09-2013/my-life-as-a-caregiver.html

Chapter Eight

What is Suffering?

The prevention of suffering near the end of life

Case Study:
*The case of Grandma, certainly dying, arms tied
so she wouldn't pull out tubes*

GRANDMA ANNA HOLM lived a hard yet good life. She grew up on a farm in Kandiyohi County, Minnesota, the daughter of Swedish immigrants. My grandmother was swept off her feet in those early years of the 1900s by a fiddle-playing farmer. He talked her into moving, as a newlywed, to a homestead near Bowman, North Dakota. Their first home, if it could be considered a home, was a humble (possibly sod) house out on the flats of the prairie. After years of hard work, they had earned success in farming purchasing several other homesteads. They eventually built a proper wooden home, complete with a wooden floor and even a few windows. Feeling blessed, after several years and three children, they sold everything for a good profit and moved to northern Minnesota. It was a radical change from the life they'd previously known. They bought a sawmill and began manufacturing their invention of table-mounted ironing boards. Just when everything was flush and promising, they lost it all when their bank foreclosed. My grandparents fell victim to that era of economic turmoil known today as The Great Depression.

All prior financial victories my grandparents had experienced were now unimportant, and everything that they had worked for was gone. After such a devastating loss, they moved their three children to Minneapolis. Grandpa found work in a hardware store while Grandma worked (until her mid-eighties) in a retirement apartment system not unlike a modern assisted living facility.

Years later, at ninety-six years of age, my grandmother endured a fractured hip and the surgery that followed. During recovery, she suffered a debilitating stroke which eliminated her ability to speak. She was also burdened by other medical complications that were a consequence of advanced age and the recent surgery. However, the stroke seemed to be the final straw, because, shortly afterward, Grandma decided to stop eating. Although the stroke had lessened her mental function, she seemed to know enough to realize it was time to quit.

Despite the objections of my dad and aunt, the nursing home doctor put a feeding tube down Grandma's nose. To no one's surprise, my independent and strong-minded grandma pulled it out. Every time it went back in, she pulled it right back out. My dad called and asked me to talk to the attending nursing home doctor. "Please leave it out," was the request my father and my aunt asked me to relay. I regret to this day my inability to stand up to that physician. He had no difficulty in resisting the request of a kid who was only in his second year of medical school, and, at the time, didn't realize his aunt and dad had the legal right to direct the care of their mother. The nursing home physician's position was that he couldn't order the tube feedings stopped because the nurses would rebel against the order. Ironically, he contended that removal of the feeding tube was cruel instead of the blessing it would have been.

Author's Grandmother Anna Holm, about ninety-three years old[233]

We didn't realize we had the right to choose a different physician, a different nursing home or the right to bring her into one of our homes to comfort her and to give Grandma the peaceful and dignified death she desired. The horrible truth is that four weeks later she died, arms restrained, feeding tube in place. This incident had a profound effect on me and is one of the reasons I have made it a personal mission to help people better understand how care at the end of life matters. In this era of advanced technology, we have a misconception of

233   From private collection

death, a misguided idea that living is always better than dying, even if that living has to be sustained by feeding tubes, artificial hydration and breathing tubes. There is a time for life support technology but not in a situation like that of my grandmother.

It is important to know when to let go and stop intervening during the natural dying process which eventually affects every one of us.

THE ONE-HOSS SHAY SYNDROME AND FACING THE FACT OF EVENTUAL DEATH

When in life does one come to the mature truth that, even with all the best that science has to offer, each of us will eventually die? I dare say, in my years of experience as an internist caring for young and old alike, when people are younger than sixty, they usually do not have the maturity of mind required to look into the eyes of death. Put it off as we may, the hard certainty is that one day we all must die. Shakespeare described advanced aging and failing in his play *As You Like It*, Act II, Scene VII (All the world's a stage):[234]

> ". . . Last scene of all,
> That ends this strange eventful history,
> Is second childishness and mere oblivion,
> Sans teeth, sans eyes, sans taste, sans everything."
> (*Sans means "without"*)

---

234   https://www.poets.org/poetsorg/poem/you-it-act-ii-scene-vii-all-worlds -stage

His description is of a man who was able to live long enough to become elderly. The death of this elderly man in the early 1600s was rather bleak. Presently I think, with the support of a loving family, we could do better. The following is a more hopeful version to end Shakespeare's *All the World's a Stage* and I share it here, asking for your forgiveness as I humbly invade great Shakespeare's realm. I believe that facing our own death should not fill us with dread:

> . . . He did not have to end his life alone,
> If over time he'd shared his caring, raised
> The worth of others, guiding kids 'till grown:
> His death would find him kindly loved and praised,
> While kin sing festive songs of joy, amazed.

I once read an editorial in *The New England Journal of Medicine*[235] that referred to medical doctor Oliver Wendell Holmes' poem, *The Wonderful One-Hoss Shay*.[236] The writer pointed to the poem as a metaphor of the aging process. The poem tells about a magnificent horse-drawn shay (carriage) that was constructed with all the finest of materials. It was so well made that, for 100 years, not a piece of it wore out. Then, as the bell tolled that day, 100 years after the shay was constructed, it all fell apart at once, leaving the rider sitting in a pile of dust. What if we could all live full, healthy lives with everything working as

---

235　James F. Fries, M.D. Aging, Natural Death, and the Compression of Morbidity. N ENGLAND J OF MED 1980; 303:130-135 July 17, 1980

236　www.youtube.com/watch?v=wiOHhhwnK6k

it should, and then one day, around 90 or 100 years of age, all our parts would wear out at the same time?

The life lesson in *The Wonderful One-Hoss Shay* is not far off from what actually happens at the end of life. The essayist states that most people, if not dying prematurely from an accident, heart attack or cancer, will live to be eighty- to ninety-years-old. One day, the person comes into the hospital with pneumonia and shortly thereafter, the dominoes begin to fall. The heart fails, there's a stroke, the kidneys quit, the person stops eating and everything falls apart at once. If we add all of our life-extending technology at this time, life is only extended days to weeks, too often with the addition of suffering.

A wonderful, (stored in the barn) dusty but still working, one-hoss shay[237]

---

237   Photo with permission of owner by author in personal collection 2/2007

There are important lessons here. Too many of these very old and unquestionably dying people receive fruitless treatments that drag them through inordinate suffering rather than help them. Treatment is aimed at cure, not comfort, and does not change the inevitable. Had my grandmother's physician understood the lessons contained within Holmes's poem, she might not have suffered as she did.

To be fair, even when care providers have appropriate motives, know when to let go and do provide simple comfort, there remain instances when some people have a piecemeal, gradual, and dwindling end. The *Wonderful One-Hoss Shay* or "All the World's a Stage" metaphors don't always happen. When dealing with an elderly person whose parts are all failing, we need to do better in understanding and accepting when it is time to quit.

WHAT DOCTORS DO WHEN THE PATIENT DOESN'T WANT AGGRESSIVE MEDICAL CARE OR WHEN THE PATIENT IS ACTIVELY DYING

There is no question that providing intravenous or feeding tube hydration to a sick patient can play an important role in recovery when recovery is an achievable goal; however, there is something paradoxical about providing fluid replacement to a person who is going to die no matter what we do. Any fluid replacement in this situation only prolongs suffering.

Intravenous fluids and liquid food through feeding tubes are both defined as artificial hydration. Providing these forms of artificial hydration are advanced medical interventions which are clearly different from providing natural food or drink by mouth. These interventions should be considered when the patient has a reasonable chance of recovery, but they have become more frequently used in terminal patients who are at the end of life instead of allowing patients to die in a natural way. Too often physicians encourage families to consent to start IV fluids or to place feeding tubes in dying patients. Uninformed families give their consent or ask for intervention rather than let go of their loved once. The busy and over-scheduled physician may not be able to take the time to advise the family about the suffering that may result from intervention. The tubes go in, and suffering continues.

Please understand this is not about withholding fluid replacement for people who have a reasonable chance of recovery, this is not about withholding any treatment for the elderly in general, and this is not about giving up on grandpa because he's old.[238] Instead, this is about determining whether his case of pneumonia is treatable. It's whether recovery to a reasonable state of function is achievable. When an elderly person has a reasonable chance of recovery and the patient or family wants full treatment, I go full bore as requested. **Withholding the starting of artificial hydration is never about withholding food and drink by mouth.** When someone is alive enough to want to take food or drink, I have always provided it, no matter what the condition.

Going past fluid replacement, there are more medical interventions that keep people alive and are commonly given to patients who are severely ill, like intubation which involves placing endotracheal tubes through the mouth past the vocal cords to protect airways and control breathing. Other aggressive care options include tubes placed into veins, arteries, bladders,

---

238   https://www.jscimedcentral.com/EmergencyMedicine/emergency-medicine-2-1032.pdf

abdominal cavities or chest cavities in order to provide medicine and remove fluids. Also, aggressive care options include
pacemaker or defibrillator wires placed into the heart to keep it
pumping, medications given through IV tubes placed to expand
or reduce blood volume, fight infection and constrict or dilate
vessels. These treatments are considered aggressive because they
are above and beyond standard supportive care. They are interventions meant to reverse the condition at hand; therapies that,
if avoided, potentially could allow a natural death.

Consider this scenario: if I were a stroke victim with enough
brain activity to drive breathing, but not enough brain function
to protect my airway from inhaling saliva and food, it would
be obvious recovery to a reasonable life is not going to happen.
Then, my wishes would be: I DO NOT WANT aggressive therapy like a feeding tube, IV fluids, a breathing tube or antibiotics.
Allow me a natural death. However, DO give me supportive and
comfort care, and provide opportunities for me to eat and drink
naturally, if I ask for it.

Treatment or supportive care should be the choice of the
patient. However, if she or he cannot direct care due to one or
more medical problems, then the family, or an assigned durable
power of attorney for health care (DPA or "substituted judgment") should step in. The patient or his assigned person to
provide a legal substituted judgment should make those choices
and NOT the doctor or the hospital. A living will (another term
for an "advance directive") is any wish that is expressed by
a competent person in written, authorized, verbal or even an
unauthorized form giving family and care providers direction
for a time when that person may be unconscious, demented

and no longer competent. A living will would allow the patient to make plans to direct medical care before a life threatening event occurred (stroke, heart attack or cancer). One example of a living will would be to assign a certain person to have the durable power of attorney (DPA) and be responsible to choose for the patient when the patient can no longer choose for her or himself. Another example would be a living will which clarifies the patient's choices about feeding tubes, breathing tubes or cardiopulmonary resuscitation. These examples of an advance directive help address tough end-of-life choices.

A famous nationwide, multiyear $29 million Robert Woods Johnson study about end-of-life hospital care titled the *SUPPORT Study*,[239] presented its findings in 1995. The study indicated how challenging end-of-life care can be. The study occurred in five large health-care teaching centers scattered throughout the United States and looked at 4,000 acutely ill hospitalized patients. They asked five important questions:

1. Did the patient have a prior expressed or written advance directive?
2. Was that directive respected?
3. What was the prognosis (chance of recovery)?
4. If the patient was certainly dying, did he or she still receive aggressive (futile) intervention?
5. How often did aggressive care result in pain and suffering?

---

239   A controlled trial to improve care for seriously ill hospitalized patients. The study to understand prognoses and preferences for outcomes and risks of treatments (SUPPORT). The SUPPORT Principal Investigators. **JAMA.** 1995 Nov 22-29;274(20):1591-8.

The results of the study were dismal. It found that many patients did not have a written, or even verbalized, advance directive. It found that, even when there was an advance directive, despite their wishes, the tubes went in and aggressive care was provided. It found that when there was not a reasonable chance of recovery, the tubes still went in, and the dying patient landed in the intensive care unit (ICU).

Did the aggressive care cause pain and suffering? The heart-breaking answer was also "yes." As later reported by family members, 50 percent of those who had died during the study were in moderate to severe pain at least 50 percent the time. The results showed that during the 1990s, significant numbers of hospitalized people were experiencing prolonged suffering as they were nearing the end of their lives. Ironically, this was because of the aggressive nature of our health-care system.

These findings were only the first half of the *SUPPORT Study*. The study was repeated after a few years, this time making every effort to provide education to the physicians and house staff caring for these dying patients. By educating hospital staff about how fruitless this effort might be, and how possible pain and suffering could result from aggressive care at the end of life, the hope was to significantly decrease the number of people who suffered needlessly before their death. The education involved prompting physicians to ask about advance directives; to properly define the patient's prognosis; and, if prognosis is poor, to inform patients about the suffering that can result from futile care. Despite those interventions, the second half of the *SUPPORT Study* found no change from the first half. There was no earlier documentation of a "do not resuscitate" (DNR) request, no improved respect for an advance directive, no reduction in days spent in an intensive care unit (ICU) before death and no reduction in the pain experienced in those last days of life. Apparently, families were not informed or respectful of the patient's living will, and physicians (or physicians in training) found the tools to prolong life too tempting not to use.

I find it a paradox that science has developed all these wonderful interventions to save lives, yet we have not been able to understand when to stop treatment. Alas, despite scientific advancements, some people needlessly suffer at the end of their lives.

It is worth noting that the *SUPPORT Study* occurred in large hospitals with rotating hospitalists (physicians who share in providing for only hospitalized patients and do so on a rotating schedule), residents and medical students. Generally, a personal doctor, a designated primary care provider or a patient-centered medical home was not involved. It is my experience that, when a personal doctor or medical team who knows and communicates well with the patient and their family are involved, appropriate comfort care is more likely to be provided and inappropriate interventions are more likely to be avoided. I also believe that since the *SUPPORT Study*, there has been a greater emphasis on palliative (comfort) and hospice care in this country. Perhaps, in those big city hospitals, end-of-life care is improving, and it is time for another study.

There are many reasons why problems persist. Payers like Medicare and insurance companies pay hospitals more money when more is done. A personal physician or primary care team is becoming less involved with hospital care because of the move toward hospitalists who are on rotating shifts. There is a move toward consulting subspecialists like cardiologists, endocrinologists and pulmonologists who have a propensity to order excessive tests. The family commonly doesn't know who is primarily responsible for directing the care of the patient who is incompetent. In addition, too many patients have not made their own living will or advance directive. The literature indicates that only 25 percent of the U.S. adult population have an advance directive.[240] Until these issues are changed, overaggressive end-of-life care will continue.

What should be done? When a physician or care provider team realizes that the patient is clearly dying, the next intervention should be to inform the patient and the family about options. If the patient is unconscious, the family should be informed that they have the responsibility and the power to direct care, and one choice might be to stop aggressive care in someone who is at the end of life. This can mean stopping cardiopulmonary resuscitation (CPR), stopping antibiotics and stopping intensive monitoring. Each complex hospitalized patient needs one compassionate and communicative medical person whose job is to know the patient well, communicate with the patient and family about progress, know when to move with aggressive care or understand when to move to comfort care. It remains the responsibility of the family, or the defined durable power of attorney for health care, to follow the wishes of the patient, to follow the spirit of that directive and to make the

---

240   Jaya Rao, et al: Completion of Advance Directives Among U.S. Consumers. Am J Prev Med. 2014 Jan; 46(1): 65–70.

decisions the patient would have made in this situation, should she or he have full mental capacity to do so.

It is the responsibility of the care team to help the patient and family understand the dire situation of a dying patient, to help bring struggling family members to face the certainty of this and to comfort the patient and the family. It is NOT the care team's responsibility to make medical decisions. In the end, it is the care team's responsibility to follow the patient's or the family's direction.

STOPPING ARTIFICIAL HYDRATION

Stopping hydration remains the most difficult challenge for physicians, as well as for families, but it is one of the most important choices either can make. As defined earlier, artificial hydration is defined as intravenous fluids or fluids given by a feeding tube to someone who cannot or will not drink. Families, and even some doctors, struggle with the idea of not giving artificial hydration to a dying patient for the mistaken fear of causing thirst and discomfort. It is important to understand that just the opposite is usually true. During the dying process, as dehydration naturally occurs, the body produces its own endorphins that numb the pain and bring comfort. If a person cannot drink or swallow and is not artificially hydrated, that human being will slip away from this earth gently over an eight- to twelve-day period. In this way, Nature has provided comfort in dying for as long as humans have walked this earth. The American Medical Association, the American College of Physicians, the American Academy of Family Physicians and the American Academy of Neurology all agree that allowing the natural process of dying (withholding artificial hydration and feeding) allows a natural and comfortable death and does not cause undue suffering. Providing artificial hydration, on the other hand, can prolong a natural dying process, worsen pain and extend the duration of pain.

When a person is clearly dying, cannot be saved and has an advance directive that especially advises against artificial hydration: families and health-care providers should provide love, not fluids. I, for one, have clearly instructed my doctor and my family about my wishes. If I do not recognize my children and cannot or will not swallow fluid and there is no reasonable chance of recovery, then let nature take its course. No tubes!

SUFFERING AND SUICIDE

The argument I have heard after such a discourse comes from the question, "How do you measure suffering?" There is no question, suffering can result from both physical and emotional pain. We will all experience enough of both if we live long enough—and living long is the hope, is it not? The animated Disney movie *Inside Out* illustrates the emotions of a little girl which are represented by five tiny caricatures depicting disgust, anger, fear, sadness and joy. The story tells how the emotions interact inside the girl's brain when she's upset about her parents moving the family to a new town. Each emotion reacts differently to the loss resulting from such a move. This wonderful story, although perhaps oversimplified, makes the point that joy alone is not enough, and all emotions are needed in different amounts at different times to form the makeup of a well-adjusted and poised individual. To become a whole person, we all need to experience, understand and even accept those experiences that are repugnant, maddening, dreadful and dismal as well as those which are delightful—we need to take the bad with the good. Balance.

Part of the mantra, or sacred prayer, of every good physician is to reduce suffering, but what is it to suffer? The dictionary explains suffering as "more than just experiencing something unpleasant or painful." The origin of the word comes from the Latin word *sufferre*, or *to bear,* as if carrying a burden. It is interesting to note that neuroimaging maps have found that a certain part of the brain fires up when we feel either physical pain or emotional distress. These two radically different kinds of suffering seem to share a single neurological space in our heads. Some philosophers believe that suffering leads to the creation of meaning in life and it helps us to know more about our world. They believe pain is not always negative. For example, heartache and overwhelming situational sadness can warn us about danger, tell us what to avoid, direct us as to how aggressive or how far to go in obtaining a certain objective without hurting ourselves and, of course, remind us of the value of someone when he or she is gone. Some great philosophers believe it is with some great loss in life that brings us to realize that "it is not all about me" and that meaning comes from caring about others. You have to have the pain of loss to get there.

To better understand the concept of suffering, I asked numerous patients and friends, "What has caused you the most suffering throughout your lives?" Surprisingly, not one described an incidence of physical pain. Rather, all the answers revolved around emotional loss. I heard about the emptiness and anxiety that followed the death of parents and siblings, about the psychological stress of having kids, and plenty about the depression that followed divorce. It seems most people tend to forget about their physical pain, but emotional scars tend to stick around.

As hospice medical director, I was recently asked to be a part of a national survey on how we treat those dying from various illnesses, and it was a long list of rather difficult and challenging inquiries. Two questions were especially challenging for me: 1. "Is pain and suffering a means for spiritual growth?" and 2. "Should physicians seek to relieve patients' spiritual suffering just as much as their physical pain?"

In response to the first question, I truly believe that experiencing some significant pain, suffering and failure in our life helps to bring us to mature thinking; to realize and accept our own humanity and failings; to love others and ourselves despite many flaws and imperfections. I have no problem with the idea that people grow from emotional suffering, but I struggle with the subtle implication that at the end of life, we should not provide comfort from physical pain lest we rob the patient of spiritual growth. On the contrary, I believe relieving severe physical pain would not rob any lives of meaning when the end is near. This is the time to let out the stops, go full speed for comfort, and do whatever possible to help. This mind-set should provide a direction for physicians, family or friends who are there for a dying person. In other words, any suffering that might be fruitful during life is no longer important at the end of life when it is no longer time for growth, but rather for rest.

To the second question: "Should physicians seek to relieve patients' spiritual suffering just as much as their physical pain?"

I would also say "yes." A good physician should treat the whole person: the spiritual, emotional and physical individual. For example, if there are unresolved emotional issues during those last times, we, as a hospice group, endeavor to bring the long-lost son home to see his dying father so they can reconcile their earlier struggles.

The suffering issue begs the question about suicide, whether it be physician-assisted when there is a terminal illness or a nonterminal person choosing to commit suicide for whatever reason. I believe that physician-assisted suicide should not be necessary if the patient's physicians, family or friends promise to allow a natural death and, at the same time, pursue every effort to make the patient comfortable. Even in the worst and most painful situations, physicians can provide profound and deep sedation to relieve suffering, and, of course, without hydration, the end will come. I see that as an intent to comfort and not to kill.

Most think it is wrong to allow suicide when a person is suffering only from depression. Depression is generally reversible and deserves treatment; not a quick, self-inflicted gunshot wound to the head, a noose around the neck or an overdose of medication. Why is it okay to allow suicide in a person who has situational depression resulting from the diagnosis of cancer? It is not surprising that many people experience depression when they face a terminal illness. Physicians, care providers, mental health professionals and family members need the wisdom and strength to help terminally ill people recover from depression, so they can savor the time they have left, reconcile or resolve any conflicts in their lives and move to some level of acceptance and comfort. Why waste that important time with an unnatural and complicating suicidal escape?

During 2013, in the state of Oregon, about 66 percent of all deaths occurred at home. This is in comparison to the rest of the country where 39.6 percent died at home.[241] The authors of the research believed that this was the consequence of Oregon having provided extensive general public education about what to expect at the end of life and ways to improve end-of-life care. This has happened over the years since physician-assisted suicide legislation was adopted. Personally, I am not a fan of suicide in any form since (reversible) depression is the root cause in, I dare say, every case. However, I am impressed how the people of Oregon have learned that, at the end of life, dying at home (away from all the aggressive interventions of the hospital) is a laudable and achievable goal.

Emotional suffering is often more significant than most of us realize. My hat is off to the psychiatrists, psychologists, counselors, pastors, family members and friends whose jobs concentrate on that part of the quest to enhance human health. In all my years of experience practicing internal medicine, I have treated the discomforting and debilitating physical illnesses or ailments that affect the body as well as the maladies of the mind and soul. The last group is definitely the biggest challenge. Everyone should have the goal of finding meaning in this crazy and sometimes hurtful life and, when it gets too painful, should realize there are professionals available to help.

---

241   Susan W. Tolle, M.D., and Joan M. Teno: Lessons from Oregon in Embracing Complexity in End-of-Life Care, N Engl J Med 2017; 376:1078–1082, March 16, 2017

THE LIVING WILL, A TOOL FOR TALKING
TO YOUR FAMILY ABOUT DYING

The following essay was written more than 10 years ago but still relates to this topic. I would highlight the third paragraph which states that a living will (advance directive) may fail as a legal document and may not prevent unwanted resuscitation. Instead, I believe a living will should be viewed as a communication tool. Certainly, kids will more likely follow the directions, when the parent, eyeball to eyeball, uses her or his living will to educate them about their wishes. In these cases, when living wills are personally and verbally provided, they have a much better chance of working.

Indeed! A living will (advance directive) is first, and foremost, **a communication tool.**

An Essay:
The prevention of suffering at the end of life

AUDIENCE EYES WIDENED as I spoke, "We will all be dead one day. We should not pretend that it won't happen, and we should all prepare for the experience rather than ignore it." I was asked to give a talk to a group of mostly retired people about the value of a living will or an advance directive. I remember that the audience became very quiet after those words.

I explained that, over 41 years of practice, I have watched helplessly while desperate, fruitless, excessive and painful resuscitation efforts were provided to people who were, without a doubt, dying. If the patient or family want everything done, then health-care providers are obliged to provide everything, even when chances of recovery are nil. It is one more paradox in medicine. The fear of death and not facing the reality of dying can be responsible for suffering that can occur at the end of life.

A living will is simply a tool to communicate how you would like to be cared for if, in the future, you are no longer able to speak for yourself. Ultimately, a living will allows an individual to influence how he or she would like to die and relieves family members of the burden of the responsibility of stopping care.[242] In my opinion, the true value of such a document is not about it being a legal document, but rather in the encouragement and opportunity the document provides to talk to your family about how you want to be treated if there is a catastrophic medical problem. There is a time to intervene with fancy medical care. . . and there is a time to let go.

Bottom line: A living will makes it easier for families to allow a natural and comfortable death when death is inevitable.

After the presentation, one guy told me his wife purposefully avoided coming because she didn't want to think about such gloomy things. He said wryly, "We are all going to die. Why shouldn't we talk about it?" Another asked, "I still don't know the definition of a living will. Does it

242   Erin S. DeMartino, MD, et. al Who Decides When a Patient Can't? Statutes on Alternate Decision Makers. N Engl J Med 2017; 376:1478–1482, April 13, 2017

have anything to do with death squads pulling the plug on Grandma?" I responded, "No, just the opposite. It is all about Grandma telling us when not to put tubes in so no one has to pull them out." I can't say it was my happiest audience, and I'm afraid I may have offended some of them by being so blunt.

In this age of external chest massage, shocking paddles, breathing machines, feeding tubes and the potential for years of vegetative bedridden life, there is hardly a more important message than letting be known your wishes about dying. I repeat this point for emphasis: a living will may not be respected in an emergency room when those accompanying the patient are requesting everything be done. If the family says "yes" to Cardiopulmonary Resuscitation (CPR), "yes" to shocking paddles and "yes" to breathing tubes, then all those activities will be done even if there is a legally certified living will document that say "no." Will the patient sue the doctor for doing CPR when the living will instructs "no CPR?" The answer is "very unlikely." Rather, it is much more likely the family would sue the doctor for not doing CPR and letting their loved one die. Thus, in this scenario, full CPR is usually done. Also, when everyone is undecided, emergency responders, physicians and essentially any health-care professional will default to actions that save lives, unless they are directed otherwise. It is imperative that your family know your treatment wishes, and these wishes may change as you age or as you develop illnesses or terminal conditions.

People of all ages, but especially the elderly, should realize that CPR is an intense effort that begins when a patient is found in an acute stage of dying or even dead in an institution and does not have an order to withhold resuscitation ("do not resuscitate" or DNR). Chest message is rigorous, often cracking or breaking ribs in elderly patients. A breathing tube is placed down the throat in between the vocal cords to control breathing, and, when appropriate, electric shock is given across the chest to return the abnormal heart rhythm back to a normal rhythm. On average, a successful return to normal life after CPR (in otherwise healthy people younger than sixty-five-years old) is about 6 percent when it happens outside the hospital and 15 percent if it happens during hospitalization. The chances of success drop precipitously with advancing age, with each additional medical problem and especially with an acute infection. The DNR order is driven by the wishes of the patient or the family, often when a patient reaches an advanced age or a condition that would make resuscitation efforts futile. When appropriate, one should give that direction on admission to a hospital or nursing home so that the nursing staff can avoid starting CPR.

The AMA Code of Medical Ethics Opinion 5.2 clarifies that respect for the autonomy and choice of the patient is a core value. When the patient is not able to make health-care decisions, the patient's representative or surrogate should make the choices the patient would have wanted.[243] That sounds well and good, but what if

---

243   https://www.ama-assn.org/delivering-care/advance-directives

the family wants to do everything even if the patient has a DNR order and even if the patient is dying and resuscitation efforts would be futile. In this same opinion, the AMA Ethics Opinion states that when conflicts arise between the advance directive and the wishes of the patient's surrogate, the attending physician should seek assistance from an ethics committee. This clearly means that everything will be done (resuscitation will occur) until a committee meets to make sure all issues are addressed. Certainly, the issue the committee will likely first address will be liability.

Bottom line: Any advance directive will be more effective in avoiding inappropriate and uncomfortable care at the end of life when the patient talks about these wishes with her or his family. Because I am such a firm believer in having safeguards in place, I have included here my own advance directive which includes the formal naming of my Durable Power of Attorney and my expressed wishes regarding my care in the event I am unable to direct my own care. I am confident that my wishes will be followed, not because I have written them in a formal document but because I have taken the time to have that difficult conversation with my loved ones.

THE ACTUAL DURABLE POWER OF ATTORNEY
FOR HEALTH-CARE DECISIONS OF RICHARD P. HOLM

Know all persons by these presents that I, Richard P. Holm, of the City of Brookings, County of Brookings, State of South

Dakota, do hereby constitute and appoint Joanie S. Holm to be my true and lawful Attorney-in-Fact with full power to make and render decisions related to my health care.

Accordingly, I hereby grant the following powers to the person named above within the limitations hereinafter specified.

1. To authorize or withhold authorization for medical and surgical procedures;
2. To authorize my admission to a medical, nursing residential or similar facility and to enter agreements for my care;
3. To arrange for my discharge, transfer from, or change in type of care provided;
4. To arrange for consultation diagnosis or assessment as may be required for my proper care and treatment; and
5. To authorize participation in medical, nursing and social research, consistent with the limitations hereinafter specified and such ethical guidelines as may appropriately govern such research.

My instructions to my Attorney-in-Fact, with respect to decisions to withhold or withdraw life-sustaining treatment, are as follows:

1. Allow me to enter into decision making as much as possible and choose as I would have chosen if I had my full faculties. But if I am incapacitated, know those decisions are not binding.
2. Allow me to be home as long as reasonably possible but transfer me to a long-term care facility or skilled care facility if I become a burden.

3. I desire that cardiopulmonary resuscitation (CPR), respirator, feeding tube of any type, intravenous fluid, or antibiotics be used only when there is a reasonable chance for long-term recovery, or survival, or to ever be able to recognize and know my family; and I further direct that any or all of these treatments be withheld or withdrawn if I do not have a reasonable chance for recovery to ever be able to recognize and know my family, or **if I have a terminal condition**, or if I have unrelenting, untreatable and severe pain.

4. I desire that if I do not have a reasonable chance for long-term recovery or survival, or I am not able to recognize and know my family, and I am incapable of eating or drinking; that I understand withholding these treatments will allow a natural death in approximately 10 days. Comfort care should be initiated if needed. In these conditions, I direct that especially IV fluids or feeding tubes be withheld.

5. If the hospital or care facility is not willing to follow the above direction, then I authorize and direct my durable power of attorney (DPA) to transfer me to a facility that would respect and follow these wishes and directions by my advance directives and by my DPA.

This Durable Power of Attorney shall become effective when my attending physician has determined in good faith that I do not have decisional capacity; shall not be affected by my disability as contemplated in State law; shall continue in effect through any period of full disability or incapacity that prohibits me from understanding and transacting activities mentioned in this Durable Power of Attorney for Health-Care Decisions; and shall be binding on me and my heirs, executors and administrations. It will remain in force up to the time of a written revocation signed by me.

In the event the aforesaid Joanie S. Holm shall predecease me, fail, or refuse to act, or become incapable to reasonably continue as my Attorney-in-Fact, then I constitute, appoint and direct that Eric Powell Holm, Carter Jackson Holm, Preston Smith Holm, and Julia Xu Holm, or any of them, act as my true and lawful Attorneys-in-Fact with all the powers and discretion set forth above.

I authorize any health-care provider to release to my Attorney or Attorneys-in-Fact, without restriction, a copy of all my medical records. This authority shall supersede any prior agreement to restrict disclosure and has no expiration date unless I revoke authority. This grants my Attorneys-in-Fact to serve as my representative under any and all HIPAA regulations.

In witness whereof, I have hereunto set my hand and seal on this ___ day of _____, at _____, _____. _____

_____
Richard P. Holm

NOTARY REPUBLIC

Witness: _____ date:_____
cc. to Joanie, Eric, Carter, Preston, and Julia
cc. LeWayne Erickson, Attorney at Law

THINGS YOU SHOULD KNOW: Q & A

Questions and Answers about:
What is Suffering? The prevention of suffering near the end of life

The following is a real case, and these questions were originally written to encourage the patient's doctor not to worry so much about liability but rather to know the accepted ethical and legal rules and principles, and, therefore, to be responsive to the mother's wishes. Details have been altered to avoid disclosing the identity of the patient and her family.

This discussion developed from the experience of a young woman who had a severe brain injury many years ago, and, since the injury, the woman has been in a persistent vegetative state. For unknown reasons, after years, suddenly the father came to realize that he wanted to stop artificial hydration and let his daughter die a natural death. This dilemma brings up several ethical questions.

Question: Are there standard Medical Ethical principles which give the father a choice in this matter?

The American Medical Association's (AMA) Code of Medical Ethics states it plainly, "Physicians are to sustain life but also to relieve suffering;[244] and where one duty

---

244   https://www.ama-assn.org/delivering-care/advance-care-planning

conflicts with the other, then the preference of the patient or her or his representative should prevail."[245] The chief executive officer of a local hospital system echoed that ruling, "The person or the person's representative should have the last say."

———— ∽∾ ————

Question: Would stopping fluid feedings be more merciful than keeping her alive for years in a vegetative state?

YES. In my opinion, a person in a permanent vegetative state would experience little if any discomfort from stopping all hydration and feedings for the ten days it would take to allow a natural death. In many people's opinion, being kept alive for years in a bed without sensing the joy of independent movement, without eating or without communicating would be dreadful. The paradox of this situation is that fluid replacement meant to sustain life can also prolong pain and suffering. In this case, there was a significant burden of suffering from severe muscle spasms not to mention the consequences of total bed rest and complete dependency day after day, year after year. This is to say nothing of the suffering endured by the family knowing their loved one is in such a predicament.

———— ∽∾ ————

245   https://www.ama-assn.org/delivering-care/orders-not-attempt -resuscitation-dnar

Question: Please reassure me that stopping fluid feedings
would NOT cause her to suffer?

Scientific research shows us that if dehydration
occurs during the dying process, the brain produces
natural endorphins that reduce pain and provide comfort. If dehydration is allowed, the patient will slip away
gently in eight to twelve days. In contrast, for someone
caught in a persistent vegetative state, discontinuing
IV fluids and feeding tube fluids/feedings can allow
for a peaceful end. Some uninformed people think
that the discontinuation of fluids would be a painful
way to go when, ironically, it is very peaceful and a
much better alternative than continuing fluid and tube
feeding treatment.[246]

—————

Question: Is there a difference between choosing not to start
fluid feedings versus deciding to cease them?

The AMA Code of Medical Ethics, U.S., and State
laws declare that there is no ethical or legal difference
between not starting treatment and stopping treatment.[247] Any treatment started to enhance health and
diminish suffering can be stopped, especially if the

---

246   http://www.nejm.org/doi/full/10.1056/NEJMra1411746

247   https://www.ama-assn.org/delivering-care/withholding-or-withdrawing
-life-sustaining-treatment

situation changes and treatment is no longer helping and, especially, if it is now causing harm.

———❈———

Question: Do I, as an individual, or someone acting on my behalf, have the right to ask for the tube to be removed?

Yes, especially where sustaining life might cause suffering. Furthermore, the physician should honor those wishes. However, if the physician believes this is not consistent with her or his personal ethics, that physician is obligated to help transfer the patient to the care of another doctor more comfortable with the choices the patient has made. If the institution is not comfortable with removing the tube, that institution is obligated to help transfer the patient to another institution more comfortable with the choices of the patient and her DPA.

———❈———

Question: What is the most important lesson from this story?

The important lesson in stopping treatment for a patient who is terminally ill, or permanently and severely brain injured, is to realize that stopping or not starting intervention is not morally or ethically wrong. Many people see this option as giving up, when on the contrary, it can be virtuous. Letting go is not easy, but what many fail to realize is that the decision to stop aggressive treatment can be a selfless gift to a loved one who is enduring constant suffering. Death is inevitable for all of us, and it is important to recognize when it is time to let go.

The overlooked beauty of the living will or advance directive is that it answers the tough questions about end-of-life care so the family doesn't have to. We should all talk to our family in advance about our wishes regarding sudden cardiac events, vegetative states and feeding tubes. It might prevent a lot of suffering.

———⌇———

Chapter Nine

A Silent Shame

Elder abuse: The new and old epidemic

Case Study:
The case of an abused and demented elderly man

YEARS AGO, A FRAIL, CONFUSED, ELDERLY MAN arrived in the emergency room with a fractured hip. He was incontinent, had poor hygiene and was covered with bruises and sores. His family explained that the patient had recently fallen multiple times. I could see his needs were overwhelming his caregivers, and, if there hadn't been physical abuse, there was at least neglect. After talking with the family, I suspected that this elderly man had been abused as a child, abused his kids when he was in power, and then, as he was failing, he was being passively abused in turn. It is described in the medical literature as "repetition compulsion," the gift that keeps on giving. (Beware the seeds you sow with your own children, for you may reap a similar fate.)

Many books are written on the topic of being a good parent.[248,249] Almost every one of them, in some manner, offers two recommendations. First, love your children unconditionally. Second, teach them discipline. With love and discipline comes fairness, a way in which to interact successfully with others while living in this world filled with rules. In a healthy family, parents provide total support for the little person who begins life completely helpless and who requires tremendous amounts of support and direction. Over time, the parents encourage self-sufficiency and independence by gradually withdrawing much of that support and direction and allowing their children to make their own decisions and start lives of their own. Eventually, parents urge the children out of the nest.

Caring for an elderly person is a lot like caring for a child only in reverse. At first, adult children give support from afar. Then, as need for help arises, the elder may live at home with support or move into an assisted living center, a nursing home or may even live with her or his children in either the elder's home or the child's. This can be extremely difficult as no one easily accepts having their freedoms taken away, especially when a younger person is the one taking away those liberties. Ideally, adult children should allow as much freedom and independence for their parent as possible until the time when the elder is no longer capable. It might be considered elder abuse when an adult child, for example, takes and insists on maintaining control of

248   https://www.goodreads.com/book/show/159760.Reviving_Ophelia

249   https://www.amazon.com/Becoming-Brilliant-Successful-Children-Lifetools/dp/1433822393

their elderly parent while the parent is still capable of caring for herself or himself.

Experts say that most people don't hurt or neglect their family members intentionally. Their actions may be a manifestation of how they were raised. Many abusers were abused themselves. Sometimes they had very young parents, often there was poverty, divorce or mental illness. Most physically normal and mentally healthy people have some low level of self-doubt, but common feelings in abusive people are excessive feelings of self-doubt and inadequacy. Abusive tendencies can manifest when such a person is put into a position of power. Examples abound when these people become higher on some totem pole and take advantage of their power over others. For example, we see it in movie directors, teachers, drill sergeants, political leaders, physicians and counselors. Abuse abounds, and so it is no surprise when abuse happens to a weakened, aging and disabled parent, especially when the adult son or daughter who was abused as a child is given the responsibility of caring for their helpless parent. Add alcohol or drugs to this mix, and severe abuse can happen.

There are those who say that you can measure the fabric of a person by how they treat others who have less power or control. Consider the corrupt king who treats all under his rule with disdain and abuse. In comparison, think of the benevolent king who treats his lowliest servant with kindness and respect. To be a good person and caregiver, please treat others, the strong and the weak, the old and the young, with fairness, unconditional love and respect. Be a good king.

Bottom line: Perfect parenting might be defined as giving loving support while providing freedoms with fair discipline.

Perfect caring for a frail, dependent and elderly person can also be defined as loving support while providing freedoms with fair discipline.

AN ELDERLY PERSON ABUSED BY EMOTIONAL CRUELTY

Another case was one of emotional abuse in which blaming, shouting and anger were imposed upon an incapacitated elder. All this came from a visiting, psychiatrically ill son who had arrived from afar and was unloading his own emotional baggage upon his frail and defenseless mother. The mother had been admitted for a medical issue, and the nurses recognized that the son's abuse of his mother continued in her hospital room. Police were notified, and the visitor was banished from visiting his mother in the hospital or visiting her when she went home.

I saw the patient in the office after she was sent home from the hospital. I documented how the mother was clearly demented and incapacitated, and I had a judge confirm her incompetence. Later, for reasons unclear to me, the judge determined the offending son would have custody and power of attorney over his mother. When the nurses and I heard about the judge's decision, we threw our hands in the air in disbelief and decided there must have been more to the story. This problem could have been avoided had the son been more considerate and responsible; had the mother made earlier financial plans while she was competent; had a bank's trust department, a CPA or a bookkeeping business been asked to pay bills; and had other family members been more observant of the patient's overall condition and the son's aggressive behavior toward his mother.

Bottom line: None of us are safe from abuse, and especially when people become frail or lose their mental capacity, they are at risk. Elder abuse can come in the form of physical harm, neglect, emotional cruelty or financial exploitation, and it is more common than one would expect.

REASONS FOR ABUSE

Another abusive man was an only child who grew up loved but overprotected. He received lots of parental praise for being a "nice guy" but had not been disciplined for his uncontrollable bouts of rage. He was protected from repercussion or disciplinary action at school because his parents would pressure his teachers. Intolerant of direction, he dropped out of group sports. His marriages failed because, whenever he felt criticized, he would fly into a rage, and gradually emotional abuse became physical and divorce followed. When it was time to care for his elderly and dependent parents, he was abusive. The parents were reluctant to confront him or call for help because they felt responsible, were terrified of his rage and physical threat or, worse, feared he would ignore them.

There are many theories to explain why people abuse others. Psychologists say that every case is different and every abuser is driven by a different monster. Carrie Askin, a clinical social worker and author who has had extensive experience treating spousal abuse says that abusers most commonly become that way because **they never learn to tolerate criticism and they**

retaliate when they hear it.[250] She states that often abusers learn during their youth that she or he is above criticism, has the right to punish anyone who violates that right and can do so without expecting repercussion.

Isn't it a paradox that the most common reason for abuse happens because the abuser did not experience fair discipline as a child? If one is to improve as a person, then **that person must learn to take constructive criticism very early in life.** Those who haven't accepted this life lesson and those who respond to every disapproval

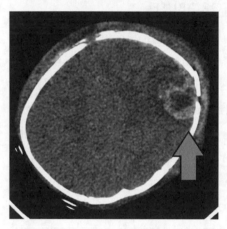

with anger and retribution eventually live an isolated, ignorant and unfulfilled life as people learn to avoid them when the abuser comes near.

Bleeding within the brain, under a skull fracture from abusive head trauma[251]

Those who were raised in environments that tolerated their bouts of temper often become adults unaware of how damaging their temper is to their social image, their communication skills and, most importantly, their capacity to be trusted. They come to believe their anger, intimidation and tantrums allow them to "get their way". They do not realize how their temper is harmful

250   https://www.psychologytoday.com/blog/hurt-people-hurt -people/201510/five-reasons-people-abuse-their-partners.

251   Photo by James Heilman, MD, May, 2016, from https://commons.wikimedia .org/wiki/File:CTheatInfantAbusiveheadtrauma.png

to others around them, and they do not realize how destructive such anger is to themselves. Paradoxically, they erroneously believe their anger empowers them when just the opposite is true. No one would dare tell them the truth because such honesty would likely bring on their wrath. People with anger issues and temper fits may never realize how their behavior results in a missed opportunity to improve. Those who eventually have to face negative consequences to this behavior can search out the many available resources to help with anger management. Such resources are often led by trained professionals and provided locally. I suggest starting with a Mayo Clinic online summary of recommendations.[252]

There are other reasons why people become abusers.[253] Some, who have never known kindness and were abused themselves, become abusive almost in self-defense. They were taught, by example, that abuse is (incorrectly) normal and deserved. About one-third of the children raised in an abusive environment become abusive adults. However, this also means that two out of three raised in a family with abuse, do NOT become abusive.

Bottom line: Abuse should never be tolerated. Children, spouses, friends and the elderly should be able to trust the people around them and live in a safe environment. If you are an abused person, please do the right thing and call for help from your physician, minister, social services or even police. You deserve the right to get some help (and so does the abuser).

---

252   http://www.mayoclinic.org/healthy-lifestyle/adult-health/in-depth/anger-management/art-20045434?pg=1

253   http://www.nytimes.com/1989/01/24/science/sad-legacy-of-abuse-the-search-for-remedies.html?

ABUSE IN ALL FORMS

More to abuse than meets the black eye
(physical abuse)

From the National Committee for the Prevention of Elder Abuse comes the definition: "Physical abuse is physical force or violence that results in bodily injury, pain or impairment. It includes assault, battery and inappropriate restraint."[254] This national committee of experts states that the perpetrators of abuse of the elderly are commonly unmarried, may live with their victims, are unemployed or employed as caregivers of the victims and may have alcohol- or substance-abuse problems. Of course, none of these descriptors may apply.

Classically, physical abuse is suspected when the elderly person appears in the ER or clinic with a black eye or other bruises. Sometimes these bruises are covered by makeup. However, bruising occurs very commonly in the elderly without abuse because of increased fragility of skin, antiplatelet (blood thinner) or steroid medications, the increased number of bumps and falls secondary to balance problems or just because older and frail people simply bruise more. Elder abuse might be suspected if the bruises are on both upper arms (possibly from shaking), on both inner thighs (possibly from sexual abuse), a wrap-around bruise encircling the entire limb (possibly from heavy and hard handling) or are multicolored (implying repeated and separate trauma over time). One might be more suspicious of physical abuse when an elderly person appears with a broken arm and handprint bruises on both sides of the fracture, when there are recurrent burns

---

254   http://www.preventelderabuse.org/elderabuse/physical.html

from any source, when there are rope or strap mark-like abrasions or when there are signs of trauma-induced hair or tooth loss. Physical abuse of the elderly doesn't have to be from violence but can be by way of neglect. Abuse from neglect becomes apparent with poor hygiene or poor living conditions. More difficult to identify is when neglect doesn't allow adequate time for recreational activities. We all need time for activity besides being plopped in front of a TV.

If any of these findings occur, there should be further exploration of the living situation for that elderly person. Physicians, care providers, caregivers and family members all should be aware of these diagnostic clues. The best action to take, should one suspect abuse, would be to get the potential victim to the emergency room, inform the care provider or ER doctor of suspicions and let them do the investigation.

Abuse isn't limited to just sticks and stones (emotional abuse)

Every individual, no matter the age, deserves to be treated with dignity and respect. Elder emotional abuse, without physical harm, can reflect acts of commission or omission, can be committed by a caregiver or anyone else, and can result in significant emotional injury. It is estimated that two-and-a-half-million older adults are abused annually, and one quarter of those abused report significant levels of psychological abuse. However, these numbers may be under-reported, and some experts say more than 50 percent of the elderly have experienced at least some level of psychological or emotional abuse.[255]

---

255 Eckroth-Bucher, M, Devious Damage: Elder Psychological Abuse, *Aging Well*, Vol. 1 No. 4 Fall, 2008. P. 24.

In nursing homes and assisted living facilities, so much monitoring now occurs that it has become rare for significant physical or emotional abuse to occur. Most emotional abuse of the elderly occurs in private homes and usually (90 percent) by family members.

Different kinds of emotional abuse include verbal and non-verbal threats, humiliation, manipulation and fear. These are methods used to control another person, in this case the elderly person. Often, these abuses result from frustrations of the at-home caregiver who is challenged by the difficulties of caring for elderly individuals. In comparison to physical abuse (thought to be perpetrated by males in 80 percent of the cases), emotional abuse has been found to be perpetrated in equal rates by females and males.[256] Research also suggests that someone who has caused psychological harm in the past is more likely to be one who will cause physical harm in the future.

To my knowledge, there is no good way to measure which is more challenging for a human: emotional abuse or physical abuse. There are differing opinions on the topic, but I hold with those who believe that emotional abuse is even more painful and that the effects last longer than physical abuse. It's been said, "You can put a band-aid on your finger but not on your heart." There is no easy answer to this problem, but there is scientific data to show that, when people experience either emotional pain or physical pain, the same area

---

256 Murphy, Christopher M.; O'Leary, K. Daniel (October 1989). Psychological aggression predicts physical aggression in early marriage. *Journal of Consulting and Clinical Psychology*. American Psychological Association via PsycNET. 57 (5): 579–582.

of the brain becomes active.[257] Both physical and emotional abuse hurt.

Caregivers, who find themselves saying hurtful words to their elderly and disabled family members, must realize that an emotional unkind word is more painful than a full slap in the face or a slam to the ground. At the same time, caregivers should not be hurt or driven to anger by a demented elderly person who is acting mean and does not realize what she or he is doing or saying. **Negative words from a demented person should not be taken seriously.** However, if anger overwhelms the provider, she or he may be experiencing burnout and should think about finding someone else to help (see **Chapter Seven**). Coping skills should include taking time to realize the joy and fulfillment that comes from the simple act of providing the gift of caring. Such a positive attitude should help bring a discouraged caregiver through periodic hard times. If this is not enough reward and anger and resentment persist in the heart of the provider, she or he should consider taking time off or even giving up the job and finding another way to get care for the one who needs help.

Financial abuse, the dirty rotten scoundrels

Financial scams targeting seniors have become so prevalent that they're now considered "the crime of the 21st century."[258] Why? Because seniors are thought to have a significant amount of money sitting in their accounts. Remember the famous bank

257   Kross, E, et. al.: Social rejection shares somatosensory representations with physical pain. vol. 108 no. 15, 6270–6275.

258   http://www.all-things-conflict-resolution-and-adr.com/elder-financial-abuse-the-crime-of-the-21st-century-case-study.html

robber, Willie Sutton? When Sutton was asked by a reporter why he robbed banks, he said, "Because that's where the money is."[259] That has become Sutton's Law and could be used to explain why scams are often aimed at the elderly. Another reason that scammers commonly target the elderly is that financial scams of seniors often go unreported. Since scammers are difficult to prosecute, their crimes are considered low-risk. Financial scams can be devastating to many older adults, leaving them in a vulnerable position and often with less working time in their lives to recoup their losses.

It's not just wealthy seniors who are targeted. Middle- and low-income older adults are also at risk for financial fraud. Also, we should all be aware that strangers are not the most common perpetrators in these crimes. Over 90 percent of all reported elder financial abuses are committed by the victim's own family members, most often their adult children, grandchildren, nieces and nephews.

Actual examples of financial fraud abound. A son of one of my patients called and said his eighty-year-old mother and her new boyfriend had recently been going to the bank and removing large sums from the mother's savings account. The son pointed out how his mother was losing her memory and the capacity to make reasonable choices. She had been spending thousands of dollars for herbal and supplemental cures for memory problems and had unpaid bills everywhere. Add to that, an opportunist boyfriend was manipulating her to have access to her savings. The son asked me how to protect his mom and her money.

---

259   https://www.fbi.gov/history/famous-cases/willie-sutton

She was encouraged to come see me in my office at which time I tested her capacity and competence. She had very poor short-term (antegrade) memory (See **Chapter Six**). She obviously did not have the capacity to make legal decisions. I asked a judge to intervene, and the power of attorney was yielded to the son. The son stopped the withdrawals and acted to protect his mother from the possible harms that a manipulative boyfriend might cause. It was a heartbreaking case because the boyfriend disappeared, leaving the mother angry and lonely. She eventually moved in with her son for a while. Over time, her memory deteriorated enough that she needed a great deal more attention than her son and family could provide. Finally, she found some level of happiness in a nursing home in her son's town.

Phone call or Internet fraud

The National Council on Aging (NCOA) has written a compendium of common fraudulent traps that result from telephone calls or Internet messages. The NCOA information is so good that I would recommend going to the Internet site referenced below.[260] When phone calls come from unfamiliar numbers or from strangers with unusual stories or incredible and unbelievable offers, you are not obligated to carry on a conversation or to be gracious. Simply hang up, or, better yet, if you have caller ID and don't recognize the number, don't answer. The caller is intruding on you. Everyone should be aware that telemarketing scams are without a paper trail and very hard to trace. In addition, once a scammer locates a

260 https://www.ncoa.org/economic-security/money-management/scams-security/top-10-scams-targeting-seniors/

susceptible senior, the senior's phone number may be shared with other fraudulent schemers who are looking for easy targets. Be aware.

Medicare and health insurance scams

Posing as Medicare representatives, the perpetrators obtain personal information. The scammers commonly promote bogus services which provide little medical help and bill Medicare for significant profit. **Government agencies, by law, cannot initiate contact by telephone with the people they serve.** All of these calls are fraudulent when you did not initiate the call and it came from some self-proclaimed "government agency." Initiate your own contact with Medicare for such questions.

Bottom line: Never trust anyone calling you saying she or he represents the government or Medicare, especially if they are **calling you** for information.

Counterfeit prescription drugs

People are often lured to purchase less expensive prescriptions from an Internet black market source. Many times, these sources for medicine provide an inaccurate dose (too much or too little) of the drug sought, and sometimes the drug is mixed with other undefined and possibly unsafe substances. There may be reasonable sources from pharmacies outside the U.S., but it is challenging to determine which source for prescription drugs is safe or helpful. I have had Canadian friends, living in the U.S., who have used Canadian pharmacies by mail that resulted in significant savings. The medicines seemed effective and there was no apparent harm. I simply advise prudent research of such pharmacies before using them and warn that it is not technically legal to buy medications from Canadian pharmacies. However, at the time of this writing, U.S. officials usually allow a three-month supply of medication to be brought or mailed across the border providing the drugs are not opioids or controlled substances. Do not purchase pharmaceuticals when someone calls you. You should be the caller.

Funeral and cemetery scams

Scammers may claim fake debts after the death of a loved one. This scam is an effort to extort money by stating that a fake bill needs to be paid or some fine or punishment will follow. Another scam tactic involves encouraging inappropriate funeral purchases such as an expensive casket for someone being cremated. Consider using your local funeral home or obtaining a second opinion before working with any companies that reach out to you. If there is a question about a large bill like this, have your trust department, your bookkeeping service or another family member address this problem.

Fraudulent antiaging products

Scammers sell herbs, supplements or even prescription medicines that they falsely claim will reduce wrinkles, reduce fat, enhance strength and energy or add years to one's life. I am aware of one wrinkle product for bags under the eyes that has remarkable before-and-after pictures. The catch is that it only lasts for less than two hours and works by dangerously causing reactionary swelling. Another risky, and possible scam, is botulism toxin (Botox) which is a potentially paralyzing and hazardous neurotoxin and should not be sought on the black market. The best antiaging plan is to get into good physical condition. Relish the fact that your wrinkles may reflect your wisdom.

The pigeon drop

In this scam, the conartist calls and promises to split a large sum of found money if the senior will make a "good faith" donation to the scammer. Sometimes a second scammer, posing as a lawyer, is involved. Call your bank's trust department and explain the situation before thinking there is free money out there. Trust officers are aware of these scammers and should advise when safe or not safe to donate. If the telephone caller is reluctant to let you hang up to discuss the offer with your family or the trust department at your bank and is offering a discount only during this one phone call, then HANG UP. If it sounds too good to be true, it likely is.

The fake accident or caught in a country without money ploy

The conartist, by phone or Internet, pretends to be a friend or family member traveling in a foreign country who is either injured, in a hospital or caught without travel money. The senior is asked to send money to help the family member or friend. Do not send money unless you have confirmation in a separate call from other family members that there is, indeed, a problem. Otherwise, just hang up.

The fake charity scam

Often, especially after a major disaster, callers talk the senior into sending rescue money which, of course, does NOT reach those affected by the disaster. If you want to give after a major disaster, YOU initiate the call to a well-known charity. Fake charities abound even without disasters. If you want to give to your **local** firefighters, police and local charities, YOU initiate the call. Do not give to someone who calls you on the phone from afar. Just hang up.

Fake antivirus computer programs

A phone call or a pop-up browser window may indicate a fake virus is invading the senior's computer and encourages the senior to purchase a fake, often expensive, antivirus program. When some of these so-called antivirus programs are downloaded, the senior's computer can be exposed to a real virus that discloses private and personal information. Have a local computer specialist advise you of an antivirus program. Ignore or hang up on anyone selling antivirus programs.

E-mail phishing (pronounced fishing) scams:

Phishing email messages usually ask the reader to go to a website to update personal information such as passwords, debit or credit card numbers, bank account numbers or Social Security numbers. Some promise an IRS refund or some other fake promise of money back. One should never give up any personal information, a debit or credit card number and especially a Social Security number to an Internet site unless you initiated the interaction yourself.

Investment schemes and scams

Anyone calling you, or e-mailing you, with a great investment opportunity should not be trusted, especially if it sounds too good to be true. Investments should start with a local investment advisor or the trust department of your local bank, never from a stranger over the phone, especially if they called you first. Just hang up.

Homeowner reverse mortgage scams

These have become very popular in recent years. The National Council on Aging warns that unsecured reverse mortgages can lead property owners to lose their homes when the perpetrators offer money or a free house somewhere else in exchange for the title to the property. Do not deal in reverse mortgages unless the person who is presenting this plan to you is reputable. Always consider first calling your bank to ask about a reverse mortgage type of plan. Just hang up.

The sweepstakes and lottery scam

The scammer first informs the mark that they have won some sweepstakes or a lottery, and sometimes a real-looking check comes with it. The only thing the senior must do now is to make some payment to the scammer to unlock the supposed prize. Of course, their sweepstakes check bounces after a few days, and the prize never appears. Don't deposit any of your money into their account unless their check to you has been cashed and money is in hand. Better yet, just hang up.

The grandparent scam

"Hi! Grandma, do you know who this is?" (Don't ever answer that question.) If you give up the name of a grandchild, the scammer now has a grandchild's fake identity. Usually the fake grandkid will ask for money to solve some unexpected financial problem like overdue rent, an inappropriate jailing, or an important car repair. Often the scam artist will say, "Please don't tell Mom and Dad, because, if you do, they will kill me." You should always talk to the parents or family member before sending any money.

A judge giving legal power of attorney to someone outside the family

Apparently, in certain states (Arizona, for example) when there is some question about the capacity of an elderly person or persons, a judge may assign a legal substituted power of attorney that may or may NOT be a family member. In some cases, elderly people have been removed from their home and placed in institutions against their will and against the wishes of the family by a substitute power of attorney. Although this situation may not seem perfectly like an abuse scenario, it does seem to me to be a loss of autonomy and thus is added to this chapter. Although I cannot personally confirm this information, I use it here to warn people of all ages to understand your state laws in this regard and to make at least a short will to define who should make legal choices for you should you become unable to make decisions on your own.

If you are tempted to give money away and have the slightest suspicion that it might be less than legitimate, call your banker, lawyer or trusted professional before writing that check. If you realize that you are susceptible to such scams, a local bank certainly has a trust department, and you can arrange for them to develop ways to protect you. Again, please define a trusted person or family member to make legal choices for you should you become demented or comatose (lose consciousness). This will actually help you preserve your independence. Please do this.

Bottom line: If you suspect you've been the victim of a scam of any kind, please contact someone you can trust like your local doctor, banker, clergy, police, Adult Protective Services in your community or go to a government-sponsored national resource line. Call 1-800-677-1116 to speak to an Eldercare Locator or visit their website: www.eldercare.gov.

An essay entitled:
Power and abuse

Think about it. Domestic violence is more about controlling than about physical injury. The American Psychiatric Association defines it as control by one person over another in a dating, marital or live-in relationship. The control might also be of a child, an elderly loved one or of anyone else for that matter. The means of this control include physical, sexual, emotional and economic abuse, as well as through threats and isolation.

All of us must admit to an unfair vying for power and control over our partner at one time or another in some manner. I believe that neither sex has the corner market on control and emotional abuse, although the male of the species certainly uses physical means more readily.

The U.S. Centers for Disease Control and Prevention estimates that, in this country, one out of every four women, and one out of every seven men, will have experienced severe physical violence from a bully in their lifetime.[261] The number of American troops killed in Iraq and Afghanistan from 2001 through 2012 was about 6,000, and the number of American women murdered by male partners during that same time was about 12,000. Bullies and abusers are everywhere.

While in medical school, I was in an Atlanta Emergency Room when a woman came in with a broken nose and other broken bones and bruises that she explained away as the result of a fall. (We knew full well they were inflicted by her spouse.) Since coming to this prairie town 37 years ago, I have seen several cases of parents who physically and emotionally abused their children and of adult children who physically and emotionally abused their parents. I remember numerous cases where women came into my office, explained that their husbands were physically beating them, and, despite my recommendations to escape and seek shelter, they stayed married to the scoundrels.

Whom can we blame for this destructive behavior? Experts say that if one is brought up in a family with any kind of abuse, the chance of being abusive, or marrying an individual who abuses, becomes much higher. The National Coalition for the Homeless estimates that ten million children in the U.S. are exposed to domestic violence every year. They estimate that children who are exposed to such violence are three to four times more likely to become abusive, or to be abused, than people raised in families

---

261   https://www.cdc.gov/violenceprevention/pdf/nisvs_report2010-a.pdf

without abuse.[262] In our power-hungry society, where our children are steeped in violent examples on TV, movies and video games (not to mention watching the evening news), it is shocking that there isn't more violence in our homes. Other experts believe that people raised without reasonable discipline are also at risk to become abusers. When raised without facing consequences for inappropriate actions, without growing to accept direction and criticism and without developing control of their temper they become potentially harmful to others.

Sometimes it's right to stand up to a bully, but, when there is danger, it's also right to escape and get help. It's always right, however, to save your children from a lifetime of abuse. Do not allow it in your family, and, if that means calling for help and finding a safe place, then call for help.

If you are the abuser, are you compelled to continue the cycle of abuse? I believe each of us must ask more of ourselves and put an end to it in our own families, our work situation and our love relationships. We must take responsibility for our own actions no matter what abuse we have had to face ourselves. It is our ethical and spiritual duty to treat our partner, our children and our parents (and for that matter, all people) with kindness and respect. When we empower and respect those around us, power and respect is returned. Real power that lasts and grows

262   http://www.goodhousekeeping.com/life/relationships/a37005/statistics-about-domestic-violence/

comes from kindness. Unknown by the abuser, while violent fits of temper and abuse may feel controlling, in reality, there is a loss of power, a loss of listening and a loss of any chance to truly communicate with others. Make up your mind to end the cycle of domestic violence. Take back control of yourself and truly expand a real influence on those around you by listening, letting go of abusive actions and letting go of an exhausting and hateful desire to control others.

THINGS YOU SHOULD KNOW, Q & A

Questions and Answers about:
A Silent Shame—Elder abuse: The new and old epidemic

Question: What should I do if I sense I am being emotionally "controlled" or "abused" by my children? Who can I turn to? I am afraid that if my son discovers I have asked for help, he will walk away from me, and I will never see him again.

We all can sometimes feel controlled and emotionally abused by our partners, our children and our parents, but often this feeling is a reaction to feeling angry or disappointed with ourselves. It may also reflect depression and self-deprecation. If you are afraid of how your son will react, likely you are receiving some level of abuse or inappropriate attempt to control you. Your first plan should be to get help and discuss it with support people such as your doctor, minister, lawyer or social worker. If, indeed, there is controlling or emotional abuse happening, these support people can help you. (They might also help you if you are experiencing depression.)

The fact that you are concerned enough to seek help might help your son analyze his behavior. If the abuse continues, you have the right to call law enforcement and leave. Search your heart and do what you think is best.

Question: When I get a phone call from a telemarketer, I find it very hard to hang up, even when I know they are trying to get money from me, and I want to hang up. How can I handle this?

You are like many good people, cordial and caring to the core. You simply must realize that, unless the callers get money, talking to you will be a waste of their time as well as yours. Do not risk their talking you into giving them money. Say, "Thank you for your call, but I am not interested," or, "I am not able to give, (or buy)" and hang up. Do not wait for a reply, because they are taught to never give up. Hanging up is the considerate thing to do for all involved, including the caller.

Bottom line: Don't feel guilty. Hanging up is the right thing to do.

Question: I was financially tricked by a telephone scam years ago and find it hard to trust people after that. Is my distrust response appropriate?

Think of it this way. Something like 90 or 95 percent of all people are trustworthy and would not scam people out of their hard-earned savings. However, there are people who never learned that we get more out of life by giving. In this case, it is "all about them, and no one else." These are a group of people from whom we need to protect ourselves. They are the vandals, the crooks, the dishonest percentage that have caused our civilized society to develop rules, regulations, laws and police action. Indeed, regulations are the result of a necessary effort to protect the whole population from a small percentage of villains. Telephone callers who are asking for money are waving a red flag. Unless they are someone you know, do not trust them and simply hang up. If you want to donate, you can initiate the giving process.

Chapter Ten

Head-to-Toe

A care guide for the aging body

Case Study:
An older gentleman with multisystem failure

Mr. X was a farmer, in his nineties, from a nearby town. He had lost his wife 15 years earlier. He had been deeply involved with his family, neighbors, community and church throughout his life. I knew him first through caring for his wife as her doctor, and, eventually, I became his doctor. After a fall and resulting hip fracture he was moved to a nursing home for rehabilitation. He never left. Over the five years in the nursing home, he had been progressively failing. It had been about three years since he had recognized his grandchildren, three months since he had recognized his children, and, over the last week, he had stopped eating.

His problem list included multi-infarct dementia, cataracts, macular degeneration, hypothyroidism, diabetes, poor teeth, multiple surgically removed skin cancers and esophageal reflux disease. He'd had a previous myocardial infarction (heart attack) with resulting diastolic heart failure (stiff and poorly functioning heart), chronic renal insufficiency (poor kidneys), chronic constipation, COPD (overexpanded and poorly functioning lungs from smoking) and prior prostate cancer diagnosed and surgically treated ten years ago after which he was burdened with an indwelling urethral catheter (tube) for the last two years. He had severe degenerative arthritis of the hips, knees and shoulders, a prior pressure ulcer (sore) of the sacrum and a history of depression. He took eight scheduled medications and six "as needed" pills prior to when he stopped swallowing.

This is not an uncommon situation, and I have cared for many elderly folks who didn't die from one event but lived long enough to have almost every system finally fail simultaneously.[263] Mr. X appeared to no longer have joy in life. I met with the two daughters, and they reaffirmed an earlier decision to avoid any resuscitation effort. They asked me to make sure he was comfortable but to provide no antibiotics or any medical interventions. They said, "It is what he would have wanted." I instructed the nursing staff to continue to try to feed him if he was willing to take food but not to force it and certainly do not place a feeding tube. My words to the nurses were, "Just make sure he is comfortable, please." When

263 https://palliative.stanford.edu/home-hospice-home-care-of-the-dying -patient/common-terminal-diagnoses/advanced-senescence/

the daughters asked how long he would last, I estimated about ten days from the time he stopped eating and drinking.

After examining him once again, I stopped all oral meds, and because I sensed he was somewhat uncomfortable, I started a very low dose fentanyl (opioid) patch. I advised the family, especially grand and great-grandchildren, to all come and see him, hang out with him for a while and try to bring some fun into his room. I thanked the daughters for the opportunity to care for him (and their mother) over the last twenty-five years. Two days later Mr. X slipped away comfortably during the night. During those two days, the nurses reported to me that the family filled the room with laughter, grandchildren played on his bed, the family sang hymns each night and, in the end, there was joyful weeping.

When filling out the death certificate, I dutifully listed dehydration and malnutrition with all the conditions listed, but the best answer would have been, "advanced senescence." In other words, almost every organ system was failing simultaneously due to advanced age.

BLIZZARD ON THE JOURNEY HOME: *VISION LOSS*

One winter Sunday, after holiday feasting with family, we ran into a blizzard while driving home from a distant city. Intermittently, the powerful wind and new snow would seem to explode between shelterbelts or when passing big trucks, diminishing all vision. The idea of coming to a stop during such blinding snow was not an option because moving vehicles were coming from behind. We pressed on as carefully as we could, white knuckled, leaning forward, staring hard onto a prairie highway that would repeat-edly appear, disappear, come back to view and disappear again, until we finally arrived safely home. Whew!

Being able to see what's in the line of sight is something most take for granted, and, yet, this will change for many as aging occurs. It's one of those unhappy surprises about growing old. If people don't lose their vision from a cataract, glaucoma, diabetic retinopathy (loss of vision) or even a misguided Fourth of July bottle rocket, many will develop age-related macular degener-ation. Although this type of vision loss only affects 2 percent of those over fifty years of age, it climbs to 30 percent in those over sixty-five.[264] Our vision may be like winter snow that can whip up into a blizzard as we get older. The macula is the central element of the retina, the center part of your vision. It provides for that concentrated part of the eyesight necessary for thread-ing a needle, painting the lips of the Mona Lisa, finding a lost button, or seeing excitement on the face of a grandchild as she discovers a new thing.

Experts advise that smoking, living without significant physical activity, eating a highly caloric diet and living with sleep apnea may bring individuals to a higher risk for macular degeneration as well as a higher risk of premature aging, heart attacks and stroke. Other ways to prevent macular degeneration might be with taking microdoses of minerals like zinc and certain supple-ments if one is malnourished and deficient in these. The science behind zinc supplements and all other supplements is weak, and one pharmaceutical company has made hay on one small study

---

264   https://www.aafp.org/afp/1999/0701/p99.html.

that showed minimal improvement of wet (bleeding) macular degeneration but none with the common (80 percent) dry form. I suggest zinc and other eye supplements **that come in food form** are a better option than pill form. Foods for eyes include beef, squash-type vegetables, oysters, spinach, mixed nuts, beans and mushrooms. I also suggest eating oily deep sea fish twice a week, a regular intake of ground golden flax seed as well as a supplement of vitamin D3 (2000 IU/day). I should emphasize that a regular exercise program such as a brisk (yet comfortable) walk for 30 minutes every day is by far the most important component on this list to prevent macular degeneration. If you already have macular degeneration, these recommendations are still important. Just don't put yourself at significant risk of falling when walking. Consider walking sticks (like ski poles).

Growing old has its challenges and sometimes is like driving home from a trip and finding yourself in the middle of a prairie blizzard.

THE SOUND OF A TROMBONE BLAT: *HEARING LOSS*

The eighth grader's new trombone made a sound like some distressed huge reptile out of some ancient forest. The loud "blat" filled the bedroom and moved into the kitchen causing a loving wince by a listening mother. The sound waves are captured by the trumpet-shaped outer ears (auricles) that funnel the sound down her ear canals. The sound is amplified by the drum-like tympanic membranes and moves onto the bones of the middle ears which, in turn, vibrate the fluid within the snail-shaped inner ears (cochlea). It is here that hair-like nerve receptors move in different ways to different pitches of different sounds, sending signals to the brain, which distinguishes the blat of a trombone from the scream of a smoke alarm.

Not everyone can hear the trombone blat. There are 11 million deaf Americans, and many more that are hard of hearing.[265] This is second only to lower back pain as the most common physical disability in our country. About a third are born that way; another third have hearing loss from high fevers, bacterial infections, viral diseases, toxins or other unknown reasons; with the last one-third losing hearing due to noise exposure or some combination of these three.

A simple method to prevent deafness would be the use of noise protection devices (if we could only get people to wear the darn things). Macho, deaf-denying boys and men are the worst, allowing themselves to be overexposed to the sounds of rock music, lawnmowers, motorcycles, firecrackers, guns, snowmobiles, saws, headsets, leaf blowers and other big noisemakers. To help prevent such noise exposure, it is well worth purchasing those large cushiony ear covering noise blockers which have a radio included. These trick the macho guy into covering his ears by providing entertainment while protecting his ears from the big-time noise he is making.

Another way to protect hearing is to vaccinate all children (especially girls who may become pregnant one day) against typical childhood illnesses. This will help prevent infections and high fevers from conditions like meningitis, mumps or measles,

---

265   https://www.mayoclinic.org/diseases-conditions/hearing-loss/symptoms-causes/syc-20373072

which can rob babies of hearing. Probably the worst culprit is simply a high fever in babies or in women during pregnancy.

Indeed, those who can hear should make every effort not to lose the wondrous sounds of a choir, the first words of a grand-child, or even the blat of that beginning trombone player!

SNEAKY LOW THYROID AND LOW ENERGY: *HYPOTHYROIDISM*

One of my favorite words in medicine is Hashimoto's thyroid-itis. The sound of it verily trips over the tongue, just like oligo-dendroglia (a nerve insulator cell) and endoscopic retrograde cholangiopancreatography (a procedure to study the gall bladder and pancreas). These are words of medicine which are totally unrelated except that they are fun to say out loud.

However, Hashimoto's thyroiditis is more than an interesting name.[266] This is a condition in which the thyroid is destroyed by the person's immune system. It is the most common cause for hypothyroidism (low thyroid) and occurs more often with advancing age. More than one in six people over sixty-five years of age have it. Hashimoto's thyroiditis takes a course which is so gradual and subtle that the symptoms of low thyroid often go many years unrecognized by the individual or the doctor.

Perhaps this is because, by nature, our bodies try to compen-sate for the environment in which we live. For example, memory loss, which might be mistakenly explained by advancing age, may be the only presenting symptom. Other warnings for possible hypothyroidism include dry skin, constipation, fatigue, poor appetite, cold intolerance, hair loss, weight gain and depression.

---

266   https://medlineplus.gov/ency/article/000371.htm.

Obviously, these are very nondescript symptoms. Any, or all of them, may have nothing to do with the thyroid, may occur with age in a normal-thyroid individual or may not be present in an individual even when hypothyroidism is present.

Illustration of butterfly shaped thyroid gland over thyroid cartilage and trachea[267]

To evaluate for this condition, a free T4 blood test is checked, measuring the level of the actual active hormone made by the thyroid gland. Another blood test, and the gold standard for how well the thyroid is working in the body, is to measure the level of the thyroid stimulating hormone (TSH). This is a totally different hormone made in the all-controlling pituitary part of the brain. The pituitary senses circulating thyroid hormone levels, and when levels are too low, makes more TSH which is supposed to stimulate the thyroid to kick in and make more thyroid hormone. When the pituitary senses the thyroid hormone is too high, it reduces the TSH which is supposed to turn down thyroid hormone production. Someone who has low levels of T4 (hypothyroidism)

---

267   Illustration by author, originally drawn for endocrine show during 15th season of On Call with the Prairie Doc®, from private collection

from a sick thyroid gland will have high levels of TSH as the pituitary is trying to stimulate more thyroid. Someone who has excessively high levels of free T4 will have low levels of TSH as the pituitary is trying to turn off thyroid hormone production. In the rare case that the pituitary is not working right, the TSH will be low and the free T4 will also be low, but that is another story.

Treatment is very simple: replace the natural thyroid hormone with just the right dose of a daily thyroid tablet (levothyroxine). To start thyroid replacement, one should start at low doses and, every four to six weeks after rechecking the TSH, adjust the thyroid (levothyroxine) dose. The doctor or care provider will gradually increase the thyroid dose until the TSH normalizes.

It is important not to move too fast in raising the thyroid dose because this might initiate a heart attack. Before angiograms (injecting X-ray dye into the coronary arteries), we used to treat unrelenting chest pain from coronary disease by causing hypo-thyroidism with radiation, and the low metabolism that resulted gave some protection from chest pain and heart attack.

Checking a TSH every four to six weeks is soon enough. The hypothyroid patient and the care provider should realize this condition requires repeated testing over time. Once stable on the right dose of thyroid replacement, a recheck of the free T4 and TSH every six to twelve months should be enough.

Bottom line: The symptoms of hypothyroid can be very subtle and the diagnosis of low thyroid is often not obvious. A blood test makes the diagnosis, and the treatment can be simple but requires patience to safely get to the right dose. Perhaps it is eas-ier to say the words Hashimoto's thyroiditis than to understand hypothyroidism.

LESSONS FROM THE AMERICAN INDIAN ABOUT LIFESTYLE:
DIABETES MELLITUS

(Much of this essay was said in **Chapter Two,** but this issue is so important I decided to include it again saying it in a different way.) In 1735, the young religious leader, John Wesley, visited Savannah in the Province of Georgia in the American Colonies[268] and described nomadic Native Americans as the "perfect example of health." He correctly believed this to be due to their lean diet and rigorous physical lifestyle.[269] It is now nearing 300 years later, and people of all races could learn from the habits of the early nomadic American Indians.

What's happened since has deeply affected not only the American Indian but also the white and multiethnic settlers of this country. As advancements in technology have taken away the need for hard daily physical activity, the American public has been taking it easy, letting the wheels and motors "do the walking." We have become a country of couch potatoes. We drive everywhere. The necessity for physical activity to accomplish the chores to survive has lessened with time, but, as we physically do less, we become weakened and less ABLE to do physical activity. The weakness then encourages us to do even less.

At the same time, diets have changed with the availability of inexpensive oil, flour, syrup and cheese. This has made high calorie, fast food and high carbohydrates the dietary staple rather than lean meat, fruits, vegetables, eggs, roots, fungi and legumes

268   http://www.umc.org/news-and-media/re-evaluating-john-wesleys -time-in-georgia

269   http://www.nytimes.com/2002/10/29/science/don-t-blame-columbus- for-all-the-indians-ills.html

which had made up the traditional American Indian and Native Alaskan diet.

The consequence of eating more and moving less is our worldwide **epidemic of obesity**.[270] Two out of three Americans are overweight, and half of these are, by definition, obese. (For a 5'9" person, for example, weighing 125–168 lbs. is normal, 169–202 is overweight, greater than 202 is obese and greater than 270 is class 3 obese.) It is no surprise that an **epidemic of diabetes** has followed.[271] Right now, 29 million Americans know they have diabetes, and about one in four people with diabetes has it but doesn't know it.[272] Although this epidemic is affecting non-Indian immigrants that have come to live in the U.S., diabetes is about twice as frequent for the American Indian population. There is no doubt that this is due to a genetic predisposition for diabetes as well as related to the severe poverty which is common in that group.

How can we address the rising diabetic epidemic? It should start with something more than developing and prescribing more medicine. Diabetes is so tied to food and fitness that most prediabetics can entirely avoid getting the disease by eating right and becoming more physically active. One study from Bosnia-Herzegovina showed that educating children and parents about eating less and moving more makes the biggest difference in preventing and treating diabetes.[273] Our job as medical care

---

270   https://medlineplus.gov/magazine/issues/sprsum10/articles/spr-sum10pg4.html

271   https://medlineplus.gov/magazine/issues/fall09/articles/fall09pg10a.html

272   https://www.cdc.gov/diabetes/data/index.html

273   http://www.academia.edu/13646344/Youth_Study_Bosnia_and_Herzegovina_2015_

providers and, as a society, should be to spread this knowledge, encouraging everyone to eat a leaner diet and to live a more physically active lifestyle.

We all could learn from the habits of the early American Indians.

THE SNORT THAT SAVED A LIFE: *SLEEP APNEA*

Mr. S was a trucker who was overweight like a lot of guys and gals who drag freight cross-country for a living. His wife came with him to my office to make sure that he told me the whole story. Mr. S described struggling to stay awake while driving. This struggle had been going on for years, but, as he had gained weight and grown older, the sleepiness had been getting worse. His wife abruptly added, "He snores loudly, and, recently, I've heard spells of not breathing followed by a snort, coughing and then he gets up to go to the bathroom." She added, "Do you think he could have sleep apnea?"

She was right, and the diagnosis of severe sleep apnea was confirmed by a sleep study.[274] I think treatment saved his life and very likely the life of someone else in approaching traffic. Mr. S's story is the classic case of the worried wife dragging her husband to the doctor and reporting worrisome symptoms of snorting during sleep.

Sometimes patients with this condition come in with less than the perfect picture. They might have only a morning headache, an irregular heart rhythm, some leg swelling, nighttime urinary frequency, anger problems, memory issues or even just a dry

---

274   https://www.nhlbi.nih.gov/health-topics/sleep-apnea

mouth. Worse, it may be the symptoms of difficult-to-treat high blood pressure, waves of fast heart rate, a new heart attack, a devastating stroke or a sleep-induced motor vehicle crash.

Although sleep apnea is more common in men, smokers, obese people, and the elderly, it can also occur in women, nonsmokers, thin people, youth and even children. It runs in families with an inherited anatomy of short necks, recessed jaws, small nasal passages and is made worse in those who take tranquilizers, sedatives or excessive alcohol. Experts now estimate that at least 12 to 20 million Americans (about 5 percent of the population), have moderate to severe sleep apnea. The number of people affected by sleep apnea could be up to ten times higher than that since this condition often goes undiagnosed and will increase as the obesity epidemic expands.

There are three kinds of sleep apnea. Obstructive Sleep Apnea (OSA) (a mechanical obstructive problem), accounts for more than 80 percent of all cases. Less than 20 percent of people with sleep apnea have Central Sleep Apnea (CSA), the brain temporarily fails to tell the body to breathe, which is a nerve communication problem. Finally, something like 15 percent of those with OSA have a combination of OSA and CSA which is called mixed or complex sleep apnea.[275] Treatment for all three may be simply a continuous positive airway pressure (CPAP) machine, but those with CSA may require a special CPAP with "encouragement to

---

275   http://www.alaskasleep.com/blog/types-of-sleep-apnea-explained -obstructive-central-mixed

breathe" components. Further information about those special devices can be found easily on the Internet.[276]

In a fourteen-year study of thirty to sixty-five-year-old Australians, researchers found that of the people in the control group (those without apnea), about 7 percent died over that fourteen-year period as normally expected. What was not expected was that 33 percent of those with moderate to severe sleep apnea died during the same period. Other, more recent studies have found the same thing.[277] There was a five-fold increase in the (all cause) death rate for those thirty to sixty-five years of age when the individual had moderate to severe sleep apnea. Fivefold!

We know there is trouble for those diagnosed with sleep apnea, but can we do anything about this condition? Studies have found that there is a reduction in the death rate from moderate to severe sleep apnea when the patient can wear a device which provides continuous positive airway pressure (CPAP) each night. There are some people who may have relief of apnea by having throat surgery. Significant weight loss can be helpful but is rarely sustained. Mild sleep apnea may be helped by mouth and jaw positioning devices and by nasal opening strips. However, if the apnea is moderate to severe, a CPAP or a similar PAP device is usually the only effective option.

Unfortunately, a CPAP machine can be difficult to wear, requires patience and persistence and usually needs collaboration of the person with sleep apnea, the prescribing physician and the

---

276   https://www.sleepdr.com/the-sleep-blog/what-is-a-cpap-machine-difference-between-cpap-apap-bipap-and-asv/

277   http://www.cbc.ca/news/technology/sleep-apnea-sufferers-have-higher-death-rates-study-1.764145.

people who provide the equipment. A CPAP machine takes some getting used to and takes a lot of determination to wear every night. I know this for sure: death rate reduction won't happen when the CPAP machine is disconnected and lying under the bed.

Bottom line: When people with moderate to severe sleep apnea use their CPAP every night, their sleepy days become less sleepy and more productive, their driving becomes safer, their sleep is comforting and their lives improve and even, sometimes, normalize. If you think you might have sleep apnea, don't wait for your wife to get you to the doctor. Ask about having a sleep study; it could save your life.

BREATHLESS: *CAUSES OF SHORTNESS OF BREATH*

Defining the causes for breathlessness illustrates how challenging it can be to make the right diagnosis when someone has a medical problem. It was a party night at college when someone's date was rushed into my dorm room. She was breathing rapidly and gasped, "Can you help me?" Someone must have known that I had asthma when younger, and that I might be able to help this anxious and desperate young woman. I remember trying, unsuccessfully, to reassure her. I think she eventually had to go to the local emergency room, and everything turned out okay.

Years later in medical school, during a lecture on lung conditions, I remembered the young lady with the rapid breathing experience and realized that she likely had breathlessness from anxiety and hyperventilation and not from asthma or any other respiratory illness.[278] Since then, I have seen hyperventilation

---

278   https://www.merckmanuals.com/professional/pulmonary-disorders/symptoms-of-pulmonary-disorders/hyperventilation-syndrome

syndrome occur in many more people, mostly while I was working in the emergency room. It is important to realize this condition is a real deal. Anxiety driven over breathing causes the body's pH (acid-base) balance to drop way out of whack, resulting in numbness and even severe spasticity of the extremities which, in turn, makes the patient even more frightened.

One common treatment is to have the one hyperventilating continuously rebreathe the air from a paper bag which causes the person to inhale higher levels of carbon dioxide which raises the pH and normalizes the acid-base balance of the blood. I prefer having the patient go for a brisk walk which also raises the pH back to normal and, in addition, reassures the patient that they are not so sick. These methods, along with reassurance and a little time, allow for the hyperventilation to settle down and the pH to raise back up.

Most of the other causes for shortness of breath (dyspnea) are not so easy to fix. The following list, which is not complete, illustrates how varied are the causes for breathlessness. Dyspnea can be from obstructive lung diseases like asthma or emphysema, infections like viral influenza or bacterial pneumonia, excessive fluid within the lung like congestive heart failure or liver failure (which induces low protein), too much acid in the blood such as out-of-control diabetes or certain kinds of poisoning and lung wall lining irritation like viral pleuritis (inflamed lining around the lung) or embolic (flipping) blood clots to the lung.[279] Think how anxiety and hyperventilation could happen in addition to, or from, one of

---

279 https://medlineplus.gov/breathingproblems.html.

these other conditions and how the combination might make the diagnosis difficult.

When you run into someone who is having trouble breathing, the one thing you know for sure is that it could be from many causes: maybe just a little anxiety, maybe something bad or maybe both.

Bottom line: When breathless, always seek help.

THE SMOKING GUN: *COPD AND EMPHYSEMA*

Mr. C, a fifty-six-year-old fellow came into my office because he was experiencing shortness of breath with any exertion and was hoping we could fix it. He admitted that he had been smoking about one-and-a-half packs a day for 40 years, and that lately he'd been trying to cut down. Multiplying 365 times one-and-a-half gives him a 547.5-packs-per-year history of smoking (which is a lot). Also, because of his farming occupation, he'd inhaled a lot of hog and hay dust over all those years, causing even more chronic inflammation in the lung.

He said his shortness of breath had been coming on over the last five years and now his heart was beating fast with any exertion. Also his cough was getting worse, and for a year he had been coughing up some pretty ugly stuff first thing in the morning. The rest of the day he just can't cough up the sputum. Lately, he's been wheezing more, and his chest had been getting tight, especially at night when he was trying to sleep.

Breathing tests showed that he could inhale okay, but he had to push hard to exhale. Blood tests showed high levels of hemoglobin (the red part of blood that carries oxygen) and low oxygen levels, and the chest X-ray showed overexpanded lungs. These are changes which indicate emphysema (commonly combined with some chronic bronchitis). Emphysema is now more frequently called chronic obstructive pulmonary disease (COPD).[280] This diagnosis was not good news for Mr. C because COPD is the third leading cause of premature death in the U.S. and a major cause of a miserable disability.

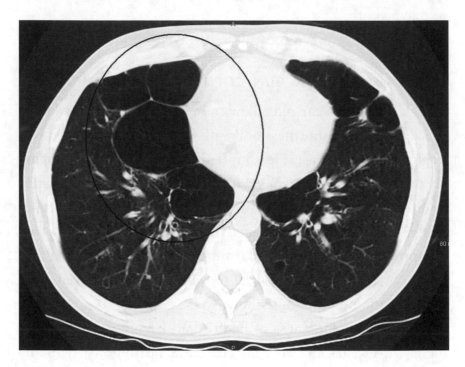

CT scan of large pockets of emphysema (nonfunctioning lung) pushing the heart to the left[281]

Normally in the lungs, airway tubes branch out, multiply and become progressively smaller until they reach tiny air sacks

---

280   https://medlineplus.gov/copd.html

281   Photo by James Heilman, MD, from https://commons.wikimedia.org/wiki/File:Bullus_emphasemaCT.png

(alveoli) which are covered with microscopic blood vessels. It is here where inhaled air comes very close to the red blood cells with hemoglobin and that's the place of an almost magical switcheroo. Life-giving oxygen is passed from air into the blood's hemoglobin in an exchange where the body waste (carbon dioxide) is passed from blood into the air. With COPD, the walls of the tiny air sacks first lose their elasticity and then are destroyed, leaving progressively larger nonfunctioning cavities. Also, airways that are supposed to carry air to the alveoli become blocked because of inflammatory swelling and mucous.

Trying to help him, I encouraged Mr. C to quit smoking, prescribed a medicine to help him quit and provided an inhaler that would turn off the inflammation and dilate the bronchial tubes. I also advised a yearly low dose spiral CT of the lung since this test is now standard for all those from fifty-five to eighty-years-old who have smoked a pack of cigarettes a day for 30 or more years.[282] He didn't do it.

The sad story is that he had a condition we could help, but not fix. If he didn't stop smoking, I predicted it wouldn't be long before he would die. He didn't quit, and it wasn't long before he died.

SEXUAL INTEREST, MOTHERHOOD, CIVILIZATION AND SUFFERING: *BREAST CANCER*

A patient came to the clinic one day having discovered a lump in her breast. Hearing her story, I suspected an infection since her earlier exams had been up to date, and the last mammogram

---

282   https://www.cdc.gov/cancer/lung/basic_info/screening.htm.

was negative. She and her doctor had taken all the right steps to keep her safe; however, her exam that day was worrisome. There was a distinct lump that was hard, fixed to the muscle underneath and the size of a thumbnail. A repeat mammogram showed a suspicious area. By the time our work-up was done, we found breast cancer that had spread to many lymph nodes and to the bones of her back.[283] What seemed like a death knell for my patient turned into bells of celebration as we observed a marvelous reversal of her condition after our cancer specialist treated her with effective chemotherapy. Many women have had to face their mortality through this malignant disease of the breast.[284]

I was surprised to learn that the human female is the only primate that possesses fully formed breasts even when not pregnant. Evolutionary psychologists believe breasts are what attracted ancestral mates seeking a healthy partner with whom to have children. Experts also conjecture that it was the female breast which encouraged woman-to-man, face-to-face interaction. Up until a few years ago, we thought humans were the only mammals that mate in this manner, but there have been rare observational reports of bonobos and gorillas mating in this way.[285] Anthropologists suggest that it is this full-frontal interface and the communication that follows which have led to the emotional bonds that brought social progress. They speculate the male's exposure to "a motherly caring attitude" brought him

283   https://www.cdc.gov/cancer/breast/index.htm

284   https://www.webmd.com/cancer/features/bone-metastasis-what-happens

285   https://www.sciencedaily.com/releases/2008/02/080212134818.htm

to search for compassion and to expect justice in all arenas of human interaction. Think about it: a woman's breast is at once the origin of intimacy, the nourishing gift of mother's milk, perhaps the foundation for civilization, and, yet, after all this nurturing, a potential source for individual suffering.

My patient worked another year before retiring, and she lived with her cancer for about three more years with the loving support of her husband, with caring siblings and with the proper direction from her oncologist. Eventually, the cancer became immune to the best available cancer treatments, and the oncologist said no more chemotherapy. We turned to providing comfort care until the end. There is no one to blame and, at the time, no alternative that would have changed the outcome except if there could have been some way to find the cancer earlier. In contrast, there have been many women who have been saved by regular self-breast awareness, regular check-ups and mammograms.

Bottom line: Our civilization has improved, not only with improved evidence-based scientific research into breast cancer diagnosis and treatment but also with men learning compassion and justice following a face-to-face exposure to "a motherly caring attitude."

BLOOD PRESSURE AND THE FEAR OF CHANGE:
HIGH BLOOD PRESSURE

The medical history books reveal secrets of circulation and blood pressure that rival the best novels of intrigue. Years ago, people hadn't figured out how blood circulates. Second century Greek scientist, Galen, had the idea that blood moved from the right side of the heart to the left through unseen pores, and that idea was not questioned for more than 1,000 years until a series of people in the mid-1500s finally broke with the old idea. After great debate among leading thinkers of the time, English scientist and physician, William Harvey, and several anatomists and scientists finally convinced local medical leaders, and later those of the world, that blood pulses through the body on a great circular journey. It was fear of change that made the acceptance of this discovery so difficult.

William Harvey (1578–1657), known as the discoverer of the circulation of blood.[286]

Harvey, and other scientists, proved that venous blood is almost sucked (returns) from the outer reaches of the body through gradually larger veins and eventually flows into the right ventricle of the heart. From the right ventricle (right lower part of the heart), blood is pumped into the lungs where hemoglobin gathers oxygen and releases carbon. From the lungs, oxygen rich blood flows to the left atrium (left upper part of the heart), to the left ventricle and is pumped out into arteries to feed almost all the cells of the

286   William Harvey. From: Arthur Shuster & Arthur E. Shipley: *Britain's Heritage of Science.* London, 1917. Based on a painting by Cornelius Jansen. Public domain, from https://commons.wikimedia.org/wiki/William_Harvey

body with oxygen. From each tiny cell the blood picks up carbon waste, and the blood is drawn back to the right heart and lungs once again. Continuous circulation happens because the heart pump squeezes and relaxes, repeating the process some 80 times a minute from birth to death. (In my mind, the marvelous truth about the circle of blood flow is pure evidence of the beauty of both evolution and intelligent design.)

Learning to measure the pressure generated by the heart pump is another great story. In 1733, the Reverend Stephen Hales first discovered how to measure blood pressure and his first subject was a horse.[287] He made the measurement of pressure by using a nine-foot-long glass tube which was held vertically and connected to the horse's artery. He measured how high the blood went up the tube, changing a foot or two with the pulse of the horse's heart and the systolic and diastolic pressure. This gave him the very first blood pressure measurement. Over time, we have learned how to measure that pressure in humans without cutting into an artery but rather with a cuff around the upper arm. The numbers we now use represent the amount of pressure generated by millimeters of mercury (mm Hg) in a glass tube (instead of millimeters of horse blood in a nine-foot tube).

The normal top pressure (systolic) is 120 to 150, and the normal goes up with age. The lower number (diastolic) measures the lowest sustained pressure. Thus, a measurement of 120 over 80 (120/80) means the pressure of fluid going through the body reaches as high as 120 mm of mercury (Hg) with every squeeze of the heart but drops as low as 80 as the heart relaxes.

---

287   http://www4.ncsu.edu/~msolufse/bpmeasurement.pdf

The diastolic pressure reflects and measures the elasticity of the arteries.

If blood pressure is elevated for too long, there is a silent sinister effect on all parts of the body. The destructive effects of high blood pressure (HBP or hypertension) happen primarily by injuring blood vessels which, in turn, eventually block blood flow and damage virtually all the organ systems. HBP can cause heart disease, kidney failure, vision loss and strokes. Most people know how large strokes can cause disabling one-sided paralysis and loss of speech, but few realize how years of prolonged and sustained hypertension often cause multiple tiny strokes. These strokes are sometimes not even noticeable except when, over time, they bring on a slow loss of the ability to reason and remember, fairly similar to that of Alzheimer's dementia. (See **Chapter Six.**)

We know that Franklin Delano Roosevelt had a BP in the 230/130 range for many months before he was in Yalta with Churchill and Stalin.[288] It is said that Roosevelt was mentally diminished by his HBP while they were bargaining to divide up Europe. It is not difficult to understand why Stalin, in his full power at that time, could out-bargain Churchill (who was said to be weakened by alcoholism and depression) and Roosevelt (who was said to be addled by HBP).[289] The West might have unnecessarily given away Poland, the Balkans, and half of Germany to the Russian expansion because of these

288   http://www.nytimes.com/2010/01/05/health/05docs.html
289   http://historynewsnetwork.org/article/126978

illnesses. Records show that Roosevelt died two months later with a BP of 300/190.

Winston Churchill, Franklin Roosevelt and Joseph Stalin meeting in Yalta, Feb. 1945[290]

It's interesting that scientific discovery over time has given us ways to lower blood pressure and thus preserve a person's capacity to think. This has allowed us the ability to live longer with an intact brain which, in turn, allows us to solve problems, to argue and, ironically, even to fear change.

---

290 Photographer unknown, from https://commons.wikimedia.org/wiki/File:Yalta_summit_1945_with_Churchill,_Roosevelt,_Stalin.jpg

THE RHYTHM OF LIFE . . . A POWERFUL THING:
ABNORMAL HEART RHYTHMS

Mr. H was a perfect specimen of health. A fifty-five-year-old man, he was physically fit because of rigorous farm work and lots of physical activity involved with hunting and fishing. One morning, he awoke with an uncomfortable chest pressure going into his neck and jaw. He arose to find no relief from stretching, drinking a glass of milk, taking a deep breath or even lying down again. Finally, after rousing his wife, they made their way to an emergency room where he was given merciful pain relief and was immediately tested to determine if it was his heart that was causing the pain.

Not long after arriving at the emergency room (ER), while talking with his wife, he suddenly slipped into unconsciousness. The ER crew immediately ran into his room and started resuscitation efforts. It was there, in that predawn hour, that he died despite their doing all the right things. Likely, due to coronary arterial blockage and an irritable heart muscle, the symmetry of his heart rhythm had changed into one of pure chaos that wasn't effectively pumping blood.[291] His heart just couldn't be converted back to a normal rhythm again. The value of rhythm is never more evident than during a cardiac arrest.

The definition of rhythm comes from the Greek root: *rhythmos* (any regular, recurring pulsing; a succession of contrasting beats occurring over various periods of time).[292,293] Think of the

---

291   https://medlineplus.gov/cardiacarrest.html

292   https://en.wiktionary.org/wiki/rhythm

293   https://www.etymonline.com/word/rhythm

rhythmic experience from words and song or drum and dance. There is something about all rhythms that calls for symmetry, and, when a rhythm is out of sync, there is a part of us that becomes uncomfortable, and we want to bring back the symmetry.

The rhythm of life is a regular and recurring pulsing; a succession of surges over time like the flow of seawater and fish meeting the shore on an estuarial tide, the birth of lambs and calves, bursting forth on an early springtime prairie pasture or even the seventy to ninety-year life-cycle of humans, moving with joy, sorrow and grace from birth to natural death.

When humans die too early, the symmetry is out of sync, the rhythm is disturbed, and we are left wanting to bring rhythm back to symmetry.

HEART WEAKNESS, NOT FAILURE: *CONGESTIVE HEART FAILURE*

This is a congestive heart failure story. Mrs. W was in her eighties and had lived a full and healthy life. Over the three days prior to coming to the emergency room, she became increasingly short of breath, even with minimal exertion, and had to sit up to breathe.

The chest X-ray, the BNP (which is a blood test for heart failure) and the echocardiogram confirmed the diagnosis. We found evidence of a silent heart attack which had occurred sometime in her past. The heart attack, a lifetime of high blood pressure and advancing age were, in combination, the likely causes for her heart weakness.[294] Our medicines, thankfully, gave her great relief over the two days she was hospitalized. We talked about what this meant as she was being discharged. She

294   https://medlineplus.gov/heartfailure.html

asked, "What, again, is my diagnosis?" My answer was, "congestive heart failure," and the sound of it left her dismayed. She countered, "failure?"

I think the word "failure" is unfortunate. To fail means to be unacceptable, to be flawed, to get worse, to break down, to fall short or even to realize that the end is near. The truth is that the medical future for one with such a diagnosis is highly variable, depending on the cause for the heart weakness, the severity of the condition, the age of the individual and, I dare say, the attitude of the individual. I would prefer to replace the word "failure" with the word "weakness." This would allow gradation of the condition such as mild, moderate or severe heart weakness. Almost more important, it would allow more hope for the individual with the diagnosis.

Bottom line: We can deal with a condition called heart weakness. We have medicinal tools that work. It is an area in medicine where suffering can be relieved and lives extended. Indeed, "failure" is the wrong word. As I explained to my patient, "Your heart is a little weak, but you're going to be okay."

THE STORY OF EDEMA: *SWELLING IN LEGS AND EVERYWHERE*

Joe was a sixty-five-year-old diabetic patient who arrived at the emergency room with his whole body swollen. Joe was very short of breath, and fluid was leaking from sores on his legs. He was so swollen that pressure from his socks left a large, but temporary, dent. Thumb pressure would leave a deep pit (pitting edema). In his case, it extended all over his body, even around his eyes.

When his kidneys were tested, we found that the kidneys weren't effectively excreting bad waste products. Instead, the kidneys were leaking and losing good proteins (albumen) into the urine that are usually captured and returned to circulation.[295] We found his diabetes was out of control, his prostate was partially blocking urine flow, he had a weakened heart and he was malnourished as his diet had been terrible. He was one sick fella with problems piling upon problems.[296] We admitted him into the hospital.

Severe edema (formerly called dropsy) is a relatively common medical problem. Edema is the swelling caused from clear body fluid leaking into the spaces between the cells. Recently, scientists discovered what might be called a new organ and labeled it the "interstitium."[297] This constitutes the space under the skin and throughout the body where much of the fluid in the body is temporarily kept when not circulating. It is interconnected to the lymph system and the venous system. Why fluid moves in and out of the interstitium is not clearly understood, and, although clinical scientists think they understand most of the causes for edema, this topic is very complicated. For example, low protein in the bloodstream usually, but not always, causes edema. It is confusing.

That said, edema is due to multiple, understandable problems, and Joe seemed to have all of them. The most challenging cause for Joe's edema resulted from blood levels of an egg white type of protein (albumen) that dropped too low. Protein is usually

---

295   https://www.kidney.org/atoz/content/nephrotic

296   https://medlineplus.gov/edema.html#summary

297   https://www.nature.com/articles/s41598-018-23062-6

reabsorbed back into the bloodstream by working kidneys, and that protein keeps the blood thick enough to keep it from leaking out of blood vessels. His low protein made the blood thin and watery so that fluid was leaking out of blood vessels into the tissue and interstitium. His low blood protein was worsened by other problems including a diet lacking in essential protein building blocks and a liver that wasn't making enough protein.

Joe was treated first with diuretics (water pills) and artery-dilating medicines to remove water and to ease the demand on the heart pump. His obstructing prostate was fixed initially with a tube (catheter) placed into his bladder and later by prostate shrinking medicines. Poor veins were treated by elastic wraps around the legs and later by support hose. Finally, we improved nutrition to achieve better diabetic control, and the protein in his diet was increased to replace the protein he was losing. His long-term kidney problems wouldn't go away, but, for now, we helped all the other organ systems work better. After a week in the hospital, Joe lost twenty pounds of water and went home without a catheter, breathing easily and with leg sores healing.

Bottom line: Edema is a very complicated and a common problem. When you find it, get to the smartest doctor you can find.

SUBTLE SYMPTOMS AND TERRIBLE DISEASE:
REFLUX ESOPHAGITIS

At first Mr. E had a subtle clue that something may be wrong, but he didn't do anything about it. "Almost everyone has had heartburn at one time or another," he thought. Gradually it became worse. He found that he could control it with over-the-counter treatments, so he felt it must not be something so bad. His wife began bugging him about eating antacid tablets day and night, and, consequentially, he began taking them on the sly.

Over time, the heartburn became less bothersome. This falsely reassured him that his condition was nothing dangerous. Then one day, food started to stick on the way down. His wife said she made him an appointment to see the doctor and told him he'd better keep it!

I know of at least five men diagnosed with esophageal cancer who have a similar story. Two are dead, two are cured, and one is in a fight for his life. They all started with symptoms of reflux esophagitis.[298] Reflux is the feeling of a burp with acid in it which starts in the stomach, comes back up the food pipe and ends in the throat.[299] The fancy name for such a disorder is gastro (stomach) esophageal (food pipe) reflux (backward movement) disease (GERD). Reflux can cause some people to have esophageal pain that feels like heart pain and is so severe that it is sometimes wrongly diagnosed as a life-threatening heart attack. Therefore, it has been called "heartburn." Sometimes the acid can roll back up from the stomach into the esophagus, irritate and even cause sores (ulcers). These ulcers may occur not only in the esophagus but also the oral cavity, the voice box and even the lungs.

On the other hand, some people with reflux may have minimal to no discomfort from the reverse movement of stomach acid, but damage can continue to occur. Over the last 10 to 20 years, we have learned that many people with GERD come

---

298   https://www.cancer.gov/types/esophageal

299   https://www.mayoclinic.org/diseases-conditions/esophagitis/symptoms-causes/syc-20361224

to the doctor's office without typical reflux symptoms but are experiencing a voice change, coughing or even asthma. These symptoms happen due to nighttime reflux resulting in acid-burned vocal cords and lungs.

Bottom line: Don't wait for your spouse to make that appointment. Esophageal symptoms, subtle or not, should bring you to the doctor.

CONSTIPATION: *CONSTIPATION CONSTERNATION*

Mr. C is an older man who has controlled almost everything throughout his life except his bowels. It seems the harder he has tried to make the bowels move, the more constipated or irregular he becomes. He is always on the hunt for the right laxative and is now using "herbal lightening" without a lot of success. He always seems to complain about feeling bloated and to be waiting for Nature's call. Mr. C often sits on the commode for long periods of time pushing too hard. Subsequently, he triples his stimulant laxative dose and becomes loose as a goose for a while, which is followed by another stint of constipation. Mr. C is one frustrated guy.

The causes for constipation are numerous and include too little exercise, too few fiber foods, dehydration, internal scars from previous surgery, pockets in the colon (diverticulosis), low thyroid, colon cancer and, most importantly, medicines. Everyone with chronic constipation needs to consider seeing a doctor for a proper evaluation. This is especially important because early cancer of the colon can be one of the causes.

There are many medications that can slow the bowels including bladder spasm meds like tamsulosin (Flomax), certain blood pressure pills like propranolol (Inderal), heart rhythm medications like verapamil, asthma medications like terbutaline, psychiatric medications like thioridazine, calcium supplements and opioid (narcotic) pain medications. Opioids are probably the most common culprits for constipation. Although the pharmaceutical industry has developed (very expensive) medications to counter this side effect, it would be better to get off the opioids.

The most common cause for constipation is from the long-term use of stimulant-type laxatives such as ex-lax®, Correctol, senna, any stool softener labeled WITH LAXATIVE (like Colace-Plus), Senna-Plus and many herbal stimulant-type combinations. People should realize that stopping regularly used stimulant laxatives causes rebound constipation or dependency. Too often people have a problem perpetuated by the very drug they use to treat it. This is the reason to gradually taper off these bowel irritants and to avoid them. I usually suggest a one-month taper, starting with skipping every fourth day for a week, every third day for a week, every other day for a week, taking one every third or fourth day for a week and then stopping them forever. During the taper, I usually start people, from the beginning, on two or three plain stool softeners a day, and that seems to get them past the rebound constipation.

Good bowel health also starts with exercise, a diet of fruit and vegetables, fiber rich foods, and, if needed, by adding ground golden flax seed. I suggest buying it whole and grinding the flax in a coffee grinder (½ cup at a time prevents it turning rancid) and mixing one or two tablespoons with breakfast cereal, yogurt or applesauce on a daily basis. If an individual is still having problems, I advise fiber supplements first (Fiber One or other high fiber cereal, Citrucil, FiberCon, Metamucil), stool softeners (docusate) without added stimulant laxatives (like plain Colace or Surfak). While using stool softeners, start with one to three capsules of generic docusate once or twice a day, adjusting the dose according to need. If necessary, and there has been no bowel movement for three or more days, try adding over-the-counter polyethylene glycol (MiraLax), milk of magnesia or sorbitol. Stool softeners and polyethylene glycol are osmotic laxatives which work by drawing fluid into the bowels instead of irritating and stimulating the bowel as happens with senna. Osmotic laxatives are effective and do not cause rebound.

Most experts have been moving toward prescribing polyethylene glycol as the first line of therapy after making sure there is no dangerous cause for constipation lurking in the bowels such as cancer. If Mr. C exercises daily, eats the right food with enough fiber and avoids stimulant laxatives, he can be back in control soon.

SPELUNKING (CAVE EXPLORING) FOR CANCER: A LIFE-SAVING COLONOSCOPY

Worldwide, more than a million people will get colon cancer this year, and about one-third of them will eventually die from it. Unless something changes, 5 percent of all babies born today will get colon cancer in their lifetime. It is the second most common cancer in women, and third in men.

How can we prevent or discover colon cancer early enough for a cure? When I started my training, an examination of the colon required a barium enema (gives a silhouette of the colon on X-ray) often followed by advancing a rigid one-foot-long steel tube through the patient's rectum, without anesthesia, while the patient was positioned over a bent table with his or her bottom high in the air. It was an uncomfortable experience for the patient and the doctor, and it missed many cancers.

Things have changed with the development of fiber-optic flexible scopes. Now it's almost like cave spelunking where, after running down to the end of a long cave, one backs out slowly, searching by powerful flashlight for stalactites and stalagmites. We explore the whole five-foot colon while the image is amplified upon a large screen. This allows the team to find even subtle lesions that can be potentially dangerous.

In preparation for the colonoscopy, a vigorous and uncomfortable cleansing of the bowel is required. There are risks from the colonoscopy, although the advantages totally outweigh the small risks. Comfortable anesthesia is provided during the procedure. In about a third of the examinations, precancerous polyps are found which can be removed. Sometimes cancer is discovered early, lives are saved and suffering is reduced. In a review of 352 colonoscopies that I performed between 1999 and 2003 on people without significant symptoms, I found 164 people (47 percent) had polyps and 8 people (less than 3 percent) had cancer.[300] Other studies have found that when a glandular type of polyp measuring greater than 0.4 inches wide is removed, the colonoscopy reduces the cancer death risk by 40 times.

A study reported in *The New England Journal of Medicine* showed that the following people are at a higher risk for colorectal

---

300   Holm, R. Personal presentation to SD State PA Convention, Rapid City, SD 2004.

cancer: People with 1. A personal or family history of colorectal cancer or polyps, 2. A personal history of ulcerative colitis, 3. A history of smoking or heavy drinking, 4. African genetics, or 5. The diagnosis of obesity. The study also showed that by removing adenomatous (precancerous type) polyps, the risk for death in those people from colorectal cancer was reduced by more than 50 percent over two decades.[301,302]

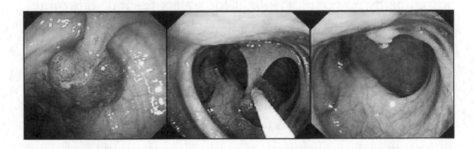

Colonoscopy: left photo: of poly on stalk; middle: loop around polyp stalk; right: polyp gone[303]

It is important to have a colonoscopy when there are obvious symptoms like blood in the stool, abdominal pain or change in bowel habits. A screening colonoscopy (screening is when people are experiencing no symptoms) can discover cancer early before it spreads. I lost my father to colon cancer, and I have had three polyps removed from my own colon. I am sensitive to this issue. When is yours scheduled?

---

301   https://www.nejm.org/doi/full/10.1056/NEJMoa1100370

302   https://www.cancer.gov/types/colorectal/research/colonoscopy -reduces-deaths.

303   Photo by Gilo1969, from https://commons.wikimedia.org/wiki/ File:Polypectomy.jpg

EGGS, SAUSAGE AND RUNNING WITH A FRIEND:
THE PROPER DIET

While running with a scientist friend, who had recently suffered a small heart attack, we talked about cardiac rehabilitation and safe running to help his recovery. He was happy to be back running, and, as I was recovering from cancer surgery, I was also happy to be running. If not overdone, we know that those with, and without, heart disease do better by exercising regularly. I could feel the run was rebuilding my strength, and I savored the social time running with a friend.

When we finished, energized and happy, a short cool down walk brought us to his home. There, his wife prepared a light morning breakfast of two eggs nicely spiced with salt and pepper, a small patty of pork sausage, sliced fried bell peppers, pieces of fresh melon and coffee. The breakfast was delicious and just the right amount.

Twenty years ago, an egg and sausage meal was thought to be a big no-no. More recently, we have learned that processed carbohydrates (like potatoes, pasta, pancakes, bread or donuts) are worse for you than fat, mostly because they seem to pile on nutrient poor calories.[304] The experts are saying that a lower calorie balanced diet of proteins, fats and nonprocessed carbohydrates (fruits and nonstarchy vegetables) is best for you. (The starchy vegetables include potatoes and corn.) Say it again, new science has discovered that it's the excessive quantity of food (excessive calories) that are more worrisome than the kind of

---

304   https://www.gaplesinstitute.org/low-carb-vs-low-fat-digging-deeper/?gclid=Cj0KCQiA2snUBRDfARIsAIGfpqGNPaJtypH2WHveCzpDlMbz-JWky5E9TCiGhnlmYJX3ltCYxxYIRRn8aApB9EALw_wcB

food we eat.[305] Smaller amounts of foods like eggs and sausage are perfectly safe. That morning the calorie count for each of us was about 300, and we both felt great.

Every day there seems to be another study that advises the opposite of what we used to think: eat less salt, now salt to taste unless the heart is weak; don't eat butter, now butter is caloric but safe; don't exercise too much, now do it every day; don't drink alcohol, now a daily glass of wine is good; don't eat fatty meals, now eat fewer calories and avoid processed carbohydrates.

Bottom line: Researchers have made headway in understanding what is good for us. May we embrace the science that supports eating fewer calories, less processed carbohydrates and eating more fruits and nonstarchy vegetables. Doing this and making time, every day, for 30-minutes of exercise and some quality time with friends, we have the perfect formula for good health.

THE BIG COVER-UP: *MALE SEXUAL ISSUES*

One day in the clinic, my patient, a ninety-two-year-old man, asked me to renew his prescription for sildenafil (Viagra). I responded with a yes and a smile, but it made me think how complex and difficult this issue can be. There is probably nothing so personal and maybe so important to any male, at almost any age, than his ability to perform sexually.

---

305   https://www.scientificamerican.com/article/the-hunger-gains
-extreme-calorie-restriction-diet-shows-anti-aging-results/

This difficult issue especially affects boys growing up. At that age, many boys develop a fragile and misguided sexual ego that wishes to be superb, hoping to be something that girls or women would want and every other guy would envy. However, the sexual ego, which is filled with expectation, doesn't seem to be something about which guys are willing to talk. Expectation is one thing but knowing what a man is supposed to do in the bedroom and what constitutes normal male sexual function is something that is all too often clouded in secrecy.[306]

When I was fourteen, the major source of information about male performance came to me in the locker room, at the roller skating rink, when camping out or late in the night from reading questionable literature with a flashlight. I don't think this type of education has improved much since that time. With such overblown expectations mixed with ignorance and inexperience, it is no surprise that many men are sexually self-conscious.[307] This makes men reluctant to seek help from a credible source like a care provider when there might be a problem.[308]

A recent study indicated that loss of erectile function or a loss of desire for sex (one or both is defined as impotence) occurs in more than 50 percent of forty to seventy-year-old men, and the

---

306   https://www.psychologytoday.com/blog/evolution-the-self/201205/the-secrettaboo-aspects-male-sexual-desire

307   https://www.psychologytoday.com/blog/married-and-still-doing-it/201708/is-how-men-really-think-about-sex

308   https://www.fda.gov/ForConsumers/ConsumerUpdates/ucm048386.htm

percentage increases with age.[309] The problem is twice as bad for smokers than for nonsmokers, three times as bad for diabetics and four times as bad for people with heart disease. Impotence also increases significantly in men with: psychosocial problems associated with hostility, suppressed anger and depression, poor physical condition, certain medications, thyroid disease, B12 deficiency or sleep apnea.

To improve sexual function, men should start by developing a reasonable lifestyle which includes walking every day, eating a lower calorie balanced diet with fruits and vegetables, avoiding smoke and establishing careful care by a care provider for diabetes, psych problems or underlying endocrine problems. Even when doing everything right, the problem may persist, and, commonly, sildenafil-like medications can help. However, the sildenafil (Viagra) should only be prescribed AFTER a medical evaluation.

Bottom line: The loss of erectile function might indicate something is medically wrong, and men should expect more from their doctor than a prescription for sildenafil. This is a problem that shouldn't be kept under the covers.

BROKEN HIP BLUES: *FALLING AND HIP FRACTURE*

Mrs. X had been a widow of 15 years and lived alone with her family nearby. She recently turned too quickly, fell sideways and couldn't get up by herself. She lay on a cold, linoleum floor for most of the night until she was finally able to crawl to a

309   https://www.mayoclinic.org/diseases-conditions/erectile-dysfunction/symptoms-causes/syc-20355776

phone and call for help. In the emergency room, we noted the tell-tale signs of a fractured hip with leg shortening and outward turning of the foot. The broken hip was confirmed on X-ray. Her hip pinning went smoothly the following morning. (See also **Chapter Two.**)

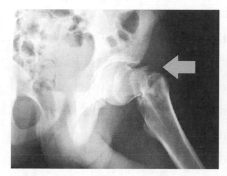

Fractured hip (femur) where neck attaches to trochanter[310]

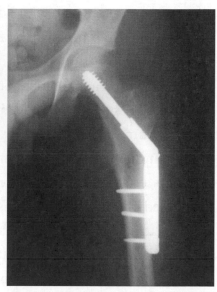

Same hip after hip pinning[311]

Lifetime risk for hip fracture is 6 percent in men and 14 percent in women. About 40 percent will require nursing home care for at least a period of time during recovery, 50 percent will permanently require a walker, and the risk of death following hip fracture is 8 to 10 percent at 30 days and 12 to 37 percent at one year.[312] In 2011, hip fractures resulted in about 30 percent of

310   Photo by Booyabazooka from https://commons.wikimedia.org/wiki/File:Cdm_hip_fracture_343.jpg

311   Photo by Booyabazooka, 2004, from https://commons.wikimedia.org/wiki/File:Cdm_hip_implant_348.jpg

312   https://www.ncbi.nlm.nih.gov/pmc/articles/PMC1615464/

U.S. hospitalizations, costing about $5 billion and immeasurable suffering. Additional studies in the U.S. and in other countries show similar results.[313,314,315]

Falls are the cause for 90 percent of hip fractures which, in turn, are the result of weakness from poor physical conditioning, softened bones, poor vision, elder abuse or advanced age.[316,317] The average age of those who fall is about seventy-five. Syncope (sudden loss of consciousness) is often the defined cause for falling. This seemingly innocuous symptom can be due to anything from an emotional stress-induced faint, a life-threatening abnormal heart rhythm or a prestroke warning sign. Syncope requires a careful and thorough cardiac and neurological evaluation. If the patient is unaware of the cause of the fall, syncope should be considered and a physician consulted.

Prior to the development of a surgical repair for hip fracture, about 80 percent of those suffering from this condition would die due to the required six weeks of bed rest and traction. These deaths would mostly result from blood clots or pneumonia. Pinning the hip with ivory pins was first tried in 1899,[318] but it wasn't until World War II that a German surgeon began regularly using metal

---

313   https://www.ncbi.nlm.nih.gov/pubmed/23872716

314   https://www.researchgate.net/publication/250924315_A_Risk_Calculator_for_Short-Term_Morbidity_and_Mortality_After_Hip_Fracture_Surgery

315   http://bmjopenquality.bmj.com/content/3/1/u205006.w2103

316   https://www.ncbi.nlm.nih.gov/pubmed/8222767

317   https://www.webmd.com/osteoporosis/news/20150915/hip-fracture-surgery-risk#1

318   https://link.springer.com/article/10.1007/s11999-017-5497-0

rods to stabilize bone fractures.[319] Shortly after the end of the war and into the 1950s, hip pinning spread throughout the world, allowing early mobilization after a hip fracture. Getting up and about quickly after hip pinning greatly reduced the death rate from a hip fracture. Now, in about a third of the cases, a new ball or total hip (new ball and socket) replace the fractured hip, but hip pinning still works in most cases and is quicker and safer than the more invasive ball or total hip surgery.

To prevent fracturing the hip, it makes sense to prevent falling. The best way to improve balance and strength is to do strengthening and balancing exercises. Walking is an excellent way to increase strength, harden bones and decrease falls. Finally, when there is a clue that the fall was caused by an unexplained loss of consciousness, one should go immediately to the emergency room whether there is a hip fracture or not.

COPING WITH RIGIDITY: *PARKINSON'S DISEASE*

Let's face it, simply to be alive is to be at risk for some degenerative assault to our brains that could be progressive and deteriorating (like Parkinson's disease). All of us will experience the natural aging process that involves at least some degeneration of the brain, and that is inescapable unless we die early from something else. Two important coping methods for dealing with Parkinson's disease will be highlighted, and these also speak to how to deal with aging.

---

319   Bong, Matthew R.; Koval, Kenneth J.; Egol, Kenneth A. (2006). "The History of Intramedullary Nailing" (PDF). *Bulletin of the NYU Hospital for Joint Diseases*. NYU Hospital for Joint Diseases. 64 (3/4): 94–97. PMID 17155917. Retrieved 2013-03-12.

The most important treatment methods for Parkinson's disease are nonmedicinal. Exercise is essential for living with most of the problems that happen with aging (as addressed in **Chapter One**), but especially with Parkinson's disease. It's true what they say: use it or lose it. Add to this, Parkinson's disease is often associated with depression, chronic pain, progressive immobility and constipation. Exercise helps not only people with Parkinson's but directly helps treat people with each of these other problems as well. Everything good about exercise seems to go double with Parkinson's.[320]

The second nonmedicinal treatment method for Parkinson's is a positive attitude.[321] Dale Carnegie and Norman Vincent Peale both recommended pushing the positive thought forward, and much has been written about how those with a glass half-full do better than those whose glass is half-empty. This is especially true for those dealing with a problem as challenging as Parkinson's disease. I've personally seen it work in several Parkinson's patients of mine who continue to convince me of the value of a positive attitude. Dealt a bad hand, they chose to make the most of it by finding purpose and humor in every moment, and to realize fulfillment within the time limit of every day. These are the people that survive the longest and with meaning.

Unfortunately, these two nonmedicinal treatments require significant effort by the affected individual and, too often, are not embraced. Their response usually is, "It's easier to take a pill."

---

320   http://www.parkinson.org/Understanding-Parkinsons/Treatment/Exercise

321   https://parkinsonsnewstoday.com/2017/10/18/parkinsons-keeping-positive-attitude/

Parkinson's patients and their families should realize that exercise and attitude are, by far, more important than the somewhat disappointing help achieved from medication for Parkinson's.[322] It should be a lesson for all who are aging and who have a degenerative assault of some kind. Please choose to exercise and choose to dwell not on the negative but on the positive.

FOOT FAILINGS: *THE CALLUS AND CORN CONUNDRUM*

Most of us foolishly ignore our feet until they give us trouble.[323] A woman in her nineties hobbled into my office complaining of an exceedingly sore foot. There was a hard, pointed callus on the sole of the foot where her fat pad had thinned with age and the bone was very prominent. The callus had progressed to the point where it caused enough pain to keep her from being able to do the activities that brought her joy, and a blood blister was starting to form under the callus. It was like walking with a large, sharp pebble in her shoe.

I have seen similar foot calluses cause blood blisters to form under them, get infected and eventually result in foot amputation. Leaving calluses like that alone is not wise. After positioning the patient on the examining table, I gently and carefully shaved layer after layer of thickened skin with a sharp scalpel until the callus was gone. That accomplished, we provided a molded foot insert that took the pressure off the boney prominence to help

322   http://forum.parkinson.org/topic/19543-sinemet-disappointing-results/

323   https://www.ipfh.org/foot-care-essentials/why-preventive-foot-health
-is-important

prevent recurrence of the callus. She left the office happy with the pebble-like callus gone.

There is a difference between a callus and a corn.[324] Calluses are the natural and usually protective thickening of skin on the palms of the hand, the soles of the feet, the knees or anywhere that there is prolonged and increased pressure or friction. Corns are smaller than calluses, form on the top or side of a toe, have a hard center and are surrounded by inflammation. (For what it's worth, it is rumored that the corn was named after the famous ancient Roman scientist and medical writer, Aulus Cornelius Celsus.) However, corns can be of similar danger to the acquirer with pain, blisters and infection.

Most of the time, calluses and corns can be prevented by wearing properly fitted shoes and removing excessive build-up of skin with sand paper, pumice stone or even fingernails during a bath or shower. Commonly, this challenging problem occurs because many feet and toes are quite deformed and therefore rub on ill-fitting shoes without causing calluses or corns. Sometimes the only solution for such misshapen and distorted feet is surgical correction.

Bottom line: Corns and calluses seem like uninteresting and insignificant medical trivia until pain begins or amputation threatens. Please don't ignore your feet.

BLUES WITHOUT A CAUSE: *DEPRESSION*

Through my years of caring for people, many seem caught in deep-down, joy-starving depression. I have seen the destruction from

---

324 https://www.mayoclinic.org/diseases-conditions/corns-and-calluses/symptoms-causes/syc-20355946

that awful diagnosis involve not only those sad and melancholy but also those around them. For people eighteen to forty-five-years of age, depression is the number one cause of disability, resulting in more than $200 billion of lost U.S. earnings per year.[325] I have been the doctor when the bodies of suicide victims came into the emergency room with their families; one dead and the rest totally devastated. I've seen too many cases where people affected by depression felt such helplessness that they would chose to escape life by suicide. There are about 40,000 deaths per year due to suicide[326] and this is about the same number of deaths per year due to breast cancer. (I am making no judgment here but should point out that despite a similar death rate, the money invested in depression research is about 1 percent of that spent studying breast cancer.)

Science has not perfectly defined why depression occurs, but theoretical causes for this malady include a genetic tendency, a learned process, a troubled childhood and adolescence, a stressful environment, a chronic medical illness, some sad or traumatic situation, an addiction or the lack of sun (seasonal affective disorder).[327] Most of us periodically have what is called "situational depression," such as an appropriate sadness that follows a severe loss such as the death of a loved one. More typical of severe and harmful depression occurs when there is no situation to cause trouble, no reason for grief, no sad story to explain

---

325   https://blogs.scientificamerican.com/mind-guest-blog/the-growing-economic-burden-of-depression-in-the-u-s/

326   https://www.cdc.gov/nchs/fastats/suicide.htm

327   https://www.health.harvard.edu/mind-and-mood/what-causes-depression

why one is filled with constant sorrow. When the patient says, "There is no reason for my being so sad," the clinician knows there is a problem.

It is not always easy to make the diagnosis of depression. We suspect depression when people experience chronic pain, find it hard to concentrate, are without energy, have flares of temper, sleep too much or too little, have a loss of appetite, have over-eating binges, have unexplained crying spells or become filled with anxiety for no known cause. People often make things worse by covering up depression with benzo-type sleeping pills, antianxiety medications, alcohol or other substance abuse which makes the diagnosis even more difficult. (See **Chapter Two**)

Two-thirds of people with depression do not seek or receive help.[328] **In the one-third that do get help and follow through with treatment, 80 percent are better in four to six weeks.** There is help and hope for those with this miserable condition, but people need to be open to the possibility of depression (men are usually the worst deniers). Treatment includes a half-hour of exercise or walking daily, someone to talk to and often an antidepressant medication which should have only minimal side effects).[329]

Bottom line: If you are possibly struggling with depression, please get help. If not for yourself, at least do it for those around you.

---

328   https://www.npr.org/sections/goatsandsoda/2016/12/02/504131307/ study-vast-majority-of-people-who-are-depressed-do-not-seek-help

329   https://www.psychologytoday.com/blog/think-act-be/201706/27 -facts-about-the-best-ways-treat-depression

THINGS YOU SHOULD KNOW

Questions and Answers about:
Head-to-Toe—A care guide for the aging body

Question: In my fifties, I was diagnosed with low thyroid. I don't know how long I had had it. Once diagnosed, I was put on Synthroid. Is it possible that damage has been done due to the delayed diagnosis and not being on proper medication for who knows how long?

As stated earlier in this chapter, there is no permanent damage from low thyroid except by the missed experience of an energetic life. However, remember that the diagnosis of hypothyroidism is challenging. People with depression, poor physical conditioning and drug abuse, for example, can present with symptoms similar to hypothyroidism, even when they DO NOT HAVE hypothyroidism.

When there is low thyroid, it can cause memory issues and depression, tiredness and weakness, a dilated and weak heart, numbness and neuropathy, enlarged thyroid gland with neck swelling, impotence and infertility and even birth defects in the babies born of women with hypothyroidism.[330] However, people with low thyroid may have no symptoms or

---

330   https://www.mayoclinic.org/diseases-conditions/hypothyroidism/symptoms-causes/syc-20350284

only minimal symptoms. In extremely rare cases, the thyroid level becomes so low that a life-threatening coma happens, although I have seen only one case of hypothyroid coma in my lifetime. Although replacement therapy with levothyroxine (Synthroid) should be done gradually over weeks and months, the good news is that once thyroid replacement happens and reaches normal levels, the dangers and symptoms of low thyroid gradually go away.

―――――⁓⁓⁓―――――

Question: Can prescription medicines have the same negative effects as over-the-counter (OTC) medicines and vice versa?

Every medication or supplement has the potential for a negative effect on some people, especially for the possibility of an allergic reaction.[331] Certain medicines such as penicillin or sulfa antibiotics cause more allergic reactions than others. Chemotherapy agents, which can beneficially poison the cancer, are known to sometimes have quite toxic side effects. The over-the-counter (OTC) nonsteroidal anti-inflammatory drugs (NSAIDs) such as ibuprofen (Advil) or naproxen (Aleve), in the right doses, are as effective as the prescription brands of NSAIDs such as meloxicam (Mobic) and diclofenac

―――――――――――――

331   https://well.blogs.nytimes.com/2015/11/30/over-the-counter-medicines -benefits-and-dangers/

(Voltaren), but can also be as toxic. Both prescribed and OTC NSAIDs are very hard on the stomach and kidneys and can cause headaches and quite dangerous allergic reactions. Whether a drug is determined to be labeled as a prescription medicine, an over-the-counter drug or a supplement depends on the choice of the manufacturer. These companies decide how to market their drug mainly on profitability rather than on how effective the medicine may be.

Bottom line: It is important to realize all three groups (prescription, OTC or supplements) are potentially harmful to the taker.[332]

Question: Can I hold off on my next colonoscopy? I had an invalid study since the "prep" didn't clean me out. The doctor recommended trying again with another colonoscopy in six months. I would like to wait for 12 months as I am not sure Medicare or Medicaid Supplement will pay for the procedure if it is done before 12 months. My brother had colon cancer, and I am concerned.

If you are fifty years old or older, and you have never had a colonoscopy, you need one. If your brother had colon cancer before his fiftieth year, you should have had a screening colonoscopy at year forty. If you had

332   https://www.cbsnews.com/pictures/12-dangerous-supplements/

a scope at forty and nothing was found, you should have had it done again ten years later and, if negative, every ten years until you are eighty or so. If an adenomatous polyp was found at any of those screening scopes, then you would have needed to repeat the colonoscopy sooner. If you have ever had blood in the stool, a change in bowel habits or even abdominal pain, you should see your doctor as you probably will need a diagnostic colonoscopy sooner than the standard screening plan.[333]

In your case, it sounds like it is time for your colonoscopy test NOW. An inadequate prep can happen in people who are on constipating medications, who have certain medical problems, who have some kind of obstruction (like a tumor) or who just happen to have long and sluggish colons.[334] Whenever my patients had an inadequate prep, I would not recommend delay but would immediately order for them a double prep that day and the next, with another day of clear liquid diet before the test. Why not do the colonoscopy as the patient was already one day into the clear liquid fast and half cleaned out? Sometimes I delayed the colonoscopy for six to twelve months if I saw at least a "pretty good" view and all was clear or if the patient wanted to delay. In your case,

333　https://www.cancer.org/cancer/colon-rectal-cancer/detection-diagnosis-staging/acs-recommendations.html

334　https://www.health.harvard.edu/diseases-and-conditions/preparing-for-a-colonoscopy

I would talk it over with your primary doctor. Usually, in this kind of situation, I would recommend a repeat colonoscopy sooner (within a few weeks) rather than later. Get it done.

Question: Is diet soda as bad for you as you hear? Is this because of the fake sugar or other reasons?

They have done studies on mice and rats and concluded that rats drinking more than the equivalent of humans drinking a case of artificially sweetened diet pop every day have more cancer than nondiet pop drinking rats.[335] In other words, we're not sure but high enough doses of diet pop might cause harm in humans. My conclusion is that two or three cans or bottles of the stuff daily is highly unlikely to be harmful. If you want to be on the safer side of things, switch to diet pop that is sweetened by stevia leaf (Splenda or Truvia). *Consumer Reports*' experts think these are safer.[336] I have switched my choice of artificial sweetener to stevia-based brands.

Studies have not found that people drinking zero calorie drinks weigh less than those drinking the cane

---

335   https://www.health.harvard.edu/blog/artificial-sweeteners-sugar -free-but-at-what-cost-201207165030

336   https://www.consumerreports.org/sugar-sweeteners/low-calorie -sweeteners-may-contribute-to-weight-gain/

sugar or corn syrup sweetened kind,[337] but this might be related to the heavier demographic of those who drink diet drinks. I believe that excess carbohydrates and refined sugars, especially in drinks, are not good for you, especially if you have diabetes. When I drink a soft drink, I pick a stevia-leaf-sweetened version.

———⁂———

Question: How can I convince my husband to take Viagra? It would enhance a level of intimacy that we already have nonsexually. Our nonsexual intimacy includes nighttime cuddling in bed, spooning and caressing. Are there health benefits related to having sex?

Your husband's reluctance to have sex could be due to a myriad of problems including low testosterone levels. This can be from testicular or pituitary dysfunction, fear of feeling inadequate in bed related to erectile dysfunction, a long-term history of excessive alcohol, a significant medical problem such as lung disease from smoking or even from many kinds of personal and emotional reasons.[338] I have had wives of many patients call me prior to their husband's visit to inform me of this problem.

---

337   https://www.washingtonpost.com/news/to-your-health/wp/2017/07/18/diet-drinks-are-associated-with-weight-gain-new-research-suggests/?utm_term=.f507aa8b4d58

338   https://www.mayoclinic.org/diseases-conditions/erectile-dysfunction/symptoms-causes/syc-20355776

When it is a new and significant short-term change, I would be more concerned that an underlying medical problem is causing it. However, long-term gradual change may also indicate a physical or medical problem. A good doctor should always see this as an opportunity to take a careful history and perform a thorough physical examination. After this, if all seems normal, standard labs should be checked to include testosterone, thyroid and B12 levels. During history taking, the doctor will ask about each part of the body (the review of systems). When each system of the body is discussed, the doctor should also explore the man's sexual history. This appears to the patient as "routine," delicately allowing the care provider to explore the man's side of the story regarding his sexual problems.[339] By the way, the care provider should not divulge to the husband any private calls from wife unless she asks the provider to do so.

If low testosterone is determined to be the problem, a further work-up and evaluation might be required, and, at this time, consultation with an endocrinologist may be apropos. Sometimes the testosterone level is borderline low simply because the gentleman is aging. Providing testosterone from shots, topicals, or patches can create some risks to an elderly patient, and this should be done carefully

---

339   https://www.ncbi.nlm.nih.gov/pubmed/6622311

only after the patient is fully informed of the risks of therapy.[340]

I believe that there are health benefits from sexual activity aside from procreation. There is an English (UK) study that shows those who have frequent (more often than monthly) sexual activity, have less dementia.[341] Most believe benefits from sexual activity are more on the side of emotional health which, in turn, reflects powerfully on one's physical health. Intimacy with another provides a special connection and a spiritual communication that is expressed in no other way. It is like having a special "best friend." Your description of your nonsexual intimacy may bring something close to that. I have heard about similar times of intimacy between elderly couples who can no longer achieve the full sexual act but who are gloriously rewarded by naked closeness (even without penetration and orgasm). I would call that intimacy! When there are two consenting, elderly people *who are not betraying a trust* and when there is very minimal chance of spreading infection, how can that hurt? How can that be anything but good?

---

340   http://www.choosingwisely.org/patient-resources/testosterone-for-erection-problems/

341   https://www.ncbi.nlm.nih.gov/pmc/articles/PMC4776624/

Question: I am facing a great deal of suffering from chronic
pain. My husband has left me and so have my friends.
How can I find help?

You are not only suffering from pain, you are also suffering from loss. I think that you should concentrate on
the loss aspect of your situation and less so on methods
for pain reduction. You are at risk for harms from aggressive pain treatments. Start by getting help for grief.[342]

In order to help you with your suffering, I will share
my own experience with the diagnosis of pancreatic
cancer and the treatments that followed. With this
experience, I have learned some ways that may help
you to lessen or live with pain and discomfort:

1. Endure the pain with as little complaining as pos-
    sible, as complaining can convince your own brain
    that the pain is worse. People helping you may have
    a natural distaste for excessive complaints and, on
    the other hand, will respect and appreciate your
    efforts to endure. After all, complaints usually do
    not make the situation better.

2. Accept encouraging words and support from any-
    one. The effort of accepting help may allow you to
    more easily get your mind off yourself. Also, it is
    an indirect gift to others to allow them the selfless
    reward that comes to many when they can help
    someone else.

---

342   https://www.ncbi.nlm.nih.gov/pmc/articles/PMC2898114/

3. Keep an attitude that you can do it. You can get through this, you can get better and you can hope for a long-term benefit. The glass half-full way of living, without question, makes the experience much easier. As an internal medicine physician, I have cared for many people going through similar tough times, and I know a positive attitude pays off. I mean that, sincerely.

4. Fifteen minutes of open-ended no-limit writing once or twice per day has helped many with chronic pain.

5. Finally, I believe in the value of deep listening. This can truly help you to get your mind off your own pain and to move into another world that is not all about pain. I found that this was the most important tool for reducing pain, for dealing with many forms of discomfort and for recovering in both physical and emotional ways. The value of deep listening cannot be overstated. (See **Chapter Twelve.**)

Chapter 11

Spirit Singing

On providing comfort at the end of life

Case Study:
The cases of the weeping widowers struggling with change

As THE SEASONS TURN, we are reminded that to survive in this life we must face change. Not too long ago, I attended two funerals in one month and wondered how both surviving eighty-year-old men were going to handle the loss of their spouses and all the changes that were about to occur? Usually people need about six months to mourn before they are expected to recover and move on. (The standard teaching in medical school is to begin being concerned when mourning lasts longer than that, but every situation is different.) I hoped that they would take this difficult transition time to connect more with extended family, friends and people in their church and community. Perhaps they could spend more time with the hobbies that were put off long ago.

There was concern that the death of the two wives, and the adjustments needed, might be too daunting for the widowers and might cause an early death in one or both. After the death of a spouse, it is not uncommon for the elderly partner to die within a month. Sometimes this comes as the result of a type of congestive heart failure called "the broken heart" syndrome (Takotsubo cardiomyopathy) which can follow severe emotional loss. Sometimes depression in the remaining partner can be so severe that it causes one to stop eating, resulting in dehydration, malnutrition and the worsening of any existing medical conditions. Unfortunately, death can also come early when the remaining spouse commits suicide. Finally, sometimes there is no explanation why an early death comes to the remaining spouse.

There may be those who perceive spouses dying so closely together as a poignant and heartwarming, romantic, elderly Romeo and Juliet-like love story. I see it as an unnecessary death that could have been prevented. No caring and compassionate person would want their partner to follow them to the grave without a reasonable cause. When love is true, they would want the one left alone to see change as an opportunity to continue in another way, to find fresh interests, to discover new joy.

Other life changes can be similarly challenging, such as learning of a new diagnosis of cancer, moving out of a home in which one has lived for many years, suffering a financial crisis or facing any crisis that might be overwhelming. I believe the ability to handle change is like working and stretching a muscle. If you don't use it, you will lose it. Stagnation can cause rigidity, weakness, despondency and death; but movement can cause flexibility, strength, happiness and life.

As of the time of this writing, the two widowers are still alive despite their period of tremendous suffering and near paralysis. In each case, their children came to the rescue and surrounded them with love and support. The sounds of playing, laughter and, sometimes, screaming grandchildren and great grandchildren brought them back to life. Indeed! family love, like a cleansing rain, gave them each hope and brought them back to living.

SURVIVING AFTER A PARENT DIES; WHEN ALL THAT UNCONDITIONAL LOVE GOES AWAY

The following is a letter I wrote for CaringBridge (an Internet site which shares information about people who are dealing with life-challenging illnesses)[343] while I was receiving radiation therapy for pancreatic cancer. (I strongly recommend use of the CaringBridge site if you ever go through a cancer-type experience.) The letter was written in late-winter, 2017:

> I'm sitting in a Sioux Falls restaurant after my morning radiation experience. It always amazes me how short those radiation visits are. The radiation experience begins with a scan to center me with any needed adjustments. The machine moves around me to six different positions and zaps me from these different perspectives for about five seconds at each position. The whole procedure is painless, and there are nice people setting it up. Still, something

about it is daunting, and I find myself repeating what I can remember of the 23rd Psalm as the machine buzzes away.

The plan is to continue for three more weeks. After some body resting time, the Whipple pancreatic cancer surgery could be performed in May. This is a scary procedure, but it is my best shot at a cure, so I am hopeful they will do the surgery. If I can survive the surgery with a fair prognosis, I aim to do the traveling my wife, Joanie, and I would like to do. I have an idea for writing a historical romantic novel that occurs during the 1400s in Salerno, Italy, the site of the first western medical school. It sounds corny, but it should be fun to write about a historical time. So, Joanie and I need to go there to research that novel.

A dear friend recently wrote to me speaking of how much confidence he had when he was growing up. Now he realizes that this must have been because of all the encouragement his loving parents poured upon him from his very beginning. His words made me think about how important love and appropriate praise is to any young, developing person.

When I was growing up, I also experienced such confidence, perhaps more than I deserved. This was clearly the result of the unconditional love I felt virtually radiating from my parents. Of course, all that support was mixed in with balanced discipline which made me a very lucky guy, indeed.

When each of my parents died, it was like in the first *Star Wars* movie when the bad guys and their death starship destroyed a good planet along with its civilization, causing the heroes to feel the sinking loss of the "force." The passing away of all that love and encouragement from, first, my dad and then my mom was like a loss of "the force." Most of you reading this likely can remember a similar loss after the death of your parents, or grandparents. When that "unconditional love giver" departs, something very good is lost, and it takes some time to recover.

The energy of self-confidence, given by our parents, might be one explanation for the force. The good news is that there is a way we can once again feel a return of the "power of the force." It can come back by simply giving it away, by providing someone else with that same unconditional love. It happens as we support our children, spouse and friends . . . but it works even when we give it away to strangers (and even to enemies). Providing unconditional love helps us to sense the God within the other guy AND ourselves.

May "the force" be with you.

CHOOSING DIGNITY

When the end of life is near, many family members struggle to let go. However, the result of such understandable denial most often does not bring an easier end but rather one of suffering and agony. Perhaps this discussion is too close to earlier chapters and feels like an unnecessary duplication. I believe the point is so important, however, that I want to relate this real case story to help prepare family and at-home caregivers about the importance of respecting an advance directive and to teach how the common condition of a severe stroke might be better managed.

I believe, in many parts of this country, too many feeding tubes are started too early, making what is an obvious and irreversible dying process become a longer and more difficult experience than needed. A gentleman in his late eighties came into the emergency room unconscious with the probable diagnosis of a new stroke. The CT scan of the head indicated there was no bleeding into the brain or around the brain. This led us to conclude that he had a blood clot forming in an artery within the brain that was causing sudden and severe brain injury. The symptoms had begun six hours earlier, and the patient and his family, for various reasons, just couldn't get him to the emergency room in time to try a clot-busting medication which can sometimes save the brain. At this point, the family and I had a long talk.

The patient had been living alone in his own home for 50 years, making a daily visit to his wife who had severe Alzheimer's disease and she was still living in a nursing home. He personally had written an advance directive a few years earlier, about which his family was aware. He had enjoyed a good life; his financial affairs were in order and his advance directive stated that he did not want resuscitation. I remember him telling me, "If I had a sudden cardiac arrest or sudden coma, that kind of death should be an easy way to go, so Do

Not Resuscitate." He also said, "Whatever happens, no feeding tubes unless I have a reasonable chance of returning to a
normal life."

A significant brain injury had occurred in this gentleman, with
the resulting loss of capacity to swallow or speak. Fortunately,
he was minimally aware of what was happening. With the
family's agreement, we did not start intravenous fluids and a
feeding tube was not inserted (which would also provide fluids)
in consideration for the brain swelling that can occur with new
strokes. Instead, we gave him time to dehydrate a little, to allow
for the swelling to reduce and to see if there was going to be any
recovery. This also bought some time for the family to absorb
the severity of the situation and to better understand what all
this might mean over time.

After the third day, he had not recovered any function and
it was very likely he was not going to recover to anything close
to independent function. His chances for a long-term life would
require putting in a feeding tube, and, likely, the tube would
never be discontinued. His chances for recovery, returning home
from a long-term care facility and becoming self-reliant again,
was just about zero. After the first three days, the family was
more comfortable with agreeing to follow his advance directive
and to allow a natural death. Over the next seven days, he gently
slipped away: no feeding tube, no respirator, no suffering.

The following list is made to summarize the points this story
clarifies with the hope that others may be spared suffering:

1. Make an advance directive and use it as a communication tool to talk about end of life choices with the family.

Realize that talking about these wishes is more important than any document.

2. Realize that the patient's choice is primary. If the patient is not capable, the family should choose for the patient, but their obligation is to respect the patient's prior expressed wishes or to do their best for him by directing his care in the way he would have chosen. Respect the prior expressed wishes of the loved one. When there is no advance directive, families commonly do not realize their responsibility to respect the dying patient's IMPLIED wishes, choosing what the family thinks the patient WOULD HAVE wanted. Too often feeding tubes are placed, and what might have been death with dignity becomes a prolonged misery.

3. In following what the patient would have wanted, if necessary, do not let the doctors, nurses and hospital bully you into doing more than what the patient would have wanted. Sometimes this is not easy, and often it means long discussions between family members regarding the family's obligation to respect the patient's rights. (There are many health-care teams who are respectful of advance directives, understand when aggressive care is potentially harmful and advise and encourage comfort (palliative) care when appropriate. However, in some places, they are not up to this level of compassion.)

Bottom line: We should all realize the value of talking to our families about our wishes, especially about feeding tubes, should the time come that we are permanently not able to recognize family members.

A BOOK REVIEW FROM *THE JOURNAL OF THE AMERICAN MEDICAL ASSOCIATION: FINAL GIFTS* BY MAGGIE CALLANAN AND PATRICIA KELLEY[344,345]

As an internist and geriatrician, often caring for very ill and dying people, and, as the director of the hospice program in our prairie community, I was pleased to review Callanan and Kelley's book, *Final Gifts*. Callanan and Kelley are hospice caregivers who listen, care and reassure people who are overwhelmed with bad news about cancer and impending death. Their book, *Final Gifts*, was crafted to do the same and succeeds.

The book is divided into three rather different parts. First, the history of hospice is described as "an old kind of hostel-like place of comfort for travelers, now adopted as a philosophy of care." Modern hospice was developed in the 1960s by British physician, Cicely Saunders, as a peaceful place "for the care of the dying on a metaphysical journey from this world to the next."[346] Also, in this section of the book, the authors give numerous examples of dying people going in and out of Kübler-Ross's stages of dying.[347] They reassure those dying, and their families, that there is no correct way to move through the stages with the exception that open communication should be encouraged all along the way. Their best

344   https://jamanetwork.com/journals/jama/article-abstract/1383214 ?redirect=true

345   https://www.amazon.com/Final-Maggie-Kelley-Patricia-Callanan/dp/ B007CK3NYG

346   Stoddard, Sandol. The Hospice Movement. New York: Vintage Books, 1978.

347   Kübler-Ross, Elisabeth. On Death and Dying. New York: Macmillan, 1969.

advice to care providers is not to give advice. Instead, they caution the readers to listen to the patient with great intensity.

In part two, Callanan and Kelley share reassuring words about dying people who have glimpses into another world. Like

other accounts,[348,349,350] which chronicle similar events, we read stories of dying people speaking about going on dream-like trips, about seeing angels and ancestors gathering around the deathbed and about experiencing very reassuring places of great light, warmth, peace and beauty. We also hear chronicles of dying people who can predict or control the timing of their death. Sometimes they wait so the last relative can get there; sometimes they wait until visitors leave the room; and sometimes they die earlier than expected so as not to inconvenience the visiting family.

Ascent of the Blessed by Hieronymus Bosch painted between 1505–1515. This painting is thought to represent a "near death experience" circa 1500.[351]

348　Moody, Raymond. Life after Life, New York: Bantam Books, 1975.

349　Osis, Karlis, and Haraldsson, Erlender. At the Hour of Death. New York: Avon Publishers, 1977.

350　Alexander, Eben. Proof of Heaven, New York: Simon and Schuster, 2012.

351　From the public domain, https://commons.wikimedia.org/wiki/File: Hieronymus_Bosch_013.jpg

Part three reveals narratives of dying people working through unfinished or unresolved problems from their lives, trying to find reconciliation before they are gone. The book urges the family or caregiver to help these dying people reconcile these problems whenever possible in order to bring them to a more peaceful place before their death. This part of the book was most innovative and helpful for me as a hospice medical director.

As a physician accustomed to reading scientific literature, initially, I had the inclination to reject the anecdotal nature of this book, especially some of the almost fairytale stories about angels at the bedside. Without delving into issues of religion and faith, I think it is fair to state that there will never be scientific proof to answer the great mystery concerning what happens after we die. The closest scientists will ever be to an understanding of heaven, or even of consciousness, will come from stories like these. Perhaps we are reassured by the fact that such similar experiences are not rare. An account by Eben Alexander, MD, neurosurgeon, (see **Chapter Twelve**) was quite powerful and certainly brings reassurance and relief if one is panicking about death.

Several years ago, I heard the following account from a nurse and family immediately after a death. The dying woman suddenly came out of her coma, looked around the room, past the family and nurse, as if seeing angels. She smiled and said, "It's going to be alright," and expired her last breath. I must confess to retelling similar stories at the bedside of other dying people through my years of trying to give comfort and hope.

Although these "life after life" or "near death experience"[352] stories are enthralling, I think the most important lessons of the book come from the encouragement to caringly listen to the dying. In the authors' words, "Your role is to teach friends and family members how to listen, understand and respond appropriately to a dying person's message . . ." Whether she or he be a spouse doing the work at home, a nurse talking with the patient in the clinic or the hospice medical director helping at the bedside, every caregiver and every one of us should appreciate those words.

Final Gifts is written in such clear and understandable language that people of all ages and educational levels should comprehend it, and, yet, the stories are so heady and thick with the depth of true human experience, that the most complex and obtuse philosopher should be challenged.

In this modern medical world of "save everyone at any cost," people have come to have unrealistic expectations of extended life and, paradoxically, have augmented fears of death. Coming to the rescue has been the hospice movement and palliative care. These are giving hope and comfort to many dying people and their surrounding families. Callanan and Kelley's book, *Final Gifts,* does the same: providing hope and comfort.

---

352   Moody, R: Life After Life. MBB, Inc, 1975

An essay
Spirit Singing

Singing for people in need had all started three months earlier after our community singing group, the Dakota Men's Ensemble, went Christmas caroling. Our leader said that it was too bad we didn't sing carols all year long, especially for those in need of comforting. At the next practice, he spoke of an article he had read about choral groups singing to hospice patients and wondered if that would be something the men would like to do. As medical director for our local hospice, it was easy to bring the idea to the next hospice meeting.

Our hospice group, besides myself, includes a pharmacist, a social worker, a dietician, a geriatric nurse practitioner and, of course, hospice nurses. Each week we review every hospice patient, discuss his or her needs and make plans to provide comfort for these people. The hospice team was very happy with the idea of our singing for hospice patients, many of whom could use something uplifting.

After making the rounds through the nursing home and hospital, we finished the evening by singing in the home of a dying friend. I stepped lightly into the dying man's bedroom, along with eight other men, and we circled around the unconscious man whose breathing was labored. His loving, almost glowing, wife was sitting beside him, comforting him and holding his hand as we began singing.

Surrounding a dying man that cold February evening, we knew we were entering a sacred space. The melodies began, and, like other hospice visits, the choral music resonated in a very spiritual way. It was as though all our souls were harmonizing with his, singing that we are together in this human experience of living and dying. I could tell that his breathing eased that evening as we sang *Beautiful Savior*. Early the next morning he died.

We've been singing for quite a few years now, and it has evolved into a mixed chorus of persons with eclectic faiths and with ages from teens to some greater than eighty-years-old. We sing for patients in the hospital, nursing home and hospice care; for people and family sitting around a dying friend; and sometimes for those just in need of a hopeful spirit or a little comforting. We have been named the Hopeful Spirit Chorale, and although we sing mostly hymns and patriotic songs, we are working on some nonreligious and nonpatriotic pieces. We sing without accompaniment, in four-part harmony, sometimes quiet, sometimes loud. I have noted that the young people in our ensemble seem to gain the most from the experience since, prior to their joining the choir, they had rarely seen people at the end of their lives. That said, those of us who are older, and more experienced with dying and death, find a wonderful sense of joy to be able to give comfort to these people.

Singers in a patient's room bringing joyous noise[353]

THINGS YOU SHOULD KNOW:

Questions and Answers about:
Spirit Singing—On providing comfort at the end of life

Question: I have heard of the "broken heart" syndrome you described earlier. Tell me more about it.

Takotsubo cardiomyopathy, first described in the '90s in Japan, occurs 90 percent of the time in women and usually happens after a severe stress situation. Quoting from an article by Scott W. Sharkey, et al, in the medical journal, *Circulation*:[354] "Emotional stressors include grief (death of a loved one), fear (armed robbery or public speaking), anger (argument with spouse), relationship conflicts (dissolution of marriage) and financial problems

---

353   Photo by author, from private collection February 2018

354   http://circ.ahajournals.org/content/124/18/e460

(gambling loss or job loss). Physical stressors include acute asthma, surgery, chemotherapy and stroke."[355]

The patient with this condition usually comes to the emergency room with chest pain, shortness of breath and leg swelling. Looking like someone with a heart attack, the patient is usually taken to the heart cath lab (where they inject X-ray visible dye into coronary arteries) and found not to be having a heart attack with blocked coronary arteries but, rather, to have normal coronary arteries with a strangely shaped heart. The left ventricle part of the heart, in this case, has a narrow neck and a ballooned lower portion which is the shape of a Japanese ceramic octopus fishing pot. In that trap the narrow neck allows the skinny and hungry octopus to enter the pot, drawn to the smelly bait within. After eating the bait, the octopus is too fat to escape. This trap is called a takotsubo pot, and this kind of heart illness is called takotsubo cardiomyopathy, related to the common shape. The good news is that heart failure medications, reassurance and time will heal most who present to the hospital in this way. Most of the time, these people recover with a heart that returns to a normal shape.

Bottom line: There is danger from not only physical stressors but also emotional stressors on one's heart. The good news: with time, people can completely recover.

───── ∿ ─────

355   https://doi.org/10.1161/CIRCULATIONAHA.111.052662 Circulation. 2011;124: e460-e462

Question: My dear niece's husband committed suicide for
absolutely no discernable reason, with no note, no
presuicide emotional problem and no clue that suicide
was going to happen. On the morning of his death, he
said to my niece, "I'll see you tonight." All members
of the family are struggling with his unexpected and
unexplained passing away. How can I handle it?

There is often no answer to why bad things happen. Often, we want to blame ourselves, or someone
else, to find a cause for tragedy. I think that in almost
every case there should be no blaming because of
the destructive nature of such a negative thought.
Instead, we should see tragedy as a hurricane, a natural
accident, a nonmoral and nonpurposeful happening
with no one at fault, even when there may be fault
and blame. I think that even goes for a malicious situation, a murder, for example. I understand this is easy
to say and hard to do. I would especially recommend
not blaming the deceased. Those left alive should have
no reason for guilt and should let go of the unhelpful,
even destructive, blame game.

As presented in the introduction, the death of my
sister left me mourning her for many years (she died
in 1964). Sometime over the last five years or so, I've
realized how harmful that attitude can be. I've found
help in realizing she would never have wanted me to
be sad when thinking about her. To help me believe
in the value of this way of thinking, I consider how I

would want people to think about me after I am gone. I would have them throw away the pity, the mourning and the sadness. I would want others to think about the fun, the good times and the joy we shared. That is how my mind wraps around my sister now. I know she is better for it and so am I.

If there is something you can do, some action you can make to help the situation, then take that action, but if there is nothing to be done, savor the good times, realize the pay it forward good effects your niece's husband has had on people's lives and then, let it go.

———✤———

Question: I simply have trouble considering the death of my spouse even though she is so disabled by dementia. I am caring for her at home, and we are so close. She is beginning to fail, and I fear I will lose her soon. Help me get through this.

Perhaps the trouble you are having facing her death may have to do with the fear you have about your own. First, read the next chapter which was written to help all of us face our own dying process. Personally, I am living with pancreatic cancer, I'm facing my own possible premature dying process and I have accepted the inevitable, even if that time is unknown at this point. A physician friend of mine often says that we all should get terminal cancer and be cured, maybe once a year.

He says it would help us to realize the value of every day. Concentrating on "value" is helpful. Concentrating on "fear" is harmful.

Let the dying process, in your wife or in you, bring you, instead, to savor the small things, realign your priorities, love others actively and stop putting off the things you want to do. If you can do these things while caring for your spouse, then it will make her dying more acceptable, even a celebration of her life.

———

Question: All this hypothetical talk about accepting death is just a bunch of words and doesn't make it easier for me. What should I do?

I would buy and read, or perhaps reread, Callanan and Kelley's book, *Final Gifts*,[356] which was reviewed in this chapter. It will do you a world of good.

---

356   https://www.amazon.com/Final-Maggie-Kelley-Patricia-Callanan/dp/B007CK3NYG

Chapter Twelve

The View Across the Water

Accepting death without fear

Case Study:
The case of a gracious death in a man with cancer

HE WAS MY NEIGHBOR, a guy my age, not my patient, a man of many talents and interests and a dear friend. He was one of those fellows who, if needed, would give you the shirt off his back. When he was diagnosed with cancer of the pancreas, which had spread to the liver, he, his daughters and his friends knew how this was likely going to end. We didn't realize, however, how graciously he would handle his dying process.

He was treated and truly helped by chemotherapy for a while, but gradually the tumor cells developed resistance to the drugs, and the oncologist suggested no more chemotherapy. My friend was ready to have only pain medicines and hospice. In the end, with the help of hospice and the caring people at the long-term care home, he "shuffled off this mortal coil" comfortably, surrounded by family and friends.

Fortunately, he had compassionate and grounded primary care and oncologist doctors. Both were realistic, knowing when to stop intervention. He had loving daughters and friends who surrounded him with support, plenty of tater-tot-like hot dishes, an advance directive that said he was to have comfort medical interventions only. Despite having an expanding belly full of cancer, when I visited him two days before his death he told me he was without pain. Most importantly, he was not fearful. Courageously, he was accepting his impending death.

In comparison, I find tragic and too common that patients and families are overwhelmed with a fear of death. Consequently, they expect modern medicine to save them even when it is a desperate and futile situation. Physicians especially struggle taking the time and challenge of helping people face their dying process, especially when the dying person and family are in denial. It is easier just to treat and retreat.

Bottom line: Too often people choose a path of unnecessary suffering at the end of their lives, and their doctors find it too easy to comply. Rather, dying people should ask, and be reassured, that enough comfort medicine will be provided. There is always something more that can be done. When therapeutic options are not good choices, they shouldn't be offered. Our profession is improving in this regard but has a long way to go. When the end nears, patient expectations should be aligned, physicians should be aware and helpful and we should all have

the opportunity to experience a gracious death, just as was the circumstance of my neighbor.

TERRIFIED OF DEATH

Swedish author, Fredrik Backman, said in his wonderful book, *A Man Called Ove*,[357] "Death is a strange thing. People live their whole lives as if it does not exist." I believe he's right. We pretend death doesn't exist because many of us are gut-wrenchingly terrified of it.

Why are we so afraid of dying?

1. Does this disabling dread come from our cultural habit of avoiding dying or dead people in the hospital, nursing home or funeral home?
2. Is it because we don't talk about death in conversations with our children and young adults? By trying to make life easier and keeping the sad truth from our youth, is our society filling them full of the fear of death? Isn't it true that the fear of the unknown is almost always worse than something known?
3. Is it because people of all ages have gotten used to such advances in medicine that we expect modern health care to save us from death even in the face of aging or terminal diseases?

---

357   Fredrik Backman, A Man Called Ove. Atria Books (Simon and Schuster)/ 2nd edition, July, 2014.

4. Is it because we see such suffering when people are inappropriately treated beyond any chance of recovery?

Understanding the reason we are so terrified and paralyzed is one thing. It's another to get past the panic and the black doom that comes over us as we consider our own death. I speak from experience while facing my own cancer. I am also a general internist who has spent all of my professional life caring for the elderly. I have seen many deaths, and I am older. With all this, I am not filled with fear.

Josie Sanderson joyously doing Yoga at Lake Poinsett
next to the sign of death[358]

One of the most powerful tools and important lessons in dealing with the fear of death comes from the experience of Dr.

---

358   Photos from private collection

Franz Ingelfinger, the famous Harvard gastroenterologist and editor of *The New England Journal of Medicine*. He was an expert in esophageal cancer, and, ironically, he was diagnosed and eventually died with that condition. It was no surprise that he had advice from many colleagues and world-renowned experts, all with various and often different recommendations. Those of us in the arena of health care like to present the image of confidence and certitude, that we understand every disease and that we have a standard and acceptable plan of treatment for each condition. Although this is often the case, at the time of Dr. Ingelfinger's esophageal cancer, good treatment for that kind of cancer was not yet clearly defined. Dr Ingelfinger became the victim of uncertainty, despite his great knowledge and wisdom.

After several months of struggling with too many doctors, too many well-meaning opinions and too much self-directed care, the good Dr. Ingelfinger found himself in deep trouble. He was without direction and became overwhelmed. He wrote later, "Finally, when the pangs of indecision had become nearly intolerable, one wise physician friend told me that what I needed was a doctor." Dr. Ingelfinger subsequently found a primary care physician he could trust, and he turned to him for guidance through this tough time. He wrote that he felt "immediate and immense relief."

This should be a huge lesson for all of us. When a severe illness, like cancer, and the possibility of dying becomes real, each of us should have one professional person who is our main advisor, one who we completely trust. Turning the responsibility over to them can provide immediate and immense relief.

LESSONS FROM MY SISTER'S DEATH

There are more lessons to learn about dying. First, I need to share with you some memories of my sister, Susan, who died at nineteen-years-old. She taught me a lot of things, but from her death there were two powerful lessons. When Susan died in a car crash, I was sixteen, just returning from a Boy Scout canoe trip. I will never forget the sadness of that moment, walking into our home filled with what seemed like half the caring and wonderful town of De Smet, to find my mom and dad grieving. It was near the end of summer but the beginning of a long period of mourning for my family.

Susan and Rick Holm 1951[359]

First lesson: I realized the importance of community support. Consolation came from our extended family, friends, neighbors,

---

church and people we hardly knew. It was like the warm wings of a mother hen as that loving and experienced community wrapped its compassionate feathers around us. It seemed more about the presence of those people than their words. The love of that community gave me strength and taught me kindness. (This is why we should stick with our home church as ministers change. I believe it is the congregation, not the preacher, that matters. Preachers come and go.) I don't think people realize the impact when they give kind- ness to others who need help. When the opportunity arises, visit your friends and family during those tough times, and don't worry about what to say. Just be there.

Susan Diane Holm 1947-1965[360]

Second lesson: Susan's death changed how I saw my own life. I had been a goody two-shoes, an overly serious young fellow. She was a person with such zest, so full of fun. She Snoopy-danced every day. Life for any of us might be brief like hers, so, it is very important to savor every moment. Why shouldn't we cherish every day? After all, what is the downside? We are all going to die one day. Enjoying every moment as well as we can will not hurry it on, and fearing death will not prevent it. Voltaire said, "I have chosen to be happy because it is good for

360   Photo from private collection

my health."[361] I'm not suggesting anyone cover up the fear of death with drugs, alcohol or the pretense of happiness while being internally bitter and angry. That might just bring death sooner. What I am suggesting is that each of us needs to find a way to savor the moments in every day.

FEARFUL AND INCAPABLE OF AVOIDING DANGER

Fear is one thing, but avoiding danger is another. Fear is hard-wired in our brains to keep us from harm,[362] but fear can sometimes do harm when it paralyzes or makes us turn from a rational approach to avoid danger. Personally, I have experienced situations when danger slapped me in the face, and the resulting fear and panic caused complete paralysis. Pertinent to this issue, I have helplessly watched some patients' fear of death bring on suffering. For example, a fifty-five-year-old woman, had observed a relative suffer from chemotherapy for cancer and believed chemo gave her relative no benefit and only suffering. The woman was subsequently diagnosed with her own cancer. Because of her fear of a similar fate, and, despite my explanations, the woman avoided appropriate and effective treatment resulting in her own death in less than a year. With standard, acceptable and effective treatment, she may have had many years of comfortable life which were lost because of her fear of suffering and her fear of death.

Another example was a forty-five-year-old helicopter pilot who came into the Atlanta Veterans Administration hospital

---

361 https://www.goodreads.com/quotes/583598-i-have-chosen-to-be-happy-because-it-is-good

362 Kunio Kondoh, et al, A specific area of olfactory cortex involved in stress hormone responses to predator odors. Nature, 3/21/16, 532, 103–196.

with back pain. When we diagnosed cancer of the lung, the malignancy had already spread to the bones of his back. With that diagnosis, he sank into a black hole of funk and sadness so deep that he avoided visits even from his loving family. His life, up to this point, was pretty much all about him with little time thinking about anyone else. Now his whole world was dying.

I know this sounds irrational, but I remember making rounds to see him and feeling the dark, empty coldness in the room which intensified as I came closer to his bed. After leaving his bedside, I felt alone, empty and weaker. He eventually slipped away, still alone, still immersed in fear and regret. Fear of death is not only dangerous, it can reduce the quality of the time one has left. If your time to live is limited, isn't it tragic to spend that precious time sad, depressed and continuously dwelling on the death to come?

In contrast, I knew a sixty-three-year-old biology professor who had abdominal pains and, after a work-up, was discovered with widely metastatic colon cancer. Chemotherapy worked for a while, but, gradually, the chemotherapy began to fail. It was time to enter hospice, to let him enjoy some time from the chemotherapy's side effects and to change the focus of treatment toward comfort care. This was when I got to know him. He loved his family, his students and his job. As a biologist and birder, he loved all living things and the world that surrounds us. His attitude was the opposite of the black hole of the helicopter pilot. He was dying, but his whole biological world around him was not dying. Everyone near him felt his warmth, his glowing spirit and his birdsong of love. This is the absolute truth: whenever I left his bedside, I felt comforted, replenished and stronger. He died surrounded by family and friends, spiritually connected to the whole world and all that's in it. He died with dignity and grace.

DEEP LISTENING

This chapter is about learning how to face our own death or dying process. It is about making our eventuality more like that of the biology professor than that of the helicopter pilot. With so much fear of death around us, there is a big question that needs answering. What can any of us do to find relief from the dread and terror about an eventual visit from death personified, the "Grim Reaper?"

I have learned from my own experience and give you an ancient formula that can help with this lifetime challenge. I believe intense listening and selflessness can help anyone let go of fear, anxiety and pain and help bring hope, especially when dealing with the paralyzing and dangerous fear of death. During my years of practicing medicine, I have realized my most important diagnostic and therapeutic tool is listening . . . listening with intensity and with all the senses. Listening carefully results in losing oneself in the patient's story, to let go of oneself and it brings the listener a step toward valuing the patient and closer to what Maslow calls self-actualization and self-transcendence.[363] Deep listening has even helped me face my own eventual death by drawing my attention away from pitying myself. I am surprised how there has been no panic, no sleepless nights, no regrets and

363 https://www.psychologytoday.com/us/blog/hide-and-seek/201205/our-hierarchy-needs

only increased joy with even mundane parts of every day. (See **Chapter Four** for more on this topic.)

Richard Rohr, a Roman Catholic priest, has emphasized that people change after significant losses.[364] He teaches that people can come to an "aha!" moment, usually in their thirties when they realize "it's NOT all about me, it's about the other person."[365] In other words, listening comes with maturity. I submit the corollary: Learning to listen enhances maturity.

Long-term care nurse with one-hundred-five-year-old competent and happy woman, 2016[366]

---

364   "The Franciscan Alternative Orthodoxy". Center for Action and Contemplation.

365   "The Intricate Dance of Our True and False Selves". Englewood Review of Books. 12 April 2013.

366   With patient's permission, from private collection

Accepting one's own eventual death brings an openness, a selflessness and a chance to savor each moment. It asks the question, "Why not open your heart and self to the world around you? What have you got to lose? Why hold back? What are you waiting for?" Remember how Dorothy threw water on the Wicked Witch of the West[367] making the witch melt away? Deep listening throws water on the Grim Reaper, melting fears and bringing freedom to see and savor our daily blessings.

TALKING TO YOUR FAMILY ABOUT YOUR DEATH WISHES

As a physician, caring for the aged or the very sick, I have been called to speak with those who are near the end of their lives. It has regularly been my job all these years to help them through the dying process when it is inevitable. I should add that I don't believe my profession always provides enough comfort in these times. I believe, too often, physicians, care providers and nurses are overzealous because they are running from their own fears of death. Besides, giving comfort takes time. It is simply easier just to do everything . . . full resuscitation, full steam ahead.

Make an advance directive and explain it to your family. No matter what your age, we all need to talk to our families about letting go when it is time to die. An official document is good, but the talking is most important. (See more on this in **Chapter Five**.)

FACING ONE'S OWN DEATH AND PREPARING FOR LIFE

What happens after we die is beyond understanding. The potential dangers of fearing death, however, are real, whether you are an

---

367   https://en.wikipedia.org/wiki/Wicked_Witch_of_the_West

elderly person dying from heart failure, lung disease, pancreatic cancer or a perfectly healthy younger person sitting comfortably in your chair reading this book. Knowing our lives are finite, that there will be an end, will help us sense the value of every life, including our own. This helps us, in turn, to act in a kinder way, a kinder way to treat others and to treat ourselves. As Picasso said, "The meaning of life is to find your gift. The purpose of life is to give it away."[368]

Bottom line: You will be better able to live and give if you can honestly face your own potential death.

After hearing of my cancer, a psychologist-minister friend from afar wrote, asking, "How is your soul with all this, and how should I pray for you?" Here was my answer:

> "I would ask you to pray that each one of us learn to better see and accept our own dying process and to let go of all that fear. Fearless, we can better learn to savor every day . . . every moment. As for me, my faith surrounds me like the wings of a mother hen. I'm okay with dying. I am trying to put it off as long as I can, but I'll be alright if it happens sooner. I am incredibly thankful for an abundant life. My job as a physician has given back far more than I could ever give. I still love and play with gusto, gather all the humor and fun I can have at every juncture and I try hard to do a Snoopy dance through every day. I'm surrounded by dear friends, the love of a wonderful spouse and honest,

---

368 https://www.goodreads.com/quotes/607827-the-meaning-of-life-is-to-find-your-gift-the

creative and joyful kids. I direct an interdenominational choir that sings hymns weekly to help people in need savor a moment."

The comforting wings and feathers of a mother hen[369]

Indeed, I've been listening as hard as I can for life . . . which helps me face my own impending death, and I believe God is listening. I realize rough seas may be coming. Still, it is well with my soul.

---

369   Photo by Michael Varun, from https://commons.wikimedia.org/w/index.php?title=User:Michael_varun&action=edit&redlink=1

Someone enjoying life. Julia and Sasha Holm
doing Snoopy dance 2017[370]

Now, savor the first and last verses of this wonderful song:

IT IS WELL WITH MY SOUL
BY HORATIO G. SPAFFORD (1873)[371]

When peace, like a river, attendeth my way,
When sorrows like sea billows roll;
Whatever my lot, thou hast taught me to say,
It is well, it is well with my soul.

---

370   Photo from private collection
371   http://library.timelesstruths.org/music/It_Is_Well_with_My_Soul/

Refrain:
It is well with my soul,
It is well, it is well with my soul.

And Lord, haste the day when the faith shall be sight,
The clouds be rolled back as a scroll;
The trump shall resound, and the Lord shall descend,
Even so, it is well with my soul.

Refrain:
It is well with my soul,
It is well, it is well with my soul.

First of three essays
Wedding Cake and Funerals

This was a big month of dying in my practice: three nursing home patients in their late eighties and nineties died with everything failing; an elderly woman, who was living at home alone, came in with a vague abdominal pain and died suddenly; a seventy-five-year-old died of complications from her cancer; finally, there was the tragic death of a college youth who died of asthma and shouldn't have had to die.

Death surrounds me. I'm not complaining because it comes as part of the job description, but I'm not alone. Death surrounds everyone, really. If you are born, you will die. What's more, you will come to experience it happening all around you, unless you die first. That's the sad truth about living.

Facing our own death is the challenging issue. Modern humanity, in this country at least, seems not built to handle the discussion about a permanent end. Does it have to be so sad? Perhaps it would be better to live our lives with some hope for a future, yet living just one day at a time.

Recently I heard that most clergy much prefer performing funerals rather than weddings. In weddings, the organizers are worried about the catering, the flowers, the photographer, the presents and so on. With all the pressures and impossible expectations of the event, one cleric said that too often a wedding can become all about fake joy.

At a funeral, however, the clergy say it is not about expectation but rather reflection. This is a time not only to consider the person who is dead but also one's own fragility, brokenness and limitations. It is a time to realize that you are not the one dead, that you still have another day . . . another day to try to fix what is broken, to show some compassion and to savor the time you have left. In a way, the funeral is an occasion to wake up those of us who are half-living, walking through life like zombies or maybe even living a fake-joy over-pressured life with wedding cake frosting on our lips.

May we all look upon the deaths around us, and our own dying process, as a chance to come alive.

Second essay
Surprise Death

The late physician poet, John Stone, MD, wrote about death:[372]

> I have seen come on
> slowly as rust
> Sand
> or suddenly as when
> someone leaving
> a room
> finds the doorknob
> come loose in his hand.

This is not a topic about which anyone likes to talk. The poignant truth, however, is that all of us will die one day, so we should consider it every once in a while. Many say they would like to die quickly and unexpectedly. "Let me go at ninety, shot by a jealous lover," or more realistically, "Let it happen to me when I am a very old person and still with all my faculties, sneaking up to me in the night during sleep after a joyful day."

As a physician, I have seen death occur in many ways. Certainly, no one wants to die slowly while suffering or after a long period without the capacity to know what is going on. In these cases, I have grown to appreciate the hospice attitude of comfort care instead of medically trying to prolong a life without joy.

---

372   http://journalofethics.ama-assn.org/2011/07/jdsc1-1107.html

I have often wondered what the ghosts of those who die abruptly must think. Is it, "That wasn't so bad!" or "Wow, that caught me off guard!" or "I wish I could have told my family one more time that I love them." or "That was a better way to go than a long and drawn-out suffering way!"

It's difficult for people to hear, "We have found cancer, and your condition is terminal." We are simply not built, as human beings, to handle well the hopeless sound of a phrase that suggests a long and dragged-out dying process. It is better to live our lives with hope for a reasonable future yet knowing that at any moment this could be our last. One friend told me, "When it's my time to go, surprise me."

Bottom line: Talk to your family about your own death wishes, finish your daily work and play like it might be your last, and say what you should say to your loved ones at the end of every day.

Third Essay
The Mystery of the Universe

Facing my own cancer, I have read a few books recently recommended by friends who are lovingly trying to comfort me. A book written by neurosurgeon Eben Alexander, entitled *Proof of Heaven*, is similar to others about "near-death experiences."[373] Alexander became deathly ill with

---

373 Alexander, E: Proof of Heaven, a Neurosurgeon's Journey into the Afterlife. Simon and Schuster, NY, NY, 2012.

bacterial meningitis and, during a seven-day coma, experienced a near-death experience like many other people through the ages. Alexander's description was wonderfully explicit. Common to many others, he found himself in a tunnel, drawn to a warm light while sensing tremendous reassuring comfort. A former skeptic of these stories, he has become a fervent advocate that these near-death experiences are evidence for our connection to all living things, Heaven and God. His final chapters discuss how inadequate science is in explaining "consciousness" and suggests that all of us are "more than our physical bodies."

Throughout the ages, some of the greatest minds in the universe have addressed the question, "What is consciousness?" From what source does our awareness come? Where does God fit into that question? Alexander states that, ". . . the greatest clue to the reality of the spiritual realm is the profound mystery of our conscious existence."

Throughout my years practicing medicine, I have tried my best to use evidence-based science to guide me in choosing the best diagnostic and therapeutic options for my patients. I define medical science as a search for truth using double-blind studies that avoid the placebo effect and preconceived biases. With advancing science, we have been improving what we can do for people. For example, we can cure certain cancers that twenty years ago would have killed those affected. We can now relieve suffering from severe shortness of breath, unrelenting heartburn, racing heart and profound depression. I am forever amazed,

and enthused, by the continuous improvements in medicine that keep happening, all because of the benefit of
the scientific method.

However, with all of our "method," science does not
bring us closer to answering the consciousness question,
the spiritual connectedness we can feel toward each
other, the question about life after death and the love and
acceptance that many of us sense coming from God or
another higher power. I agree with the neurosurgeon. The
answers to these questions must come, not from science,
but from another place.

THINGS YOU SHOULD KNOW: Q & A

Questions and Answers about:
The View Across the Water: Accepting death without fear

Question: I know I'm supposed to accept the truth that I am
going to die, but I just can't do it. It makes me panic.
I have enough burdens in life, and I can't think about
dying. You can't expect this of me.

(First, know that, in answering this question, I am
trying to set aside spiritual thinking, not knowing from
where you come on that subject. I am also answering
your question in a nonreligious way to provide something
that should fulfill all religious and nonreligious thinkers.)

Dear friend, please do not think that facing the
eventuality of death is a morbid and awful thing. See it

as something that will help you realize what is important in life. Specifically, facing the dying process should help anyone fully absorb the truth that this whole experience is *not just about you*. Fearing death is dangerous to our health, and the opposite is true: not being afraid of dying allows us to better avoid dangers as we are better able to make rational choices. Accepting the limited time we have left brings us to realign our perspectives. I advise that knowing our lives are finite, and that there will be an end, raises the value scale of every life, including our own. This, in turn, helps us act in a kinder way . . . a kinder way to others and to ourselves. This makes it easier to, "live on by the repercussions of our good deeds."[374]

Accepting our limited time on this earth is like an exercise program to improve wellness. It takes time, patience and perseverance to get into shape. Of course, it is a process, something that takes practice to do well, something into which you can grow. I see it as a daily process of making EACH DAY as good as it can be.

The story, *A Christmas Carol*, by Charles Dickens, the movies, *It's a Wonderful Life*, with Jimmy Stewart, *Groundhog Day* with Bill Murray and *Pay It Forward* with Kevin Spacey, are all examples of how the heroes in those movies finally realize that "it's not about me." Self-doubt and sadness go away when one starts considering how to help others. This concept is not

---

374   https://www.webmd.com/balance/features/science-good-deeds#1

new and is older than the Bible. The concept of pay it forward, for example, was used in an ancient Greek play entitled *The Grouch* by Dyskolos[375] and has been repeated many times by the artistic work of people like Ben Franklin, Ralph Waldo Emerson, Robert Heinlein and Ray Bradbury. To love one another is basic to the teachings of all the major religions of the world.

Bottom Line: Value others by actions (acts, deeds or accomplishments). More than superficial well wishes, action is making the well wish move, happen and be actualized. That is powerful stuff. We entirely underestimate the aftermath and influence of doing the right thing even when it's just a little thing. Living each day as if it could be our last benefits each of us because, almost paradoxically, it encourages us to focus on others and not on ourselves. This should take away the panic one might have with the thought of facing death.

Question: You say your faith surrounds you, and, yet, you don't speak about heaven and the belief that there is life after death. What do you believe?

I believe what happens to our souls after we die is an unanswerable question, and I do not think it is sinful to doubt the standard answers that religious leaders commonly provide. There is no good scientific data that

---

375   https://en.wikipedia.org/wiki/Pay_it_forward

can help. There are numerous accounts of survivors of motor vehicle crashes, cardiac arrests with resuscitation and near-death experiences where people have a common recollection of a warm and reassuring light or an unrolling of a scroll that played out the individual's life story. Most significant is the loss of the fear of death in these individuals after near-death experiences. The stories are very similar and reassuring that there is something more after we die. We simply have not found a way to provide scientific proof of anything in the spiritual realm.

What is most reassuring to me of the presence of God (Creator, Great Spirit, God Within Us) comes from the obvious spiritual presence that emanates from individuals. It's that twinkle in her eyes as she speaks of her grandchildren. It's that jumping up and down he does when the tight end catches the football and runs in for a touchdown. It's that tear that rolls down her cheek when she is asked about the love and support she received during her cancer treatment.

Don't get me wrong, I embrace my religion. I was raised a Congregationalist (UCC), and now our family attends the Methodist Church. I especially cherish my adult Sunday School class where we watch and discuss videos of leaders from all religions and beliefs. It is an inclusionary form of Christianity rather than one of exclusion. I don't claim to have the only true way, and I respect everyone's right to worship in their own way. I would encourage everyone to join some belief group if only because, at least weekly, attending a church, synagogue, temple or mosque leads the participant to think about the meaning of it all. I sense it is most important to think about the value of metaphor and story. Finally, I believe that religion is best when we can celebrate the right to question and change.

That said, I would ask you to treasure your religious beliefs, especially if it gives you succor and comfort. This is not about trying to sway you into my way or any way of thinking. It is about kindness and comfort; about honesty and truth; about acceptance, inclusion, and respect for everyone's right to choose; and about finding your own way to believe. (See **Chapter Four** for more on such ethical thinking.)

Maybe, to best explain how I feel about the topic I will share part of an essay I wrote a few months after being diagnosed with cancer:

I am reassured of God's presence when watching Teen Challenge, a religious-based rehabilitation program, successfully help men find their way back from drug or alcohol abuse.[376] The leaders who fill a mentor role, teach "It is not about you . . . it is about loving others and loving God." I am reassured when studying the complexity of the human heart and the way the heart muscle, valves and arteries interact while sending blood with oxygen and nutrition to every cell in the body. I am reassured when our Hopeful Spirit Chorale sings and brings Spiritual

---

376 http://tcdakotas.org/?view=mobile

connection to the hearts and tears to the eyes of those listening and singing. I am reassured when a church, mosque or synagogue full of people saying the Lord's Prayer (or any prayer in unison) resonates in sync with the souls of the congregation. I am reassured when watching a flock of birds or a school of fish move together and change direction as if they are one organism in sync by some ancient and Holy Spirit.

As a medical doctor caring for people through the years, I have had to rely on science with which to try to help resolve the health problems people face. In caring for people, especially at the end of their lives, I have realized that often science is simply not enough. There is another place where people need to go for help when the end is near. The Spiritual realm, in my view, is all around us if we listen very carefully for it. This Divine Essence provides, for many, great meaning and help. We need to acknowledge the force and power within and outside our scientific understanding.

Epilogue

IT WAS WITH GREAT OPTIMISM that I wrote this book for you. I hope it brings you to value yourself more and helps you become comfortable caring for others while caring for your own DAILY exercise and BALANCED dietary needs. I hope you learn of the dangers in relying on too many pills; the benefits of defining your end-of-life wishes with a living will; the value of listening and caring for another who is aging, or losing memory or dying; and I hope you find relief from a personal fear of death.

I am facing my own cancer with the knowledge and independent thought that I have lived a life dancing a Snoopy dance at almost every turn; feeling forgiveness for my transgressions; trying to do my best to help others; savoring every moment possible; and not wasting any time with a useless and joy-reducing fear of dying. When it becomes your time of dying, I wish the same for you.

With the following prayer, I bow to our unrealized connectedness (you and me) and to the miracle mystery of the universe.
—Rick

Rick and Joanie, May 4, 2018

Years ago, I was captivated by the American Indian medicine wheel while reading the book *Black Elk Speaks*. (This was an interview with an Indian medicine man from the late 1800s and early 1900s, translated and interpreted by Black Elk's son, and made into book form by author John Neihardt.) Dear friend, Amiel Redfish, also brought me to appreciate the ancient medicine wheel and how it gives honor and respect for Nature-God represented by Father Sky, Mother Earth, the four directions, the colors, the seasons and the central tree of life. I interpret the sacred circle as part of many spiritual traditions: the study in Christian theology of resurrection and rebirth; the Buddhist idea of reincarnation; and the Jewish old testament of the changing seasons (to everything there is a season and a time for every purpose under the heaven). Everything comes around, as seasons turn, turn, turn.

The circle is a universal spiritual symbol, but the Indian medicine wheel has particular complexity and power for me, as a person caring for the elderly, living and practicing a lifetime on the prairie. Through the centuries, the American Indian wheel has given a bearing, a route, a road, a sense of position, an objective and simultaneous understanding of both the infinitude and the limitation of life.

Some of the power and energy of the circle, from all traditions, comes as it rejects the duality and judgmentalism of "right and wrong." The wheel brings a conscious spirituality and a high wisdom that recognizes and accepts all things. The hoop explains aging and dying in a way that, for me, brings comfort from the fear of death and closes the gap between the cynical scientific part of me and the inclusive spiritual part. By spiritual, I mean that unexplainable part of the soul that savors music, art, poetry and the divine; the part that grows to love all those living and nonliving things around us, sometimes as much as we cherish our families.

After several revisions to the prayer in open form and free verse, I decided to put it into iambic pentameter which is a five-beat poetic rhythm that matches the lub-dub rhythm of a pulsing heart. I found great joy in the challenge. Whether this is your cup of tea or not, it was pure fun for me, and I hope you can at least sense and take pleasure in that.

AN ANCIENT PRAYER IN SACRED CIRCLE FORM

(Consider reading/singing this out loud)

From every land and culture lore we learn
That ancients found the sacred circle form;
For seasons always turn, and turn, and turn,
And with the hoops, and circles, rounds: transform.

This ring disowns the dual poles, it claims
That 'black and white' or 'good and bad' are wrong;
The blessed circle turns away the blames
For storm of nature, fair skies, lightning, flames.
No fault for love or hate with swaying throng,
We pray in harmony, as love consoles.
O sacred hoop of life, please touch our souls.

We get down on our knees and feel the soil,
The womb of life, the cherish'd Mother Earth,
From where good food and sustenance is made
To feed all creatures/persons living now
That gaze upon the prairie, peaks, or glade;
For mud brings life: foundation is the Earth.

We stand upon the dirt, this hallow'd ground,
We raise our arms to sacred Father Sky
From where vitality flows down to Earth;
We see the sun which brings us light and warmth,
A cloud brings breath of wind, and rain brings sips
To quench our thirst so life with roots are nursed;

While dark brings out the stars, bless'd time to rest.
With hands in air, infinity is Sky.
Beginning and the End: Turn Earth and Sky.

We pray in harmony as love consoles.
O sacred hoop of life, please touch our souls.

Around the fire, within the blessed round
We turn and bow to East, red rising sun,
The red of blood and birth, the morning star,
And springtime, infant, toddler, blameless youth;
For may we nourish renaissance and fun,
And hope for fresh and novel growth to come.

Around the fire, within the blessed wheel
We turn and bow to South, the midday sun,
The yellow strong abundance, summer hue,
The sensuality of youth love-kiss'd,
False sense of might—invincible? Untrue.
Still, may we have the strength and right to fight
For justice, truth, and freedom when at risk.

Around the fire, within the blessed hoop
We turn and bow to West, the setting sun,
The black of looming thunderclouds and night,
The autumn feel of ripeness, full alert
To loss from death, and war, and drawn-out fight.
May we have sense enough to face our flaws
And honest eyes to see how others hurt.

Around the fire, within the blessed ring
We turn and bow to North, short winter sun,
Of brilliant snow and nighttime, starry sky,
Of old age, wisdom, cleansing-ending winds,
The old sage-elder, teaching fearless death.
O may we understand how blest we are
For chance to love, and listen, reconcile;
So we may face our ending with a smile.

We pray in harmony as love consoles.
O sacred hoop of life, please touch our souls.

O tree of life within, since all began,
Please help us know of folks beyond our clan,
Most people everywhere are good and true,
And skies in every land are just as blue.

O Mother-Father God, now hear our prayers,
It's you who lives where rising sun brings hope,
Where summer sun brings growth, and might to fight,
Where autumn storms give range for full-grown sight,
And winter, old sage wisdom gives us worth.
We thank you for your blessings and our roles
And for the strength to face time's change, to cope.

We pray in harmony as love consoles,
O sacred hoop of life, please touch our souls.

Medicine Wheel, Bighorn National Forest, Wyoming[377]

Acknowledgments

I AM DEEPLY GRATEFUL for the many people who provided help for this project. We are what we are because of those that raised us. My mom and dad, Jody and Earl Holm, along with my sister Susan, gave me unconditional love and the important discipline I needed. My sister-in-spirit Jeannie Van Dyke Cecil not only gave me emotional support through my high school and adult life but provided important editorial direction and encouragement as I wrote this book. Love you, Jeannie.

I needed plenty of help editing this book. While I am an experienced physician, I am a writing novice. My forgiving and tolerant wife, Joanie Smith Holm, has always been my first editor, teaching me to incorporate compassion in everything I write.

Bette Gerberding, an adjunct professor of English, inspired theater director and a dear friend, inserted and removed more commas than Carter has little liver pills as she tried to "teach this old dog new tricks." Thank you, Bette. As we worked together on this book not only did our friendship become even more important to me, but your direction made my writing better.

My student, now my teacher and my friend, Kyle Hain, also helped edit this book and wrote the beautiful foreword. He is a trusted guide and editor of my weekly essays as well. I truly appreciate Gail Widman who provided wise and valuable input on the book from her perspective as a retired school teacher.

Thanks for editorial and production advice from fellow authors Ellen O'Donnell and Maggie Callanan. My friendship with Maggie sprouted as we discovered our similar compassion for hospice care following my reading, *Final Gifts,* a book written by Maggie and another hospice nurse, Patricia Kelly. (Read that book.) Thank you, also, to Ronda, Bob, Bill and Kathryn of 1106 Design for their editing, design and guidance.

I thank all my teachers (grade school on up) and the State of South Dakota for giving me the opportunity to be a doctor. Also, I thank the teachers, many of whom were also students and residents from Emory University School of Medicine in Atlanta who molded my love of evidence-based science. I try my best to pay it forward to people in need.

My professional friends in medicine are dear to me. They include the people that run the organization and my colleagues of the South Dakota State Medical Association (docs of all kinds), the South Dakota College of Physicians (internists), and the physicians, physician assistants and nurse practitioners working alongside me at Avera Medical Group Brookings Clinic (AMGB). Collegiality brings quality and meaning. Thank you.

My serious writing began with and continues as host of our weekly call-in health education television show, *On Call with the Prairie Doc®*. Each week for the past 16 years, physician and scientist guests volunteer to bring unbiased honest science to our viewing public. They come with gracious courage and I thank all of them. Special thanks to the Prairie Doc® "heroes," my AMGB physician friends who fill in as hosts for the show when I am unavailable. Kelley Evans, MD, Deb Johnston, MD, Jill Kruse, DO, and Andrew Ellsworth, MD will carry on the program if, and when, I am gone. They are indeed heroes!

I also appreciate the production team for our television programs, including the many SDSU students who work the cameras, sound equipment and all those behind-the-scene activities to make a show happen under the careful watch of talented director, Lowell Haag. Our artful producers, Jay Vanduch and Ginger Thomson, provide the panache that brings personality to the show. I thank Judge Kelley with all his creative enthusiasm for establishing the Prairie Doc® Assistants, a preprofessional student group from SDSU who answer the phone calls from viewers each week along with a myriad of other duties. Joan Hogan my radio partner and host at KBRK (1430 on your AM dial), along with radio announcer Bob Wayne, brought me to realize the value of public health education through our radio programs and it remains great fun. I am also grateful for Jim Wooster who shares some of his weekly time with me on WNAX-AM radio.

Joanie and I founded the nonprofit 501c(3) Healing Words Foundation (HWF) in 2011 thanks to encouragement from Jay Vanduch. This foundation is the funding mechanism for our public health education mission. I thank Laura Ellsworth, our funding coordinator and all the underwriters. Thanks, also, to Doyle Estes, JD, fellow brothers (alums from LXA at USD) Louie

Hogrefe, MD, Ed Pluimer, JD, Gary Davis, JD, Bill Bowen, JD and Doug Estes, MBA and Harry Christianson, JD who financed the costs of preparing this book for publication. You helped make it happen and I am thankful.

I also appreciate those who have unselfishly served on the HWF board including Joanie Smith Holm, RN, CNP, Mark Bubak, MD, Jim Engelbrecht, MD, Dave Hyink, PhD, Tom Luzier, MD, Stephanie Herseth-Sandlin, JD and Jennifer May, MD. I especially appreciate the steady and essential organizational guidance provided by friend Barb Anderson who served on the HWF board prior to her current position as our executive administrator.

As I write this, it's been 22 months since my cancer diagnosis. I am alive due in large part to my AMGB internist Dan Cecil and surgeon Theresa Oey, Mayo Whipple surgeon Mark Truty, Avera oncologist Mark Huber and the oncology nurses at AMGB, Lindsay Hawks and Sarah Bowen. My humbling cancer journey has brought me to be thankful for all my blessings, especially those of THIS day.

The Brookings Health System Hospice team of nurses, pharmacists, social workers and pastors taught me about compassion, caring, and acceptance of death with their weekly stories and discussions. If my cancer progresses, I know I will be in good hands with that group. Hospice team, YOU ROCK!

Thank you to all the singers past and present whose voices join with mine as part of the Hopeful Spirit Chorale. Let's keep singing for those who are in hospice or need of cheer. To my dear friends who make up the Lake Poinsett Sailing Academy, thank you for helping keep my boat steady and my sails full. As our mission statement declares, a smooth sea never made a skillful sailor.

I salute my family. My two cousins, Bob McDonald Sr. and Mark Powell, comprise the living members of my extended family. They continue to fill the roles of older and younger brother to me. Bob and Mark became especially important to me after the childhood death of my only sibling Susan. Their families are my family.

Our children, Eric, Carter, Preston and Julia give us the responsibility of parenthood, bringing joys for their successes, grief for their failures and reasons to try to be good examples. Joanie is my best friend and wife. When someone asked how to build a good marriage my response was: "Find someone with common active interests; and for the rest of your lives treat each other with the common courtesy of kindness, honesty and respect for the other person's choices." Thank you, Honey, for "hanging in there" with me all these years, especially now when I'm ill. It's been great fun and a wonderful adventure.

Finally, I thank you, the reader, for your interest. If you and a family member are wrestling and rolling in the mud with the mythical monster of aging and death, may the words within help you win the match with grace.

About the Author
Richard P. Holm, MD, MACP

RECENTLY INDUCTED into the South Dakota Hall of Fame and cited as "South Dakota's Voice of Healthcare," Dr. Richard (Rick) Holm, MD, is founder and volunteer host of *On Call With the Prairie Doc®*. This weekly call-in television show offering health information has aired on South Dakota Public Broadcasting most Thursdays at 7:00 PM for more than 16 years.

Holm's musings on health, *Prairie Doc® Perspectives* are currently published as weekly columns in 57 South Dakota newspapers. A contributor to four medical textbooks and numerous articles published in national medical journals, Holm is a regular writer for the *South Dakota Journal of Medicine*. Holm and illustrator Judith Peterson, MD are authors of *The Picture of Health: A View from the Prairie*, a book published by the South Dakota Agriculture Heritage Museum in 2008.

Practicing medicine for nearly 40 years in Brookings, SD, Dr. Holm is Clinical Professor at the University of South Dakota Sanford School of Medicine and Adjunct Professor of Journalism at South Dakota State University.

Rick was raised in De Smet, South Dakota, the *Little Town on the Prairie,* home of Laura Ingalls Wilder. After two years of medical school at the University of South Dakota, he completed his medical degree and internal medicine residency at Emory University School of Medicine in Atlanta, Georgia, where he later taught and practiced for three years before returning to South Dakota.

Rick and his wife, Joanie Holm, RN, CNP (pediatrics) raised four children and are active in their community. They live in Brookings, where he is surrounded by friends, enjoys walking, running, sailing on prairie Lake Poinsett, directing a hospice choir and writing.